Sybil Rides

The True Story of Sybil Ludington
The Female Paul Revere
The Burning of Danbury and Battle of Ridgefield

The Expanded Edition

By

Larry A. Maxwell

Larry A. Maxwell

Dedicated To
The Unsung Everyday Heroes Among Us

Special Thanks to Jonathan O'Hara

Cover Designed by Matthew R. Maxwell
Featuring a 13 Star American Flag
And the Sybil Ludington Monument
on Route 52 in Carmel, NY

1775 Productions

599 Route 311, Patterson, New York 12563
1130 Perry Rd., Afton, New York 13730
GoodInformation.US

ISBN-13: 978-1-949277-01-2

Creative Non-Fiction
New York History; Connecticut History; History of the American Revolutionary War; Military History; Biographies of Women; Biographies of Adolescents; Biographies of Military History

Reenactors in pictures in this book belong to the Brigade of the American Revolution, Continental Line, British Brigade and/or the Living History Guild.
These organizations help keep history alive.

All illustrations in this book are either in the public domain or used by permission. Photographs by Larry A. Maxwell and Gary Vorwald are copyrighted with this book. All rights reserved.

© COPYRIGHT 2018 – Larry A. Maxwell

Table of Contents

Chapter   **Page**

List of Illustrations   5
Introduction   9
Information to Understand Before Reading   12
Chapter 1   Paul Revere's Dangerous Ride   17
Chapter 2   War Begins   31
Chapter 3   Meet Sybil's Family   43
Chapter 4   A Plan to End the War   49
Chapter 5   Enoch Crosby the Spy   67
Chapter 6   The Loyalists Plot   79
Chapter 7   Crosby Warns Ludington   89
Chapter 8   Attempt to Capture Ludington   99
Chapter 9   Conflict at the Ganong's Home   110
Chapter 10   Sybil's Birthday Party   116
Chapter 11   British Fleet Embarks for Norwalk   130
Chapter 12   Shooting Muskets   134
Chapter 13   Crown Forces Land at Norwalk   142
Chapter 14   Conflict Between Father and Son   148
Chapter 15   Confrontation at Bethel   151
Chapter 16   Danbury Attacked   157
Chapter 17   American Officers Meet at Redding   166
Chapter 18   Messenger Arrives at Ludington's   175
Chapter 19   Sybil Arrives at the First House   182
Chapter 20   The Looting and Burning Continue   185
Chapter 21   Sybil and the Bandits   188
Chapter 22   Americans Arrive in Bethel   191
Chapter 23   Sybil Arrives at Another Home   194
Chapter 24   Making Ammunition   197
Chapter 25   Sybil Faces an Obstacle   202
Chapter 26   Militia March off to Battle   205
Chapter 27   Sybil at the Ganong's   210
Chapter 28   Crown Forces Leave Danbury   213
Chapter 29   Sybil Rides as the Sun Rises   217
Chapter 30   American Officers Plan Response   219
Chapter 31   Opposition South of Danbury   223
Chapter 32   Sybil at the Last Home   226
Chapter 33   Wooster Attacks the Crown Forces   229

Chapter 34	Sybil Returns Home	235
Chapter 35	Barricades in Ridgefield	241
Chapter 36	Battle in Ridgefield	246
Chapter 37	Crown Forces South of Ridgefield	253
Chapter 38	Ludington Meets Arnold	258
Chapter 39	Back at the Ludington's Home	266
Chapter 40	British Officers Before Last Battle	269
Chapter 41	Battle in Norwalk	274
Chapter 42	The Smoke Clears	280
Chapter 43	The Return	283
Historical Background		289
Suggested Study Strategies		376
Projects and Questions		377
Some Vocabulary Words & Terms		382
Fun Facts and Trivia		383
Bibliography		385
About the Author		393

List of Illustrations

Illustration	Page
Sybil Ludington Monument	Cover
Portraits of Sybil Ludington	8
Royal Naval Ships in Boston Harbor	16
1775 Map of Boston and Surrounding Area	18
H.M.S. Somerset	21
Paul Revere Being Rowed to Charlestown	24
Paul Revere's Ride	30
Battle of Lexington	38
British Regulars Advance on Concord	40
Minutemen Fire on Retreating Regulars	42
Retreat of the British from Concord	42
Ludington Mill	44
225th Anniversary of Sybil's Ride	45
1776 British Map of New York City	50
Portrait of The Lord William Howe	52
Portrait of General William Erskine	53
Portrait of Governor William Tryon	54
Van Wyck Homestead - Fishkill Supply Depot	60
Colonial Log Church	68
Portrait of Enoch Crosby	75
Drumming Out of Town	80
Inside a Colonial Tavern	83
An Integrated Militia	90
Loyalists Seek to Apprehend Colonel Ludington	102
Colonial Two-Story Home	105
Colonial Bedroom	108
Home of Loyalist Beverley Robinson	111
Hanging of Nathan Hale	114
Rev. John Gano	117
Haym Salomon Silver Medal	118
Sketch of a Stockbridge/Wappinger Indian	121
Route the British Fleet Took to Compo Beach	133
Loading a Musket	141
Compo Beach Photographs	143
Crown Forces Landing at Compo Beach	145
Tory Tax Collector	150
Crown Forces Wait for Enemy to Attack	153
1796 German Map of Connecticut	156

Portrait of Colonel Joseph Platt Cooke	159
Musicians Play as Crown Forces Enter Town	161
Danbury Raid Monument	165
Portrait of General Benedict Arnold	168
Portrait of General David Wooster	170
Take Notice Recruitment Poster	174
Simple Colonial Home	183
Militiaman Prepares to Respond to the Call	184
Crown Forces Raid and Burn	192
Colonial Home	195
Colonial Militia Respond to the Call	196
Inside a Typical Colonial Home	200
Overflowing Stream in Putnam County	204
Sybil Rides on Through the Night	210
Crown Forces Leaving Town	213
1777 Map of Tryon's Raid on Danbury	216
Colonial Fairfield County Connecticut	220
Colonel Jedediah Huntington	222
Loyalists Return Fire	225
Kitchen in a Typical Colonial Home	227
Historical Marker for Sybil's Ride	228
Monument to General David Wooster	233-234
The Minute-Men of the Revolution	238
Militia at the 225th Anniversary of Sybil's Ride	238
Colonial Militia Assemble	240
Fight at Ridgefield	243
Battle of Ridgefield Historic Marker	247
Cannon Crew Fires	248
Exploit of Benedict Arnold	251
Continentals Attack from Woods	254
Continental Artillery Fire Cannon	259
Portrait of Colonel John Lamb	264
Colonial Dining Area	268
Continental Army and Militia on the March	270
Continental Soldiers Maneuvering to Battle	277
Patriot's Monument at Compo Beach	279
Friend Helping Wounded Soldier	281
Soldiers Return from Battle	285
Opposition to the Stamp Act	291
The Boston Massacre & Crispus Attucks	294
The Boston Tea Party	295
Paul Revere's Ride	296

The Public Advertiser, May 30, 1775 edition 301
First Continental Congress Opens in Prayer 302
Raising of the Continental Grand Union Flag 303
The Birth of New York State 304
Engraving of Battle of Bunker Hill 307
Peter Salem at Bunker Hill 308
General Howe Evacuating Boston 309
British Fleet Arrives in New York 310
Enoch Crosby Historic Marker – Fishkill 314
Enoch Crosby Historic Marker – Carmel 314
Affirmation of Loyalty 316
Oath of Loyalty to the King 317
Rev. John Gano Baptizing George Washington 321
Contributors to the Cause U. S. Stamps 322
Daniel Nimham, Sachem of the Wappingers 323
Prison Ship H.M.S. Jersey 324
New York City 1776 325
17th Light Dragoons' Emblem 326
Cannonball in Keeler Tavern 327
Grave of Luther Holcomb 332
The Liberty Flag 335
The Dutch East India Company Shipyard 339
Paul Revere's Bill for His Messenger Service 341-342
Approximate Route of Sybil's Ride 345
Sybil Ludington Monument Dedication 346
Capture of Major John Andre 348
18th Century Musket Ball Mold & Tool 351
Revolutionary War Militiaman on Horse 353
Sunrise Over the Hills 355
Militiamen Attach Crown Forces 357
Historical Marker of Wooster's Death 358
Sybil Ludington's Ride Ends 359
Battle of Ridgefield 362
Soldiers Return Fire Under Cover 363
Crown Forces Fall to Militia Attack from Woods 365
Cannon Monument at Compo Beach 368
Battle of Compo Beach Bas Reliefs 369-371
Newspaper Advertisement for Lost British Army 372
Tombstones of Sybil and Colonel Henry Ludington ... 375
Edmund Augustus Ogden 375
Larry A. Maxwell 393

Larry A. Maxwell

Historically Accurate Portrait of Sybil Ludington

This image by Hal Bailey is based on an original image of Sybil. This appeared on a First Day Postal Cover for Artcraft in 1975.

Incorrect Portrait of Sybil Ludington

This portrait was displayed in the National Women's Museum In the late 1800's, identifying this person as Sybil Ludington. It is an 1801 Watercolor on Ivory of Eliza Izard Pinckney . by Edward Green Malbone.

Introduction

*S*ybil Rides tells the inspiring true story of events during the American Revolution which resulted in sixteen-year old Sybil Ludington becoming known as the *Female Paul Revere*. Her ride took place during a significant event in American History designed by the British Commanders to bring an end to the Revolution.

As a teenage female heroine Sybil Ludington is part of many school's history curriculum yet many people never heard of her. Even fewer know what led to Sybil's ride or the intense drama and events connected with it.

On a cold rainy night in the spring of 1777, the British Regular Army, along with a regiment of Loyalists, bent on revenge against their Rebel neighbors, plundered and burned Danbury, Connecticut. That raid was part of Lord William Howe's plan to end the Revolution. During the raid a messenger was sent to the home of Colonel Henry Ludington appealing for help. The Colonel's sixteen-year old daughter, Sybil, disregarded the danger and bravely rode forty miles on that cold rainy night throughout the Hudson Valley to call the Militia to action.

On her ride Sybil stopped quickly at each home, banged on the doors and windows, and yelled, *"Call to arms! The Regulars and Tories are burning Danbury! The Militia is* needed! Call to arms!" Families awoke. Men dressed quickly, grabbed their muskets, and headed out into the night to face a powerful foe. Sybil's courageous ride earned her the nickname, *The Female Paul Revere*.

A larger than life monument honoring Sybil Ludington, stands in Carmel, New York along the route where she made her historic ride. It portrays her dramatically riding on her horse as she rode to call out the Militia.

The United States Postal Service issued a special stamp to honor Sybil during America's Bicentennial celebration.

This story starts at the beginning of the Revolutionary War with Paul Revere in a rowboat in Boston Harbor, two years before Sybil's ride. From there it goes to Lexington, Massachusetts, where we see the Militia who responded to Revere's call, facing the might of the British Army. We learn what really happened and are there as the *shot heard round the world* is fired and the Revolutionary War starts. We then watch the war shift with a vengeance to New York.

All the events and characters in this book are historical. Some of the dialogue in this book is verbatim. Some of the dialogue is conjecture but based on historical events.

This story not only tells the true compelling story of Sybil Ludington but also of her father, Colonel Henry Ludington, his family, and other unsung heroes.

In this book you meet British officers and their Loyalists allies and see the conflicts between them.

You will see the brave, yet humorous way Sybil and her siblings foil the Loyalists attempt to capture their father, Colonel Henry Ludington.

You will meet Enoch Crosby, a friend of the Ludingtons, who disregarded the danger and served as a spy in the struggle for independence.

You will meet Jacob Angevine, a former slave who earned his freedom and that of his family, by serving in the French and Indian War. You will also meet Joseph, his teenage son who is a friend of Sybil Ludington and a brave member of the Colonel Ludington's Militia.

You will also meet John Gano the famous *Fighting Preacher* and his friend, Haym Salomon, a Jewish immigrant who helped secure funding for the Revolution.

You will meet Daniel Nimham, Sachem (chief) of the Wappinger Indians and his son Abraham, true unsung American heroes who sacrificed everything during the war.

You will see how Luther Holcomb, another brave young unsung hero, helped delay the entire British Army and its attack on Danbury.

One of the surprising characters you will meet is Benedict Arnold who later becomes America's most notorious traitor. He was once an admirable hero and played an inspiring important part in this story.

The *Historical Background* section at the end of this book provides important details, explanations, and historical information to enhance the learning experience.

Suggested teaching strategies, questions, strategies, and an extensive bibliography are included for educators.

Hopefully this book will help bring history alive and inspire you as you read this true story about Sybil Ludington and some unsung American heroes.

Larry A. Maxwell

Information to Understand
Before Reading This Book

Terminology

It is important to understand the correct meaning of some terminology as you read this story. At the beginning of the Revolution people in the colonies were part of the British Empire and were still considered British. That is why Paul Revere and his companions did not say, *The British are coming,* as they rode. They also did not say, *The Redcoats are coming,* because. Firsthand historical records tell us they said, *The Regulars are coming!*

Many people use the term *Patriot,* when discussing the American Revolution, in a different way today than some people used it during the Revolution. The word *Patriot* means loyal to one's country. During the Revolution the word *Patriot* was used by some to mean those loyal to the Crown. Those loyal to the Crown often referred to themselves as *Loyalists* or *Royalists.* Their enemies called them *Tories.* Those who opposed the Crown were sometimes called *Americans* but more commonly *Rebels* because there were *Americans* on both sides. It was not until after the war that only those who opposed the Crown were called *Patriots.*

Another term to understand is *Continental.* Sometimes

it referred to those who opposed the Crown, but it usually meant a soldier who served in the Continental Army instead of a soldier who served in the local *Militia*.

Militia is the correct term for Sybil's father, Colonel Henry Ludington, and his men. In most towns all men ages 15 to 55 belonged to the *Militia*, unless exempted.

Many stories incorrectly portray the *Militia* as untrained rabble. That is not true. The Militia in every colony drilled regularly. Most drilled using the same military manual of arms as the British Regular Forces

Locations

The Ludington's lived in what was then known as *Fredericksburg*, Dutchess County, New York. You will not find Fredericksburg on a modern map of New York. In 1812, Dutchess County was divided into two counties: Dutchess County to the north; and Putnam County to the south. The Town of Fredericksburg is now the towns of Patterson and Kent, as well as part of the Town of Carmel and Southeast, which are all in Putnam County. It also included a small part of Pawling, which is still in Dutchess County.

Variant Spelling

The modern spelling of places is used in this book instead of the historical spellings used during the American Revolution. *Ridgefield* was spelled *Ridgfield* back then. *Redding* was spelled *Reeding*.

Some places mentioned in this book are now separate towns but were called *parishes* during the Revolution. *Bethel* was called the *Parish of Bethel* in the *Town of Danbury*. Wilton was the *Parish of Wilton* in the *Town of Norwalk*.

Compo Beach, where the Crown Forces landed for the Danbury Raid, was in the *Town of Norwalk* during the Revolution. It later became part of the *Town of Westport.* Part of Compo Beach was called *Cedar Point.*

There were variations of spelling personal names back then. Colonel Henry Ludington's last name appears spelled, *Ludenton* in some colonial records.

Sybil Ludington's name was spelled numerous ways in historical documents. When she was a widow and applied for a Revolutionary Pension for her husband's service, she signed her name as *Sebal*. Her sister Mary, in her 1838 Widow's Pension Application, also wrote her sister's name as *Sebal*.

Her tombstone lists her as *Sibbell*. In the 1810 United States Census she was listed as *Sibel*. In some books her name is listed as *Cybil*. In this book we use the spelling, *Sybil*, which was used in most newspaper accounts and by the United States Postal Service.

Chapter Length

The length of the chapters in this book vary significantly. Each give details and conversations which occurred during different events. Some events lasted longer than others, or contain longer conversations, so those chapters are longer.

Dates and Times

The dates and times used in this book are based on extrapolations from contemporary historical records, such as newspaper articles, journals, and letters.

Historical Background Section

A large *Historical Background* section is included in this *Expanded Edition*. It looks in detail at the causes of the Revolution and at significant events before and during the first two years of the war and in relation to each chapter.

This section is provided for educators and those who want to know more details about the historical background for each chapter. It makes this book an excellent tool for learning more about the Revolutionary War and for teaching details related to each chapter.

Some may want to read the corresponding historical background before, or after, reading each chapter. Some may want to wait until after they read the entire story.

Projects and Questions

A section called *Projects and Questions* is included to provide educators, and those who want to learn more, with some suggestions to enhance the learning experience.

Larry A. Maxwell

Royal Naval Ships in Boston Harbor
Drawing by Paul Revere.

Chapter 1

Paul Revere's Dangerous Ride
Boston Harbor
April 18, 1775 – Tuesday Evening

An almost full-moon arose on a cloudy, cold spring night in Boston, Massachusetts. The date was April 18, 1775. Dark dreary clouds, heavy with ugly unrest, filled the chilly air and surrounded the many warships docked in Boston Harbor. That night each ship was filled with British Regulars who huddled together trying to keep warm. They could tell something very important was about to happen.

The British commanders in Boston planned to send a large force of Regulars to Lexington, Massachusetts, to arrest Samuel Adams and John Hancock, leaders of the dreaded *Sons of Liberty*. The plan was an attempt to end what they feared could be a possible revolution. Instead of preventing a revolution they were about to start one.

The *Sons of Liberty* in Boston discovered the British commander's plan and set in motion a plan of their own. Around nine-thirty that evening they sent William Dawes, out on horseback, across Boston Neck to warn Samuel Adams and John Hancock.

1775 Map of Boston and Surrounding Area
By J. DeCosta, Published in London, 1775.

At the same time a local silversmith, who was one of the *Sons of Liberty,* closed his shop and tried to leave the city undetected. He quietly headed up the street toward the harbor. He had to be careful because the British Military leaders expected trouble and imposed restrictive military curfews and posted British Regular soldiers all around town. Anyone out on the street at night would be arrested.

The silversmith proceeded quietly through Boston streets, seeking to evade detection. He finally made it to the docks. There he saw the Regulars boarding war ships.

There was a foreboding feeling in the air. The soldiers did not know where they were going. They knew they were not sailing back to England. That would have been welcomed by both the colonists and the soldiers. The soldiers were not being treated well by people around Boston and would rather be back in England. Unbeknownst to the soldiers they were preparing to take part in something which would change not only their lives but the entire future of the colonies, and ultimately the world. Their leaders did not give them any details. They wanted them to be unaware of the impending action lest any mistakenly revealed their plans to the *Sons of Liberty.*

As the silversmith tried to stay undiscovered he looked for two men with a small rowboat. Those men were to carry him across the Charles River to Charlestown. Once there he would begin his mission, a dangerous ride that would help propel him into the annals of history.

Suddenly he heard footsteps and slinked back into the shadows. The sound of the footsteps grew louder and louder. It was clear someone was approaching. He held his breath afraid the beating of his heart would betray him. He leaned closer to the building trying to disappear. He wondered, *will his mission end in failure before it started*?

A large dark figure approached. He strained his eyes to

see if it was wearing a military uniform. When he saw the man was dressed in workman's clothes he breathed a big sigh of relief. As that man drew closer the silversmith recognized him as his shipbuilder friend, Joshua Bentley.

Joshua quietly asked, "Paul Revere, is that you?"

He replied, "Yes, it is I. And I am so glad to see you, Joshua."

They shook hands. Then Joshua motioned for Paul Revere to follow him. "Come this way Paul, Thomas Richardson is waiting for us in the rowboat."

The two men walked quickly and quietly to the rowboat, carefully looking around as they went, doing their best to make sure they were not detected.

Joshua spoke with great concern to Paul Revere, "There has been a lot of activity around here. I hope we can get you across the river in time to warn Adams and Hancock."

They cautiously walked down the dock and finally arrived at a large rowboat. They saw Thomas Richardson nervously waiting next to a boat, holding a set of oars.

As Joshua stepped into the rowboat, Thomas greeted Paul Revere, "Paul it is good to see you."

As Paul Revere entered the boat, Thomas said, "I hope you do not get seasick."

Paul Revere nervously smiled and responded, "I will gladly take sea sickness over being spotted and shot by a musket from a British war ship."

As Joshua helped Paul Revere to the back of the boat, Thomas teased, "Is that a target I see on your back?

Paul Revere tried to look at his back, then stopped when

he realized Joshua was teasing. He smiled and replied, "I believe all of us Sons of Liberty have targets on our backs."

Joshua boldly spoke up, "That is because the only way they will get us is if they shoot us in the back."

"Or in a rowboat," Thomas said apprehensively.

They pushed off from the dock and began to quietly row across the Charles River.

H.M.S. Somerset
18th Century Engraving.

The river was filled with British war ships. On each ship, were British Regular soldiers dressed in red wool regimental coats. They huddled in groups trying to keep warm on that cold chilly night. They were glad they brought black woolen blankets, which they huddled under.

Joshua and Thomas worked hard to row the boat, while trying to be as quiet as possible, so they would not be discovered. That was not an easy task.

As they came close to the H.M.S. Somerset, a British Warship, Paul Revere was concerned they might be detected. He softly admonished the others, "Try to be extra quiet. We must not let the sentries discover us."

Joshua quietly responded. "We are doing our best."

Paul Revere spoke again, with concern, stressing the urgency of their situation. "Lives depend on us."

Thomas whispered, acknowledging the danger of their situation. "I imagine it will be our lives, if we are caught!"

Paul Revere nodded his head in agreement and quietly responded "I am sure you are right about that."

As the row boat quietly passed the H.M.S. Somerset, up on the deck, a British Marine private stood guard. He was holding his musket in his right hand. The butt of his gun rested on the deck while he leaned on the edge of the ship.

The Marine looked out over the harbor and watched as an almost full moon rose over Boston. That beautiful sight kept him from looking down at the water below, where the men were rowing by. He moved and let his musket rest in the crook of his arm, while he tried to warm his hands by holding them close to his mouth and blowing on them.

A British Marine sergeant, making his rounds, came up almost undetected and asked, "How goes the watch?"

The private was startled. He was so caught up watching the moon he did not notice the sergeant approaching. He grabbed his musket firmly and quickly turned his head. When he saw the sergeant. He composed himself and replied, "Everything appears to be quiet, sergeant."

The sergeant came and stood next to him. For a moment

he looked over the railing out across the harbor toward Boston. Then he spoke, "Quiet is a good thing."

The private nodded his head in agreement as he too looked out over the harbor. "Yes, I suppose it is."

They continued to look across the harbor toward Boston. There was a chill in the air. The sergeant blew on his hands to warm them. The private did the same.

After reflective silence the sergeant looked away from the city. He stepped back from the railing with a serious look on his face and said, "I do not understand these people, why are they being so difficult?"

He paused and again blew to warm his hands. Then, with contempt in his voice he said, "They should be grateful they are part of the greatest empire in the world!"

The private hesitantly responded. "They must not see it that way."

The sergeant pondered that thought for a moment. Then he said. "I suppose you are right. It does not make sense to me. After all the Crown has done for them. How can they be so ungrateful?!"

The private turned away from the railing, looked at the sergeant, then spoke apprehensively, "Sergeant."

He hesitated, knowing he probably should not ask what he was about to, but his curiosity stirred within him and he had to say something. He paused between each phrase, "Some of the men told me, they heard we are going to do something tomorrow to stop the Sons of Liberty, those trouble makers who are trying to incite others to revolution. Do you know if, umm, if there is any truth to that?"

Larry A. Maxwell

The sergeant changed his posture. He looked intently at the private and responded sternly. "Private! It sounds like someone knows more than they should!"

The private got nervously defensive. "Sergeant, I ... I am just saying, what I heard."

The sergeant continued with his rebuke, "You better be careful what you hear and say! If those Sons of Liberty troublemakers get any idea of what we have planned for them, that would not be good at all. No, not good at all!"

While the sergeant and private were having this conversation, Joshua Bentley and Thomas Richardson were rowing past the H.M.S. Somerset, with Paul Revere in their boat. They could faintly hear the sergeant and private talking up on the ship.

Once they rowed safely past the ship, Joshua was greatly relieved. He whispered, "That was close."

Paul Revere Being Rowed to Charlestown

By A. Lassell Ripley.
Paul Revere Memorial Association

"That was very close," Paul Revere said. "Well done!"

As they rowed further away, Paul Revere looked intently toward the shore and said, "If we can find Deacon Larkin, and if he has a horse ready for me, I should be able to reach Lexington in time to warn Adams and Hancock."

Thomas Richardson said, "As long as no one takes a shot at that target on your back," That remark made them smile.

Back on the H.M.S. Somerset, the private and sergeant leaned on the railing as they talked. Obviously we missed some of the conversation but that does not appear to be relevant. The sergeant said, "All I am saying is, I will be glad when tomorrow is over."

The private listened as he looked towards Boston. All evening the city looked tranquil, but he became alarmed as he noticed something different. He saw a light in the steeple of the North Church which was not there earlier.

He pointed toward the light and said, "Look sergeant! I do not remember seeing a light in the steeple of that church before."

The sergeant looked intently at the church. His disposition changed to deep concern, "Are you sure?"

The private and sergeant both looked with intense scrutiny towards the steeple. The private boldly replied, "Yes, I am quite sure. There was not a light in that steeple."

He asked, "Do you think it is some kind of signal?"

The sergeant looked very concerned. He knew this might have an impact on the important events scheduled to take place in the morning. With urgency, he said, "I must go report this!" He turned and quickly went to make a report.

The private stared at the steeple. He felt the chill of the night. He blew again on his hands to try to warm them.

The rowboat was now a safe distance past the ship and undetected. It came to the shore near Charlestown. Just as it landed another lantern appeared in the steeple of the North Church behind them.

Deacon John Larkin, a member of the Sons of Liberty, was waiting along the shore. He has been waiting for Paul Revere and was watching for a signal from the Church.

The Sons of Liberty knew the British planned to arrest their leaders in Lexington, as well as attempt to confiscate the muskets and ammunition they stockpiled in Concord. They knew the Regulars would either march out across Boston Neck, or cross the harbor to Charleston on ships. It was important for the Sons of Liberty to discover which route the Regulars would take so they could rally their Militia to oppose them at the right places. They pre-arranged a signal. If they discovered the Regulars planned to attack by land, they would place one lantern in the steeple of the North Church. If they discovered the attack would come by sea, it would be two lanterns. When Deacon Larkin saw the two lanterns he knew the attack would come by sea.

William Dawes set out earlier for Lexington across Boston Neck. Soon Paul Revere would set out on horseback from Charleston, to Lexington and Concord. He would take a different route in case one was stopped along the way.

Deacon Larkin brought along a horse, which was saddled and ready for Paul Revere. As he held the reins of the horse, he was pleased when he saw the rowboat approaching. He was very sure the only one who would be coming by rowboat across the Charles River that night would be Paul Revere.

As the rowboat landed Paul Revere looked intently up and down the shore. He finally saw the figure of a man standing near the shore with a horse. He was relieved when he could tell the figure was his friend, Deacon John Larkin.

Paul Revere stepped out of the boat, anxious to get to his task. He turned to Thomas and Joshua, "Thank you so much for rowing me across, you will probably be unsung heroes in the story which is about to unfold."

Joshua and Thomas tipped their hats. Joshua proudly said, "We are willing to do anything for the sake of liberty!"

Thomas and Paul Revere echoed his sentiment, as they both enthusiastically said, "For the sake of liberty!"

Paul Revere then spoke again, with a sense of urgency, "Now, get that boat out of sight, or it will be the death of both of you."

Thomas and Joshua responded, "Yes, Sir!"

Though they were very tired, Joshua and Thomas quickly pushed off from shore and rowed away. Paul Revere quickly headed towards Deacon John Larkin.

Deacon Larkin extended his hand. As they warmly shook hands he said, "Paul Revere! I am glad you made it."

Paul Revere responded enthusiastically, "Deacon John Larkin! I am so glad to see you too."

Deacon Larkin's tone quickly changed to one of concern, "Paul, there are more sentries and patrols out tonight, than I have seen in weeks."

Paul Revere agreed with his concern, yet said with confidence, "John, that is because, the time has come."

He looked more intently at Deacon Larkin, "We received definite word from sources close to General Gage. The Regulars are heading out in force, in the morning, to try to arrest Samuel Adams and John Hancock at Lexington and to confiscate our muskets and cannons at Concord."

Deacon Larkin apprehensively said, "I am sure they would love to capture the leaders of the Sons of Liberty. That would be a serious blow to our cause."

He paused to ponder the severity of the situation, then said, "What would we do without Adams and Hancock?"

Paul Revere put his hand on Deacon Larkin's shoulder as he spoke with reassurance. "John, I do not think they realize how many of us there are."

Deacon Larkin responded a bit hesitantly, "Paul, I hope there are more of us, than even we think."

"We shall see," Paul Revere said, with hopeful optimism.

Deacon Larkin then turned toward the horse he brought with him and offered the reins to Paul Revere. "I have this horse all saddled and ready for you, just as you requested."

Paul Revere took the reins and looked at the horse. He was obviously pleased. He smiled as he said, "Excellent!

Paul Revere continued to speak, "William Dawes set out earlier on his horse, across Boston Neck for Lexington. I must also head to Lexington. We are expecting opposition along the way. With God's help, by taking two different routes, one of us is sure to make it."

Deacon Larkin helped steady the horse as Paul Revere

stepped up and sat in the saddle. He then spoke, "The other riders have been ready for days to head out and summon the Militia from surrounding towns and villages. We have been waiting for your arrival and for news to see if the Regulars would be coming by land or sea."

Larkin paused and pointed towards the North Church. "I see the two lanterns in the North Church. So, it looks like they will be coming by sea."

Revere pointed towards the ships he safely passed in the rowboat and said, "Those ships are full of Regulars!

Larkin shook his head. He did not like the idea of ships full of Regulars, but firmly said, "I will let the other riders know the Regulars are coming by sea, and they will ride and let the others know the time has come to take a stand."

The horse moved about. Paul Revere pulled on the reins and spoke with a sense of urgency, "I must be on my way to call out the Militia and to warn Adams and Hancock!"

He then quickly and purposefully rode off on his mission and Deacon Larkin shouted, "God speed!"

Paul Revere galloped off down the road. He quickly came to the first house where a man was carrying a load of firewood. Paul Revere stopped for a moment and shouted, "The Regulars are coming! The Regulars are coming!"

The man was startled. He stopped and stared at Paul Revere, half in disbelief.

The man's wife heard the commotion. She came to the door and stood and yelled to her husband as Revere rode off, "William!"

William dropped the wood he was carrying and ran

towards his wife, yelling as he went by her into the house, "I have to get my musket!"

William's wife stared down the road as Paul Revere rode on. In a few moments William ran back out of the house with his musket in one hand and his frock coat in the other. He kissed his wife as he ran off.

Paul Revere continued riding past other houses. He paused briefly and shouted, "The Regulars are coming! The Regulars are coming!"

Men came out of their homes carrying their muskets. They were followed by their families, who sent them off in the direction Paul Revere rode.

Paul Revere rode on issuing the call to arms, "The Regulars are coming! The Regulars are coming!"

Paul Revere's Ride

Engraving by Charles Green Bush (1842-1909).
New York Public Library

Chapter 2

War Begins

Lexington
April 19, 1775 – Early Wednesday Morning

It was about one-thirty in the morning, on April 19, 1775, when Paul Revere and William Dawes rode into in Lexington, Massachusetts, fourteen miles northwest of Boston. They gave the dreaded news that the Regulars were approaching.

A messenger called upon Captain John Parker, head of the Lexington Training Band. Captain Parker previously served under British officers in Rogers Rangers during the French and Indian War. He was now head of the Lexington Training Band, the local Militia. Now his task was to oppose the very army he once served.

After getting the message, Captain Parker ordered the ringing of the bell to summon the Militia. The quiet of the evening was pierced. All around town, men responded. They rose from their beds, grabbed their muskets, and quickly joined Parker on the town green.

Hearts were beating like drums in anticipation of what was about to take place. Everyone nervously waited for the arrival of the British Regulars. They were told to stay in formation and let the Regulars pass by without a confrontation. The tension was so thick it filled the air.

Some eight hundred British Regulars, Marines, and Grenadiers were approaching but no one had any idea how many of them were heading to Lexington.

Scouts were sent to determine how long it would be until the Regulars arrived. When the scouts returned they told Captain Parker the Regulars were a few hours away. He allowed some of the men to go back to their homes to get some rest and wait for further word. Some remained and went to John Buckman's tavern. They waited restlessly.

At about four-fifteen in the morning, Thaddeus Bowman, one of the scouts, returned after he spotted the British Regulars approaching on the road from Boston. Captain Parker sounded the alarm again and had the drummer play the call for the Militia to assemble.

Men grabbed their muskets and poured out of the tavern and onto the green. Some ran to summon those who returned to their homes. As quickly as they could, all the men in the Lexington Training Band came with haste to the town green. Captain Parker had them assemble on the right side of the town green, parallel to the road.

British Light Infantry from the 4th, 5th and 10th Regiments, split off from the main body of Regulars and were proceeding swiftly down the road, toward Lexington, while the rest of the force headed to Concord. The troops bound for Lexington were led by forty-four-year-old British Marine Lieutenant Jesse Adair, riding boldly on horseback.

Lieutenant Adair and his men made the long all-night march from Cambridge to Lexington. Rain from the two previous days made the roads muddy, causing streams to run high, making the march more difficult. They were thankful when the rain ended late the previous day. Now after hours of marching through a cold chilly night, morning finally arrived. When the warm sun rose, it was a welcome relief.

Lieutenant Adair was coming to apprehend Samuel Adams and John Hancock. If those two rabble rousers could be apprehended and silenced, then the obnoxious, ungrateful Sons of Liberty would be neutralized, and people would once again see subservience and obedience to the Crown and Parliament were best for everyone.

Adair intended to swiftly carry out his task. He was angry with how the people in Boston mistreated him and his men. How dare those, who were chosen to act as their hosts, treat them so uncourteously! His men were cursed at and even spit upon by ungrateful malcontents. He and his men were anxious for an opportunity to put an end to this annoying conflict. Some of them hoped they would meet resistance as they marched. They relished the idea of finally being able to physically strike back at the rabble.

The Local Militia was more prepared for armed conflict than the Regulars realized. For decades, each town had its own Militia, which drilled regularly to defend their town from danger. If called to action, they would answer first to their town, then to their colony and finally to the Crown. After recent disparaging events, very few were willing to answer to the Crown.

Though all the members of the Lexington Training Band trained regularly, and knew the drill, most of them had never been in a battle, nor ever fired a musket at another person in a conflict. The ones who had been in battle, and had experience firing at other men, had not done so since the war with the French and Indians. That war ended twelve years ago. Now the army, which they once fought alongside with, were sent to oppose them. That gave them a strange uncomfortable feeling.

Now, some seventy men nervously waited with Captain Parker, on one side of the Lexington town green, with muskets in hand.

Parker looked intently across the bridge, and down the road, straining to see if he could detect any movement. Finally, the unwelcomed moment he anticipated arrived. The dark reality of the situation gripped Captain Parker's heart when he saw a large force of Regulars coming down the road, led by a British officer on horseback.

Captain Parker quickly turned to his men and shouted, "Here they come! Form a line!"

The men quickly formed a line, not behind the stone fence, which lay behind them but on the town green, with no cover, parallel to the road where the British Regular's would soon arrive. They lined up that way, so they would not block the Regulars from passing. Parker hoped the Crown was making an intimidating show of strength and would pass through, without any confrontation.

Once Parker's men formed a line, he did the proper

thing and prepared his men for a possible armed confrontation, yelling out the command, "Prime and load!"

Each man quickly shifted his musket to his left hand and with his right hand, grabbed a cartridge from his pouch. As fast as he could, each one bit off the end of the cartridge and primed the pan of his musket with some black powder. Some were so anxious their hands shook, and they spilled some powder on the ground. They nervously continued the loading sequence.

Once their muskets were primed, they cast them about and put the rest of the cartridge down their barrels. They quickly withdraw their rammers and rammed the charges down tightly, then returned their rammers, and stood ready and loaded, with their muskets held in front of their faces.

British Lieutenant Adair arrived on horseback with the infantry behind him. He and his men advanced briskly with firm resolve, until they were about thirty yards away from Captain Parker and the Militia.

Adair then pulled out his sword, held it up above his head and shouted to his men, "From column into line!"

The Regulars, who had been marching down the road in two columns, smoothly formed two rows, opposite from and parallel to the Militia. The sea of red coats, and their precision of movement, was an impressive sight and terrifying to some of the Militia.

Lieutenant Adair struck fear in the hearts of the Militia when he yelled the dreaded command, "Prime and load!"

Like a well-oiled synchronized machine, the Regulars loaded their muskets. As soon as they were loaded, they stood with their muskets held firmly in front of their faces, waiting for the command to *Fire*.

Now, both groups were loaded, facing each other. Parker's men apprehensively looked across the field at the Regulars, who clearly outnumbered them with significant fire power.

To make matters worse, Lieutenant Adair waved his sword in the air and shouted "Huzzah!" Hoping to have his men intimidate the Rebels. Immediately, his men shouted out in a frenzy, loudly echoing his call, "Huzzah! Huzzah! Huzzah!"

Captain Parker and his men were indeed intimidated but nervously held their position as the situation threatened to explode.

Then, suddenly the ground rumbled as Major John Pitcairn, Lieutenant Adair's superior officer, came riding at a gallop to the front line, waving his pistol in the air.

When the Regulars set out earlier from Cambridge for Lexington and Concord, Major Pitcairn put Lieutenant Adair in the front of the line. Adair and his men proceeded at a brisker rate than Major Pitcairn anticipated.

When Pitcairn and his men drew near to Lexington, he was troubled when he could not see Adair. He quickly rode ahead and was greatly alarmed when he saw Adair's troops in formation across from the Militia. He was concerned his Lieutenant was going to initiate a conflict.

Pitcairn rode with haste to the front of Adair's line and took command. The troops with him formed lines alongside Adair's men and enthusiastically joined the other Regulars and yelled, "Huzzah! Huzzah! Huzzah!"

Major Pitcairn waved his pistol in the air, signaling his men to stop shouting. They responded to his signal and quickly stopped. A deadly silence filled the air.

Pitcairn was angry to see the Militia defiantly loaded and standing with muskets, in the *Ready* position, across from his men. That was totally unacceptable to him.

He looked directly at Captain Parker and his men and forcefully yelled, "Throw down your arms! You damned Rebels, or you are all dead men!"

In response to Pitcairn's threatening words, some of the Militia fearfully looked at each other. They clearly wanted to run.

Captain Parker sensed their apprehension and fear. He yelled with great resolve to his men, "Stand your ground!"

His boldness and courage made those who looked ready to run a moment ago, stand firm. They held their muskets tighter and bravely faced the Regulars.

Parker yelled again to his men, "Do not fire!"

After yelling that command, he paused for a moment.

After hearing Parker's words, a look of relief came across Major Pitcairn's face. He thought he and his men successfully intimidated the Rebels into submission. He nodded his head to Lieutenant Adair with an arrogant smile.

That smile quickly disappeared when he heard Parker continue his admonition "... Unless fired upon!"

Pitcairn menacingly looked across the field at Captain Parker.

Parker steadfastly looked back at him and defiantly yelled to his men, "If they want a war, let it begin here!"

Pitcairn was outraged. He thought, *How dare these insulant, ungrateful colonists oppose the might of the King's army!*

A thick, tense hush filled the place. Each side nervously looked at the other with apprehension, and anticipation.

Suddenly, the quiet was broken, and everyone was startled as the loud blast of a single musket was heard, *Boom!* The blast echoed across the green.

Battle of Lexington, April 19, 1775

By John H. Daniels & Sons, Boston, printed 1903.
Library of Congress, Washington, D.C.

It was not clear where the shot came from. It became known as, *the shot heard round the world.*

In sworn affidavits, submitted to the Continental Congress after the battle, locals swore the first shot came from the Regulars.

That first shot did not hit anyone. It was followed by a very brief dramatic pause, but the silence was broken moments later, as a few of the Militia fearfully fired their muskets. Then, afraid that they were being fired upon by the Regulars, all the Militia fired their muskets.

One of the Regulars was hit, and Major Pitcairn's horse was struck twice.

When Lieutenant Adair saw Pitcairn's horse was hit, he yelled urgently to his men, "Make Ready! Present! Fire!"

The ground shook as the Regulars fired a thunderous volley in unison. The bullets flew across the field, striking some of the Militia causing them to fall to the ground.

After that deadly blow, Captain Parker yelled to his men, "Fall back! Take care of yourself!"

His men started to flee. Many fell back behind the stone wall scrambling for cover.

Adair struck further fear in the hearts of the Militia as he quickly yelled the dreadful command, "Fix, bayonets!"

In a swift synchronized motion, the British Regulars took out their bayonets and firmly fixed them to the end of their muskets.

Adair then gave the command, "Advance!"

The Regulars leveled their muskets and loudly yelled a long sustained, "Huzzah!" as they marched forward across the field. Their bayonets gleamed in the morning sun as they fiercely pursued the Rebels. The Regulars' advance quickly dispersed the Rebels.

The Regulars were about to enter the homes and pillage Lexington, when they heard *Assembly,* played on the drums. They quickly abandoned their pursuit and reformed their battalions.

Amazingly, in that first battle of the Revolution, only eight of the Militia were killed and ten wounded. The Regulars were emboldened because none of the Regulars were killed and only one was wounded.

Major Pitcairn ended the conflict by leading his men to Concord, to destroy the Rebel's arms. They were joined, on the way, by additional troops. When the Regulars arrived at Concord, there were more than eight hundred of them.

British Regulars Advance on Concord

By Amos Doolittle (1754-1832).
Doolittle visited battlefields and interviewed survivors.

They were confronted there with significant opposition from a force of some two hundred and fifty Militia.

The Crown Forces advanced, and the Militia quickly

withdrew, when they saw they were vastly outnumbered.

The Regulars marched into Concord and searched the town, to confiscate the Rebel's weapons. They looked diligently but were unable to find any of the supplies they expected because the warning from the riders reached the Sons of Liberty in Concord, before the Regulars arrived, enabling them to move and hide the supplies.

Once the Regulars learned the weapons and supplies they sought were not at Concord, their task was completed. They began their long march back to Boston.

It was during the return march to Boston, when the most intense fighting took place.

Many Militia, from the surrounding area, responded to the alarm, swelling the numbers of the resistance. They did not let the Regulars leave quietly. They pursued them all the way back to Boston, firing upon them from behind walls and trees.

The Regulars suffered many casualties. By the end of that first day of the war, there were ninety-five casualties among the Rebels and two hundred and seventy-three killed or wounded among the British Regulars.

Many scholars agree, the action by the British Regulars that day started the Revolutionary War.

Lieutenant Jesse Adair survived the war, but Major John Pitcairn died less than two months later at the Battle of Bunker Hill.

Larry A. Maxwell

Minutemen Fire on Retreating Regulars
Engraving 1800's.

Retreat of the British from Concord
1874 painting by Alonzo Chappel.

Chapter 3

Meet Sybil's Family
Fredericksburg, New York
April 22, 1775

It was now April 22, 1775, three days after the Battle of Lexington and Concord. News in Colonial times travelled slowly. It took a number of days for the rest of the colonies to receive the news about Lexington and Concord and to learn the Revolutionary War had begun.

Colonel Henry Ludington ran a mill and farm in Fredericksburg, Dutchess County, New York. At that time, he and his wife Abigail had seven children. Their first three children were girls. The oldest was Sybil, age fourteen; then came Rebecca, age twelve; and then Mary, who was almost ten years old. They also had four sons: Archibald, who was almost eight years old; Henry, Jr. who was age six; Derick, age four; and Tertullus, age two.

There was a lot of work to do with a big family. The fact that the Ludington's oldest son was only eight years old meant a lot of responsibility fell on their daughter Sybil, the oldest child. Henry often complimented Sybil saying, she was better than having an oldest son.

Ludington Mill in Kent (Fredericksburg) New York

This mill was built in 1776 and burned down in 1972.
Putnam County Historian's Collection, Brewster, N.Y.

Working alongside her father, Sybil became a very good horseback rider. Whenever a chore or errand involved using a horse, Sybil was the natural choice. She often took messages, to the Militia, for her father.

On that spring day, Colonel Ludington's wife, Abigail was inside the house doing some needlework, with Tertullus playing next to her. She was startled as the door to their home came flying open with a loud, *Thud!*

Sybil pushed the door open and came running inside. She was obviously excited, as she yelled, "Mother! Mother!"

Abigail stopped her needlework, looked up at Sybil and asked, "Sybil, my child, what ever has you so excited?"

Colonel Ludington entered the house right behind Sybil. Abigail saw her husband holding a notice in his hand.

Sybil quickly turned and looked at her father. She was so excited she could hardly contain herself, "Oh, Father! You must tell Mother the news!"

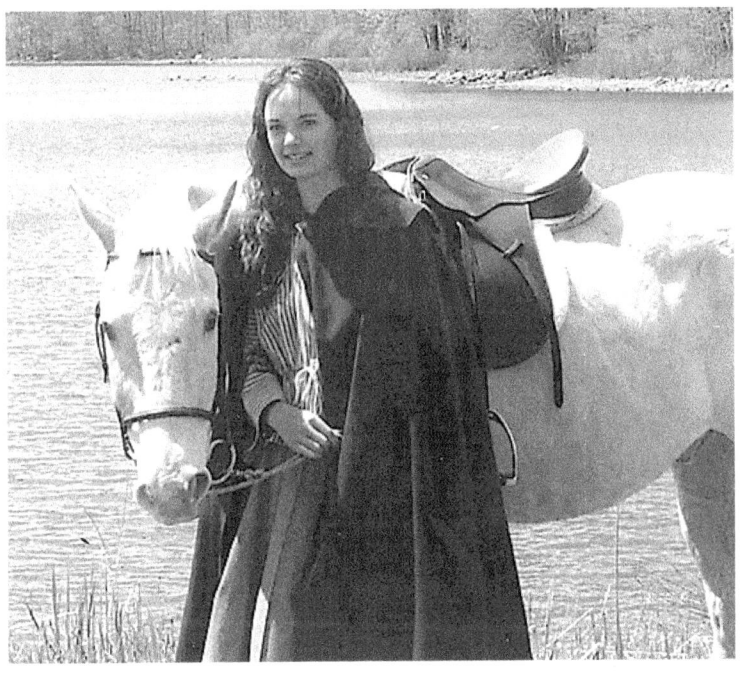

225th Anniversary of Sybil's Ride

Risa Scott portrayed Sybil Ludington for the 225th & 230th Anniversary Celebrations of Sybil's ride. She is standing next to Lake Gleneida, Carmel, N.Y., on the route Sybil Ludington rode.
Gleneida Ave., Carmel, New York – Photograph 2002

Abigail looked at her husband with a questioning expression as she curiously asked, "Henry, what is Sybil so excited about?"

Sybil's father appeared excited but was much more

composed than Sybil. He came closer to Abigail with the notice in his hand. He placed his hand on her shoulder and enthusiastically gave her the news, "Abigail, the Regulars marched on Lexington and Concord!"

Sybil could not contain her excitement. She interrupted, "And the Militia sent them running back to Boston!"

Sybil's father looked at her, smiling at her energetic enthusiasm and said, "Sybil!"

Abigail looked intently at her husband. She was very concerned about what she just heard and wanted to know more details. Inquisitively she said, "Henry?"

He was going to explain what happened, but he could see Sybil was very excited and wanted to give the details. He gave in, looked at her and said, "Go ahead Sybil."

Sybil was extremely elated her father allowed her to explain what happened. She spoke hurriedly and quite enthusiastically, "Oh Mother, Paul Revere!"

She paused and asked her mother, "You do know who Paul Revere is?"

Sybil looked at her, waiting for a response. Abigail shook her head in agreement, as she listened, while trying to take care of young Tertullus at the same time. She responded, "Yes Sybil, Paul Revere is one of the leaders of the Sons of Liberty in Boston."

Sybil could hardly contain herself. She started walking around the room as she continued speaking passionately, "Yes Mother! That Paul Revere!"

Sybil became more animated as she described what happened, "Paul Revere, and some other men, rode throughout the whole countryside, warning everyone!"

She looked at her mother and with a big smile on her face said, "Oh! Mother that is so exciting!"

Sybil's father managed to get in a few words, "Yes, Sybil. And because of those riders, Samuel Adams and John Hancock, two of the most prominent leaders of the Sons of Liberty, escaped."

Sybil interrupted. She was very animated, gesturing with her arms, as she said, "And the Militia drove the Regulars, all the way back to Boston!"

Abigail looked at her husband and responded in a positive but very concerned way, "Henry! Does this mean the war, which you said was coming, has started?"

Colonel Ludington put his hand on Abigail's shoulder then held her close to him as he said, "Yes, Abigail, it looks like war has started."

Abigail put a hand to her head in concern.

Henry continued, "The Sons of Liberty have asked all the colonies to send help to Boston."

Abigail looked up with great alarm and said, "Oh, My!"

Sybil paced about excitedly. She looked at her father and said, "Oh, Father! I wish I could have been there and been one of those riders! You know I am a good rider."

She paused, then spoke acting like she was riding, "And I, I would have ridden so hard and told everyone, The Regulars are coming! The Regulars are coming!"

Abigail looked intently at Sybil. She was flustered and could barely say anything but one word, "Sybil!"

Colonel Ludington called Sybil over to him and Abigail.

He put his other arm around Sybil and said, "Abigail, you know Sybil has always wanted to be a heroine on horseback ever since she heard how our friend Mehitable Prendergast rode eighty miles from up here all the way to New York City, in one day, to save her husband William's life, back during the Settler's Revolt."

Sybil spoke excitedly. "Oh yes, Father. I know I would make a great heroine! I can ride faster and harder and longer than any boy I know!"

Her father agreed and smiled as he looked proudly at Sybil, "Sybil, you are a wonderful daughter. And, I am sure you would make a wonderful heroine. And, it is true, I have not met many boys who can ride as good as you."

Colonel Ludington smiled as he drew Sybil closer to him. He continued speaking. "I am sure you will do a fine job when you are needed."

He got more somber as he continued speaking, "There are surely going to be dark and dangerous days ahead for us. And, I would not be surprised that one day, you may need to make such a ride, here in New York."

He looked at Sybil and proudly smiled as he said, "And you will be my special heroine!"

Sybil glowed with pride and joyfully replied, "Oh Yes, Father! That would be wonderful!"

A look of intense concern came across Abigail's face as she exclaimed, "Oh, Henry!"

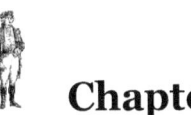

Chapter 4

A Plan to End the War

British Headquarters in New York City

March 1, 1777

Almost two years ago, the Crown Forces were humiliated at Lexington and Concord. In response to that event, a call was sent throughout the colonies for people to come help drive the British Forces back into the sea.

Hundreds of men from the surrounding colonies responded to that call. On June 17, 1775, they made a valiant stand on Breed's Hill. The battle became known as the Battle of Bunker Hill. Though the Rebels were pushed off the hill by the Crown Forces, they were emboldened by the serious damage they inflicted on the enemy.

The Continental Congress responded to the hostilities and formed an army. They appointed George Washington, from Virginia, as Commander of the Army. Soldiers from the new Continental Army came from many of the different colonies and helped the Militia surround Boston, keeping the Crown Forces under siege.

Larry A. Maxwell

1776 British Map of New York City

*Published in the London Gazette in 1776.
After the British Took Control of New York City.
Lord William Howe's Headquarters were in lower New York City.*

One year ago, in March 1776, the Crown Forces withdrew from Boston. Some people rejoiced thinking the conflict was over. George Washington knew better.

Three months after withdrawing from Boston, those who thought the conflict ended discovered they were wrong. In June 1776, just nine months ago, the Crown Forces invaded New York with the largest fleet ever to set sail from England.

In just a few months the Crown Forces overpowered the poorly equipped Rebels, occupied New York City and successfully drove the Rebels all the way across New Jersey.

It was now March 1, 1777. The British Commander General, The Lord William Howe, came up with a plan to end the war. He called some of his key officers to his headquarters in New York City to discuss his plan.

General William Erskine, Quartermaster General of the British Army, a career military officer, was walking with two of his aides to see Lord Howe. He was met by Governor William Tryon, who was also on his way to the meeting. Tryon was accompanied by two of his junior officers.

It is interesting to note, the Lord William Howe, General William Erskine, and Governor William Tryon, all had the same first name.

Before the war, Tryon served as the Royal Governor of North Carolina, then as Governor of New York. When the Rebellion started, he was deposed by the Rebels, who appointed their own governor. The Crown gave him a commission as a general in the British army. He relished the idea of ending the Rebellion.

Larry A. Maxwell

Portrait of The Lord William Howe

Portrait by Richard Purcell. Published May 10, 1778. This bears a very strong resemblance to the portraits published by Thomas Hart in 1776 of other famous Americans during the Revolution. All of Hart's portraits are considered fictitious. It is possible Hart copied Purcell's work.
On Display at the National Portrait Gallery, London

Portrait of Sir William Erskine

*Portrait by Samuel William Reynolds.
Unlike most military uniforms, which had only decorative button
holes, Erskine's uniform had working button holes.*
On display at the National Portrait Gallery, London.

Portrait of Governor William Tryon

*Some scholars believe this is not William Tryon.
The regimental coat is incorrect.*
From display in Tryon Palace in New Bern, North Carolina

When Erskine met Tryon, he touched the tip of his hat with a small bow toward Tryon and said, "Greetings Governor Tryon."

Though *General* is a respectful military title, *Governor*, was one of utmost respect, and one Tryon preferred.

Tryon replied with a subtler tip of his hat and replied, "Thank you General Erskine."

Erskine told his aides, "That will be all."

Erskine's aides nodded their heads, touched their hats in reply, and walked off together.

Tryon and Erskine continued through the camp to the headquarters with Tryon's two aides walking behind them.

"How is it with you Governor Tryon?" Erskine asked.

Tryon could not help but reply by expressing his disgust at the Rebellion, "General Erskine, I will be much better when we can put an end to this dreadful Rebellion."

General Erskine showed he understood how Governor Tryon felt, "It must be difficult, having these ungrateful Rebels reject you as their rightful governor."

Tryon nodded in agreement and continued about how much he hated the Rebels. "General Erskine, if I had my way, I would burn every Rebel's home to the ground, while I sat by smiling and drinking a cup of tea."

That reply made Erskine smile. He put his hand on Tryon's shoulder and said, "Would you like milk with your tea?"

They both smiled and continued walking.

When they came to the door of the Lord Howe's headquarters, the guards outside came to the *present* position with their muskets.

Tryon and Erskine nodded their heads at the guards, which was the proper way of saluting an enlisted man back then. Tryon dismissed his aides, then he and Erskine entered the building.

A junior officer greeted them inside, taking off his hat and bowing his head in a salute. He then led them to the room where the Lord William Howe was located.

The junior officer opened the door and stepped inside. Tryon and Erskine waited at the door.

The Lord Howe was standing at a desk looking at a map with two other officers, General James Agnew, and General Montfort Browne.

The junior officer addressed Howe, "Begging your pardon, Lord Howe."

Howe looked up and responded, "Please enter."

The junior officer motioned for Tryon and Erskine to enter the room. He then made the introductions. "Lord Howe, may I present, Governor Tryon and General Erskine."

Tryon and Erskine removed their hats and bowed their heads in a formal greeting to their superior officer.

Howe nodded his head and extended his greeting. "Welcome Governor Tryon, General Erskine."

Tryon and Erskine both reciprocated the greeting, "Lord Howe."

Howe then introduced General Agnew, "Gentlemen, you know General Agnew."

They acknowledged each other with a tip of their hats.

Howe then introduced General Browne, "May I introduce to you, General Montfort Browne, Royal Governor of the Bahamas and Commander of the new Prince of Wales Loyal American Regiment."

Browne smiled with pompous glee. He took off his hat

and bowed with a big sweep of his hand. Tryon and Erskine nodded their heads in respect, to an officer of equal rank.

Browne loved to talk and loved to meet anyone he believed might help advance his career. He said, "Gentlemen, it is a pleasure to meet both of you."

Erskine flattered Browne as he revealed his knowledge of Browne's unique accomplishment, "Governor Browne, I heard you raised the Prince of Wales Loyal American Regiment while the Rebels were holding you as their prisoner."

It was obvious Browne was pleased with Erskine's words. He gloated as he said, "Yes, that is very true. Though I was a prisoner, under circumstances quite beyond my control, I made the best of, shall I say, a bad situation."

Browne loved to speak about himself, he continued. "And, after all, I am very wise and cunning, so what better thing to do but raise a regiment to oppose the Rebels, while being their prisoner. I think that is so fitting for a man of my rank and stature."

He then paused for a moment to clarify his new title, "And, oh yes, you may call me *General Browne*, now."

Tryon and Erskine looked at each other unpleasantly surprised by Browne's attitude and remarks.

Tryon was Governor of New York until the Rebels took over and deposed him. Though he was commissioned a *General*, he preferred the title, *Governor*. On the other hand, Browne, who was still a Governor, thought his military title was more prestigious especially during a time of war, so he preferred people called him, *General*.

Tryon and Erskine both feigned a smile and politely replied, "General Browne."

Howe spoke, moving from pleasantries to business. "Governor Tryon, General Erskine, please come join us."

Tryon and Erskine immediately proceeded to the table.

Howe got right to business. He pointed at the map on the table, "I believe the best way we can end this conflict, is to divide the Rebels right here, along the Hudson River."

As the others looked at the map Browne interrupted pompously with a big smile and said, "Their own Liberty Song says, *by uniting we stand, by dividing we fall.*"

Tryon and Erskine looked at each other, they were clearly not impressed by Browne's remark.

Howe continued speaking as he pointed at the map, "It is time to divide the troublemakers in New England, and that blasted rabble on the east side of the Hudson River, from the rest of the Rebels on the other side of the Hudson."

He smiled and continued, "With their forces divided, they will not be able to last for long."

Erskine was an experienced officer. He saw the logic in Howe's plan and responded with approval, "Lord Howe, that sounds like a truly excellent idea!"

Howe continued, "General Browne has secured some very important information, information I believe will help us reach our objective and help bring an end to this infernal Rebellion."

Tryon responded with passionate anger when he heard the word, *Rebellion*. He squeezed his fist as he said, "I would love to crush this Rebellion, as soon as possible!"

Browne patted Tryon on the shoulder.

Tryon looked at Browne showing he was uncomfortable with that physical contact from him.

Browne then spoke, calling him *General Tryon,* because of his personal affection for military titles, "I could not agree with you more General Tryon. I too would love to end this insidious Rebellion as soon as possible."

Browne always had more to say, "It is simply too cold here in New York. And I do not know how anyone in their right mind can live here. I would really like to get this whole affair over with, so I can go back to my old post in Bermuda."

Tryon and Erskine were both uncomfortable with Browne's arrogant attitude. They looked at each other, rolling their eyes.

Howe addressed Browne, "General Browne, perhaps we can get you back to Bermuda as soon as our task is completed."

Howe then motioned to a man who had been seated quietly off to the side with a drink in his hand, and said to Browne, "Would you please introduce your guest?

A big pompous look came across Browne's face as he introduced his guest, "Gentlemen, may I introduce to you the honorable Dr. Jonathan Prosser from Fredericksburg, New York. Dr. Prosser is a very loyal subject of the Crown, and one of my most trusted informants."

The generals nodded their heads acknowledging him.

Prosser stood and lifted his cup to the men, making a small bow, "Gentlemen, the honor is all mine."

Howe spoke, "Dr. Prosser, come over here and show my generals what you showed General Browne and I earlier."

Prosser put down his drink and came over to the table.

Browne spoke with that pompous look on his face, "Yes, Dr. Prosser, please tell these men what you learned for us."

Prosser leaned forward and pointed to the map as he spoke, "I am sure you are aware of the Rebel Supply Depot, over here at Fishkill."

Van Wyck Homestead – Fishkill Supply Depot

*Located on Route 9 in Fishkill, New York.
During the Revolutionary War, the Van Wyck Homestead was the headquarters for the Continental Army's Fishkill Supply Depot.
Photograph by Larry A. Maxwell - 2017*

Tryon nodded in an almost annoyed manner, indicating he already knew that information. "Yes, I know, Fishkill very well. It is very close to the Hudson River. And is a very important Rebel Supply Depot."

He then added, "And it is very well defended."

Browne had an arrogant smile on his face the whole time. He thought he knew something Tryon did not know.

Unlike Tryon, who as governor of New York was very familiar with the area, Erskine was from Scotland and was not familiar. He listened and looked intently at the map.

Prosser continued speaking as he pointed to the map, "I am not sure if you are aware of this, but the Rebels have another supply depot."

He pointed to another place on the map as he said, "Over here in Danbury, Connecticut."

Tryon nodded in agreement, as he dismissively said, "Yes, I am familiar with that depot in Danbury, it is small and insignificant."

That response made Browne smile. He was elated he knew something Tryon did not know. He arrogantly said, "That is exactly what they want you to think!"

Tryon got a puzzled look on his face.

Browne smiled as he eagerly encouraged Prosser to continue, "Dr. Prosser, tell them what you discovered."

Prosser continued, "The Rebels know you know Fishkill is their main supply depot, and that you know Danbury is insignificant."

He then looked up with an arrogant smile on his face as he pointed at the map and continued, "So, assuming you would ignore Danbury, they moved a very large amount of supplies from Fishkill to Danbury."

Browne was elated as he continued, "And, they have no idea we know this!"

Tryon and Erskine came to dislike Browne in this brief encounter because of his arrogant pompous attitude, but both nodded in approval at what they could see was important information, which he helped provide.

Howe stepped forward and said, "Gentlemen, as I said earlier, if we are going to end this Rebellion then we must take control of the Hudson River."

He added firmly, "To take control of the Hudson we must cut off the Rebel's supplies."

Tryon agreed but expressed a concern, "I agree that striking the Rebel's supplies is an excellent idea but what about Henry Ludington and the Dutchess County Militia?"

Colonel Henry Ludington, Sybil's father, and his Militia were not far from Fishkill and proved to be an annoying obstacle to Tryon and his Crown Forces.

Tryon pointed to the map and said, "They are situated here, between Fishkill and Danbury."

He had an angry look on his face as he said, "They have been a terrible thorn in our flesh!"

Howe responded to Tryon with a question. "Ludington was one of your officers, was he not?"

Tryon responded, disappointed that fact was brought up. "Yes, I appointed him myself, but then he lost his mind and embraced the Rebel cause."

Browne further alienated Tryon, interjecting in his annoying arrogant way, "If I were in charge of the other Loyalist Regiments in this area, we would have apprehended that Ludington and crushed his Militia, a long time ago!"

Tryon gave Browne a disapproving glare.

Howe continued addressing Tryon, "Governor Tryon, you did place a bounty on Ludington's head, did you not?"

Tryon passionately replied, "Yes, I did, I offered three hundred guineas to anyone who captures that scoundrel, dead or alive!"

The mention of that reward made Prosser's eyes light up with greed. He had an affection for financial gain. He asked, "Did you say you are offering a bounty of three hundred guineas for the capture of Colonel Ludington?"

Tryon nodded affirmatively and said, "Yes, I did, three hundred guineas, dead or alive!

Prosser rubbed his hands together at the idea of possibly getting that reward. He spoke, almost astonished at the size of the bounty, "That is almost a whole year's wages!"

Tryon agreed enthusiastically with Prosser, showing his desire to capture Ludington, "Yes, it is!"

He continued, "And it will be worth every guinea to get that blasted Ludington off our backs."

Tryon paused and then pointed at both places on the map as he said, "If we had him out of our way we could easily take both Fishkill and Danbury!"

There was an evil glee in Prosser's eye as he spoke, "For three hundred guineas, I think I can assure you a new guest on one of your prison ships."

Tryon was pleased at Prosser's response, "I would be delighted to give you the three hundred guineas, if you deliver that scoundrel Ludington to me!"

Prosser was anxious to set about his evil deed. He asked

to be excused, "If my services are no longer required here, I would like to get to work on my next task, capturing the Rebel, Colonel Henry Ludington!"

Howe looked at Prosser and said, "Time is of the essence. We must attack at least one of those Rebel Supply Depots within the next month. If you can apprehend Ludington, it will make our job much easier."

Browne smiled as he added, "And it will make your pocket a lot fuller!"

Prosser was happy to pursue his new task. He spoke again as he started to leave, "Yes, Sir! I will do my best!"

He then offered the salutation, "Long live the King!"

The others responded, "Long live the King!"

Browne escorted Prosser to the door, speaking to him on the way, "Thank you Dr. Prosser, you have been quite helpful, and I know you are going to be even more helpful."

Browne smiled, then said, "Perhaps you could do two tasks at the same time."

He exhorted Prosser, "Why not gather your friends, capture that Rebel Ludington, bring him here and join my regiment at the same time?"

He placed his hand on Prosser's shoulder as he said, "I could use more officers like you."

Prosser was delighted at the offer and replied, "That sounds like a very good idea General Browne."

He grabbed the edge of his hat, nodded his head in a salute, and then exited.

Browne went back to the table to join the other officers.

Howe continued, "Gentlemen, I have given much

thought to what General Browne and Dr. Prosser have shown us."

He spoke with a strong positive attitude as he pointed to the map, "I did not want to be too specific with Dr. Prosser here, but I believe, with all this information before us, the next step to ending this Rebellion is to strike them right here, at Danbury.

Tryon looked to Howe and asked for clarification, "That sounds like a very good idea. What do you have in mind?"

Howe turned to Browne, "General Browne, tell them what we discussed."

Browne was gleaming with pride, "Danbury is about twenty-five miles north of the coastal town of Norwalk."

He pointed to the map identifying places as he spoke, "There is only a small contingent of Continentals and Militia on guard at Danbury. If we land here at Compo Beach in Norwalk, we could march to Danbury in one day."

He smiled as he said, "We then take, or destroy their supplies, and return to the beach and our ships before the Rebels know what hit them."

Erskine interrupted in agreement, "I like that plan. The Rebels would be unaware and unprepared for a strike like that. They would never even consider the fact we would march that far inland for an attack."

Howe continued, "General Browne has many subjects loyal to the Crown between Norwalk and Danbury, so it presents a fairly easy target."

Browne spoke with pompous assurance, "My Loyalists know that country well, and with the help of me and my men, we will be able to get those supplies out of the hands of the Rebel scum and deliver them safely back into the hands of our King!"

They all laughed.

Howe pointed to the map and said, "If we can cut off those supplies, here in Danbury, then we will drive a wedge between New England and the rest of the colonies."

He paused and then emphatically said, "And resistance will crumble!"

Tryon responded enthusiastically, "Lord Howe, I do believe that will work!"

Howe placed his hand upon Tryon's shoulder. He paused, then said, "Governor Tryon, I know you deserve vindication, especially since the Rebels stopped recognizing you are their lawful governor over New York."

Browne agreed with Lord Howe's comment. He was indignant the Rebels would dishonor another British official. He exclaimed, "Indeed!"

Howe continued addressing Tryon, "Yes, and so Governor Tryon, I am putting you in charge of the attack on the Rebel Supply Depot at Danbury."

Browne was dumfounded. He looked extremely offended. He thought he would be leading the attack. He said, "But ... I ..."

Tryon looked at Browne with a smile, then turned and looked at Lord Howe as he responded, "Sir, I would be honored."

Chapter 5

Enoch Crosby the Spy
Fredericksburg, New York
March 2, 1777

It was now March 2, 1777, a cold, chilly winter day in the Hudson Valley. People were gathered in a log church in Fredericksburg, New York. A song just finished, indicating the church service was ending.

A few moments later the minister opened the door. Sybil Ludington and her sister Rebecca came outside quickly outside followed by Jesse Ganong. The three of them headed off together toward an old tree.

Jacob Angevine and his son Joseph exited the church. Jacob was a freed slave who earned his freedom, and freedom for his family when he nearly died saving the life of his former owner, during the French and Indian War,. He lost partial use of his left leg from the injuries he sustained. He told everyone he would rather walk with a limp as a free man than be a healthy slave.

There were many free slaves in Dutchess County but there were still many who sadly, were still owned by others.

Shortly after returning from the war Jacob's joy turned

to sorrow when his wife Sarah, and his daughter Elizabeth, were taken ill with the cholera. Those were dark days, but Jacob found hope and strength in his faith and from friends like the Ludingtons. Abigail Ludington helped take care of Sarah and Elizabeth right up to the end.

Jacob joined Colonel Ludington's Militia but because of his bad leg he was not able to go off to battle. Each time the Militia went off to war, Jacob stayed behind helping the Ludington's and took extra turns patrolling around town.

Colonial Log Church

The Ludingtons attended a church similar to this.
National Register of Historic Places

Jacob taught his son the importance of freedom and the necessity of being willing to fight for it. He was very proud when Joseph joined the Militia.

As they came out of the church, Jacob stopped for a

moment and spoke to his son, "Joseph, my son, I am very proud of the way you joined the Militia and are helping to fight for our liberty and freedom."

Jacob stopped speaking for a moment. He looked up toward Heaven, nodded his head, and smiled as he looked back at Jacob and said, "Your mother would have been very proud of you too."

Joseph was glad he made his father proud. He looked at his father and said, "Thank you father. I will never forget the way you served this country and how you almost died to win our freedom."

Joseph paused, looked up toward Heaven for a moment, then back at his father, and continued, "And I think of Mother and Elizabeth often. I know one day we will all be together again."

Then with resolve he said, "And until then, I will never take freedom for granted!"

Joseph then noticed Sybil, Rebecca, and Jesse, near one of the trees. He stared in their direction with a longing look.

Jacob noticed how Sybil and her friends caught his son's attention. He smiled, then faked a cough as he leaned on his walking stick and weakly spoke, "I imagine you would like to leave your crippled old man and go over to your friends."

Joseph turned around to make sure his father was okay. He saw the smile on his father's face which made him frown, then he smiled when he realized his father was teasing.

Jacob waved his walking stick, pointed toward Sybil and the others as he said, "Get yourself over there."

Joseph cheerfully replied, "Yes father!" He started to

run towards the others, then stopped a moment and said, "I will be home in a little while!"

The rest of the Ludington children, as well as a few other children, exited the church and headed off to play.

Sybil was now sixteen years old, Rebecca was fourteen. Joseph and Jesse were both seventeen. The boys were both friends with Sybil and Rebecca. They both had an interest in being more than just friends with Sybil. She also liked the idea of being more than friends with them, she just did not know which one she liked better. She also liked to tease them, a trait she picked up from her father.

Joseph joined Sybil, Rebecca, and Jesse as they talked and played near one of the trees. It was obvious Joseph was excited about being in the Militia. Jesse wanted to join the Militia, but his father would not allow him.

Sybil picked up a stick and spoke as she walked around the tree, "So, what did you think about the preacher's sermon about Queen Esther today?"

Jesse's expression changed to one of anger as he answered indignantly. "Whenever I hear anyone say the word *King* or *Queen,* it reminds me of King George, and I get so angry I cannot think of anything else except of the injustice that *King* has put us through!"

Joseph stood next to Jesse. He also got an angry look on his face and agreed with Jesse, "I feel the same way!"

Sybil stomped her feet with disappointment, looked at the boys and said, "Is that all you can think about?!"

Jesse smiled, then spoke as he looked at Sybil, "No, Sybil, sometimes I think about a pretty girl I know, who loves to ride horses."

Sybil and Rebecca smiled and giggled.

Joseph wanted Sybil to know he was interested in her too, he quickly interjected, "Me too!"

Jesse continued, sarcastically, "Yes, I do wish I could see that girl come back around these parts sometime."

Rebecca giggled, while Sybil stuck out her tongue at Jesse.

Sybil got back to what she was saying before Jesse reacted. "Well, I did listen to the preacher today and I love the story of Esther. She was a real heroine! She was a woman who made a difficult decision and helped save her people just like I will do one day!"

Joseph agreed, "Oh, and I am sure you would be a lovely heroine!"

Then he smiled and in jest, bowed to Sybil and said, "Queen Sybil!"

Jesse laughed and joined in the fun, "Ah, but you know what we do to royalty around here?"

Joseph grabbed a long stick from the ground. He found another long one and threw it to Jesse.

Jesse pointed the stick at Sybil and said, "We shoot them!"

Joseph and Jesse pretended the sticks were muskets and shot at Sybil and Rebecca. Rebecca smiled and ducked. Sybil ducked, then shook her head and laughed.

Sybil then acted like she was riding her horse, as she said, "There will be no shooting royalty until the heroine rides and calls out the Militia!"

Jesse and Joseph laughed and fell in like Militia, holding the sticks at their shoulders, as though they were muskets. Rebecca lined up next to them.

Jesse got a big smile on his face, "Yes, Miss Revere!"

As Sybil, Rebecca, Joseph, and Jesse continued to laugh and play, Henry and Abigail Ludington, Sybil's parents, came out of church followed by John and Mary Ganong, Jesse's parents.

The Ganongs had mixed loyalties. They were business people who had dealings with others who were favorable to the Crown. They did not consider themselves Loyalists yet wished the Revolution would end and things would go back to the way they were before the conflict started.

John Ganong tipped his hat, greeting Henry and his wife Abigail, "Greetings, Colonel Ludington, Mrs. Ludington."

Abigail gave a small curtsey. Henry responded with a sign of respect, taking his hat off, "Greetings John." He bowed slightly to Mrs. Ganong as he greeted her, "Mary."

John had something troubling him. He quickly got down to business. With a serious look of concern on his face, he said, "Colonel Ludington, I heard Governor Tyron placed a bounty on your head!"

Henry responded, appearing serious but being somewhat sarcastic. He said, "Yes, John I did hear that. I wonder what took him so long?"

John was not amused at Henry's comments. He sternly replied, "Henry!"

Henry acted like he was apologetic, but was not, "Sorry John. And did you say Governor Tryon? May I remind you, he is now the *former Governor*."

John was upset with Henry's comments, "But Henry! Governor Tryon is a general in the British Army, and he has the whole weight of the Crown behind him!"

Henry acted a little penitent. "That is true." Then he continued in jest, "So John, were you thinking of collecting the bounty? I am sure three hundred guineas would be a nice prize for you to collect!"

John was offended. He responded, "Henry! You know I would not do that!"

Henry gave John a friendly slap on the back, then got a little more serious and said, "Yes, I know, John, after all you and I did fight side-by-side in the French and Indian War."

That sparked another comment from John, "Yes, we did! But we fought as loyal subjects of the Crown! Against the French and the Indians!"

Henry prodded John somewhat sarcastically, "John, are you trying to persuade me to switch sides? Do you want me to become a Tory?"

John skirted around Henry's question. He did not consider himself a Loyalist but was very concerned with the actions of Henry's friends in the Continental Congress.

He said, "Henry, please be serious. You know I signed the Oath of Allegiance, just like you. But I am concerned! I am concerned where this is going! It was one thing to want representation, but now! Now, we have the whole British army here!"

John was clearly concerned for their future. "Remember what they did to New York City?"

He was alluding to the fact the British Forces occupied New York City, arrested those they considered Rebels, confiscated their homes, and even burned their churches. He was fearful the same thing may happen where they were.

John continued, "And now, the Continental Congress has sent Benjamin Franklin to France, seeking to form an alliance with the very people you and I fought against! "

Henry smiled at the part about France, "That is true. Franklin is in France negotiating with our old enemy. Could you imagine if he could get the French to join us? The French on our side? Now that could make a big difference."

Henry's words upset John, "For God's sake Henry! It seems like everything is getting out of hand! I have always held out hope that somehow we could peacefully reconcile our differences with the Crown, but now!"

He paused briefly to gather his thoughts, then continued, "Now, they have placed a reward of three hundred guineas on your head! And, they say the reward is dead or alive! I fear for you and your family! And for mine! And for where all this is headed!"

As they were speaking, Enoch Crosby rode up. Crosby's clothing revealed he was a modestly successful businessman. He rode slowly past Sybil, Rebecca, Jesse, and Joseph. He tipped his hat as he passed by the children.

Joseph looked at Crosby with a sneer, then spoke to the others with disgust, "Oh! I cannot stand that man!"

Jesse asked, "Who is that?"

Sybil answered in a very matter of fact way, "That is Enoch Crosby."

Joseph wanted to make sure Jesse knew Crosby was a bad person, so he said, "He is one of those awful people with Tory sympathies!"

Portrait of Enoch Crosby When Older
By Samuel Lovett Waldo & William Jewett, 1830.
Smithsonian National Portrait Gallery

An angry look came across Jesse's face as he said, "You mean like my father?"

Joseph was concerned he offended Jesse. He said, "Sorry Jesse, I did not mean to offend you."

Jesse reassured Joseph he was not offended at Joseph

but at Crosby and all the Loyalists and their sympathizers.

He said, "Joseph, you did not offend me. It is those Tories, and people who try to sit on the fence, like my father, who offend me!"

He was clearly angry as he said, "And, if that Enoch Crosby is one of them, then this is what I think of him." Jesse then spit on the ground.

Sybil was concerned. She tried to defuse the situation. She knew Crosby was not a Loyalist. She knew he was a spy for the Continentals, but could not say that, so she changed the subject and said, "He sure does have a nice horse!"

Joseph looked at her angrily and said, "Sybil! Is that all you think about? Horses?"

Sybil smiled back in a flirting manner as she spoke teasing him, "What else is there to think about? Boys?"

She then pushed her way past Joseph and Jesse. She and Rebecca laughed as they walked away. The boys smiled and shook their heads.

Enoch Crosby dismounted and walked toward Colonel Henry and Abigail Ludington, who were still talking with John and Mary Ganong.

As Crosby came closer, Henry extended a welcome to him, "Greetings Enoch!"

John Ganong believed Crosby was sympathetic with him. He warmly welcomed him, "Greetings, Mr. Crosby! It is so nice to see someone with some good sense here."

Crosby responded to them politely, nodding and bowing, "And greetings to you, John, Colonel Ludington and your lovely wives."

The Ladies smiled and did a small curtsey in response.

Crosby had something important on his mind. He looked at the others and said, "Would you please excuse me, I need to speak with Henry for a moment."

John was hoping Crosby would try to convince Henry to rethink things and see things his way. He said, "Enoch, see if you can talk some sense into him."

Knowing John's divided loyalties, Crosby smiled, acting like they were on the same side and said, "I shall, John."

As Crosby and Henry stepped aside to talk, John said, "Have a good day!"

As John and Mary left, Abigail Ludington went with them speaking to Mary.

Crosby and Henry Ludington stepped aside and spoke in confidence, "Enoch, it must be hard having everyone think you have Loyalist sympathies."

Crosby nodded in agreement but explained his position, "Yes, Henry. Sometimes it is hard being misunderstood, but we need eyes and ears in the enemy camp and that role has fallen upon me. Let them think of me what they will, I am willing to be misunderstood for the sake of liberty."

Henry nodded that he understood. He then looked around making sure no one else was listening and then said, "So, I assume you have some news for me?"

Enoch showed a great amount of concern on his face as he said, "Yes, Henry, and it is not good news."

Crosby leaned closer and said, "Governor Tryon has put a bounty of three hundred guineas on your head."

Henry already knew that news, so he was not affected

the way Crosby expected. In a calm, matter of fact way, he said, "John and I were just discussing that."

Crosby was surprised. He asked, "You already heard?"

Henry nodded his head in acknowledgement of the fact, then said, "Yes, Enoch, that kind of news travels fast!"

Crosby showed his extreme concern as he emphasized the significance of the bounty, "Henry, a bounty of three hundred guineas! Dead or alive! That is almost a whole year's wages!"

Henry smiled and sarcastically said, "I am honored!"

Crosby exclaimed, "Henry!" He was concerned Henry did not understand the significance of such a large bounty.

Having just come out of church, Henry made a Biblical parallel to Judas betraying Jesus, "I thought the bounty would have been for thirty pieces of silver!"

Crosby urged concern. He built on the Biblical parallel Henry made, "Henry, you are going to have to be very careful. I know some Judases in these parts who would gladly have betrayed you for thirty pieces of silver, but now for three hundred guineas! I think now they will surely seek to collect that reward."

Henry showed he understood and appreciated Crosby's concern, "Yes, Enoch, that is true. I will be on my guard."

Henry smiled and spoke again, flattered the bounty was so high, "Three hundred guineas!"

Enoch punched Henry knowing he was being sarcastic.

Chapter 6

The Loyalists Plot
March 4, 1777

After learning of the large bounty on Colonel Henry Ludington's head, Dr. Jonathan Prosser was determined he would find a way to collect that reward and earn himself a commission as an officer in General Montfort Browne's Loyalist Regiment. He imagined he would receive additional benefits if he did that and was on the Crown's side when they put down the Rebellion.

Dr. Prosser went back to Dutchess County as fast as he could. He knew he needed help to successfully carry out his nefarious plan. It would have been easier to recruit Loyalists if he was in Westchester County, which was closer to British occupied New York City. There were many more Loyalists down there. Recruiting help in Dutchess County was going to be more difficult. There were not as many Loyalists up there. Colonel Ludington was a member of the Committee of Safety in Dutchess County and that committee rounded up most of the Loyalists and convinced the others to sign an Oath of Loyalty to the Rebel cause.

Drumming Out of Town

*18th Century Engraving.
Loyalist were arrested or drummed out of many towns.*

Dr. Prosser realized there were others like him who feigned allegiance to the Rebel cause because they were too far away to receive help from the Crown and did not want to be imprisoned for refusing to sign the oath. He believed some would rather have the Crown, rather than the Rebels in control. He just had to locate those like-minded people.

He knew some, who were not true Loyalists, could be convinced to side with him if they were provided sufficient financial incentive such as a share in the bounty or the chance of acquiring their neighbor's land.

Prosser knew he had to act quickly, so he was very persistent enlisting help. He also knew he could be arrested so he was very careful. He finally arranged a meeting at a tavern with David Chase and Roger Cutler, two men he knew were true Loyalists but managed to evade detection.

When the three of them met they sat in the far corner of

the tavern. They tried to make sure no one else could overhear them. When Prosser felt it was safe, he spoke.

"I am sick of these Rebels!" he said. "This revolution of theirs has made life extremely difficult for us loyal subjects of the Crown!"

Chase and Cutler muttered in agreement, "Here, here!"

Prosser clearly showed his disgust for the Rebels as he said, "I have seen those disloyal scoundrels throw too many people in jail and piously say it is in the name of liberty!"

He spit on the ground and said, "Liberty! All they want is the liberty to ignore our gracious King and liberty to take away our land and our homes!"

That stirred up Cutler, who said, "If I had my way, they would all be hung!"

Chase was inspired to join in, expressing his contempt for the Rebels, "Dr. Prosser, I do not see why the King does not send his forces up here and crush them once and for all."

Prosser nodded his head in agreement, then leaned in close and said, "I have some news I know you will like."

He got a sinister smile on his face as he looked at each of them and said, "David, Roger, the Crown Forces have a plan to come up here and crush the Rebels!"

Chase was surprised by what Prosser said. He asked inquisitively, "Really?"

"Yes, David," Prosser said, affirming what he said.

Prosser looked around again to make sure no one else was listening, then quietly said, "They plan to attack the Rebel depots and destroy their supplies."

With a look of surprise, Cutler asked, "Dr. Prosser, are

you sure?"

Prosser smiled pridefully, adding validity to his words, "Yes, Roger, I am quite sure. I personally brought the information about the Rebel Supply Depot at Danbury to General Browne, of the Loyal American Regiment."

He paused, then with arrogant glee said, "And he brought me before the Lord William Howe!"

Cutler and Chase looked at each other with their mouths open in awe. They never met anyone who had personal contact with a British officer before and were very impressed to learn Dr. Prosser personally met The Lord Howe, Commander General of the British Forces.

Prosser continued with a big grin on his face, "The Lord Howe then summoned Governor Tryon, General Agnew and General Erskine and had me tell all of them about Danbury. They discussed both the Fishkill and the Danbury supply depots and said they must launch an attack."

Cutler and Chase were very pleased to hear this. Cutler was so excited to hear that. He said, "That is great news!"

Prosser continued to speak with a big arrogant smile on his face. "Roger, it gets even better. That attack will take place, within the month!"

Cutler and Chase were so pleased they could hardly contain themselves. They eagerly took another drink from their mugs.

"The day has finally come," Prosser continued. "General Browne wants us to gather as many men as we can and wants us to come to New York to join his Loyalist Regiment, so we can help them defeat the Rebels and reclaim our country!"

This is better than either Cutler or Chase expected.

Prosser prodded them, "Are you with me?"

Cutler and Chase looked at each other, then at Prosser, then each of them gleefully and loudly said, "Yes!"

Inside a Colonial Tavern

Published by Carrington Bowles, 1766-1799.

Prosser looked around the room and motioned for them to be quiet. He leaned in closer and spoke a little quieter, "Now, there is one last very special thing I need to tell you. Lord Howe and General Browne, would like us to do one more thing, before we go join General Browne's Regiment."

They listened intently. Cutler asked, "What is that?"

Prosser replied with excitement. "Governor Tryon has placed a bounty of three hundred guineas on the head of that blasted Rebel Colonel Henry Ludington."

The large size of the bounty excited Chase and Cutler. They could not imagine a bounty being that large. Chase said in awe, "Three hundred guineas?!"

Cutler added, "That is a whole year's worth of wages!"

Chase smiled as he thought about that very large bounty, "I would love some of that money."

"Yes, David, I would too," Cutler said. He looked at his mug, then said, "That would buy me a lot of rum!"

They all laughed at the thought of having all that money.

Chase got a serious look on his face, leaned closer to Prosser, and asked, "So, Dr. Prosser, what were you thinking?"

Prosser looked very seriously at them, then said, "Roger, David, I have a plan."

He got a devious smile on his face as he explained his plan. "We can capture Colonel Ludington and bring him to New York as our prize when we go to enlist!"

Chase and Cutler were elated at that idea. Chase thought about that for a moment, then got a serious look on his face as he said, "I like that idea, but how do we do that?"

Prosser revealed the details of his plan with a very sinister look on his face, "I have muskets hidden safe in the Great Swamp. I want you both to gather as many men as you can, those loyal to the Crown."

He paused, leaned in close and said, "We will meet in the swamp, get the muskets and then go to Ludington's house at night, overwhelm the guards, capture him and take him with us to New York City as our prize!"

Cutler and Chase were very pleased to see Prosser had a

very specific, well thought out plan.

Cutler smiled as he picked up his mug and said, "I can almost taste the rum of victory!"

They all laughed and took another drink.

Prosser knew they must act fast. He urged them to take immediate action. "Now, get to it! Find others to help us! We have no time to waste!"

Cutler and Chase were so excited they almost tripped over each other as they got up to leave.

Prosser was quite pleased with the way that meeting went. He stayed at the table to finish his drink.

As Cutler and Chase were leaving the tavern, Enoch Crosby arrived. They both believed Crosby had Loyalist sympathies, so they politely but quickly nodded to him and left as quickly as they could. They had smiles on their faces because they were thinking about getting a big share of the bounty.

Prosser noticed Crosby enter. He called him to come over to his table, "Enoch! Come over here!"

Crosby walked over to Prosser. As he approached, he tipped his hat, "Greetings, Dr. Prosser."

Prosser replied to Crosby with a friendly nod of his head, "Enoch, it is so good to see you. Please, have a seat."

Crosby sat down at the table and said, "Thank you, Dr. Prosser, the pleasure is all mine."

Prosser was glad to see Crosby because he believed Crosby had strong Loyalist leanings, just like him. He did not know Crosby was a spy for the Continentals.

A sinister smile came across Prosser's face as he said to

Crosby, "I have some great news for you, my friend."

Crosby responded inquisitively, "Yes?"

Prosser smiled, took another drink, then said, "Enoch, this Rebellion will be over soon."

Crosby smiled, acting as though he liked what Prosser was saying, but inquisitively asked, "That is good news, but what makes you say that?"

Prosser looked around the room, to make sure no one was listening. He then leaned in closer to Crosby and softly said, "The British army is going to launch a raid to destroy the Rebel's Supply Depot."

That serious news troubled Crosby and made him look intently at Prosser, yet he calmly asked, "Are you sure?"

Prosser shook his head, leaned in closer and said, "Yes! I heard it directly from The Lord Howe and General Browne!"

Crosby looked surprised at what he heard Prosser say. He asked for clarification, "Directly?"

Prosser was proud of the meeting he had and the news he bore. He pompously said, "Yes! I had the honor of meeting with them personally and I brought them information about the Rebel Supply Depots."

Though Crosby was quite upset at that news, he acted very pleased. He looked at Prosser and said, "Oh, you did? I imagine, they must have been pleased with that."

Prosser gloated, "Yes! They were very pleased, and they told me they plan to attack within the month!"

Crosby was listening intently. He wanted more details. He asked, "Any idea where they plan to attack?"

Prosser was unsure but answered. "I am not sure about that. It could be Danbury or Fishkill. They are both Rebel Supply Depots."

Crosby was concerned as he contemplated what he heard. He was hoping for more information, but replied, "Yes, they are."

Prosser expressed his opinion, "Though I gave them more information about Danbury, I would not be surprised if they strike at Fishkill."

Crosby wanted to know which depot the Crown Forces intended to attack. He asked inquisitively, "What makes you think they will attack Fishkill?"

Prosser took another drink, then answered, "Governor Tryon was there, at that meeting with me. He said he knows Fishkill is the bigger depot. He said this attack would deal a major blow to the Rebels seeing their depot attacked."

Prosser attempted some humor using a play on words, "Why not kill the fish at Fishkill?!"

Crosby forced a laugh, "Oh, yes."

Prosser leaned closer to Crosby to tell him about his plans. "Enoch, a number of us are going to go join General Browne's Loyalist Regiment, so we can help with the attack and finally put an end to this infernal Rebellion."

Prosser put his hand on Crosby's arm, smiled and said, "Enoch, you are such a fine Loyalist. I would be honored to have you come with us."

Crosby was repulsed but acted honored at the invitation. He was pleased Prosser had no idea about his true loyalties. He replied, "Dr. Prosser, that is very tempting."

Crosby stroked his chin, trying to come up with a good response to not participate. He apologetically said, "But, someone needs to stay behind and keep an eye on things."

He then winked and smiled as he looked at Prosser and said, "If you know what I mean?"

Prosser smiled at Crosby's reply, which he considered delightfully sinister. He said, "Excellent idea, Enoch, excellent idea!"

They both laughed. Prosser leaned in close and spoke softer, "Now there is one thing more."

Crosby listened more intently, "I pray, do tell me."

Prosser gloated as he told him of his plan to capture Colonel Henry Ludington. "We are going to apprehend that wretched Rebel Henry Ludington and collect the three hundred guineas reward on his head!"

Crosby acted like he was taken back but he expected something like this. He acted pleased with Prosser's idea and said, "Oh, my! That is quite a lot of money."

Prosser smiled with his sinister smile and said "Indeed it is. Capturing that blasted Ludington will dishearten his band of Rebels and it will be a due reward for those of us who have been faithful to the Crown, we who have suffered such indignity at his hands!"

Crosby feigned pleasure at Prosser's plan, "You really are quite a Loyalist!"

Prosser gloated with pride as he gave his sinister laugh and agreed, "Yes, I am!"

They laughed again. Prosser missed the glimpse of concern on Crosby's face.

Chapter 7

Crosby Warns Ludington
March 5, 1777

It was now March 5, 1777, a cold winter day outside of the Ludington's home. Colonel Henry Ludington was working hard splitting wood. Wood was the only source of heat in their home back then. There always seemed to be more wood that needed splitting.

Jacob and Joseph Angevine, the Ludington's good friends, stopped by to help. Joseph was young and strong and very good with an axe, so he started splitting wood with the Colonel. Jacob wanted to help split the wood but was not able to do it effectively because of his disabled leg. Instead, he helped pick up and stack the wood.

Joseph was very good at splitting wood. The Colonel did not want to be outdone by someone as young as Joseph, so each time Joseph split a log he also split one. Soon, it looked like they were having a log splitting contest, trying to see who could split the most logs. One would split a log and almost immediately after that, the other split a log.

Sybil, Rebecca, and Mary picked up the pieces of wood, which Joseph split. Jacob, Archibald, and Henry Jr. picked up the wood the Colonel split. Some of them went back and forth, taking wood inside the house.

An Integrated Militia

The Militia and Army on both sides were integrated during the Revolution. After the Revolution, the stupidity of segregation became a part of the military until the Korean War.
Living History Guild Photograph

The Colonel stopped splitting wood and wiped the sweat off his brow. He looked at Joseph and said, "Joseph, you are very handy with that axe!

Joseph stopped. He was tired and glad the Colonel took that break. He pointed his axe at his father and replied, "I had a good teacher."

Joseph's comment made his father smile. Jacob paused, holding an arm full of split wood. With a big smile on his face he said, "And if my leg had not been shattered at Fort

William Henry, I would have split twice as much wood as both of you!"

The Colonel smiled as he looked at Jacob and Joseph and said, "Jacob, I really appreciate you and Joseph coming by to help us split this wood. We used up most of our wood this winter and the war has kept me away from home more than I would like."

Jacob replied, "I wish I could do more to help with the fight. I am so glad I earned my freedom from slavery. Now I look at this war as a struggle to help others become free from tyranny."

Henry said, "This war is indeed a struggle and you do more than your fair share Jacob. And It means a lot to me to know I have someone brave and reliable like you, to help keep things safe around here while I am gone."

Sybil was picking up wood near Joseph. Her father's last remarks made her speak up, "And what about me? Are you glad you have me around to help, when you are gone?"

Rebecca was picking up a piece of wood and stood up next to Sybil and quickly asked, "And me too?!"

Soon all the children chimed in, "What about me?!"

The Colonel smiled, looked at each one and said, "Yes! I am very glad for you, and you, and you, and you and for you.

That made them all smile.

As this exchange was taking place, Enoch Crosby came riding up the road with a look of urgency on his face.

Sybil saw him coming before her father did. She called out, "Oh Father, Look! It is Mr. Enoch Crosby!"

Everyone in the Ludington family knew Enoch Crosby.

He was a good friend of their father. They always liked it when he came for a visit.

Crosby had a very important message for Colonel Ludington, which made him come riding more quickly than he usually did. He rode up close to where the Colonel was, dismounted and tied his horse to the fence.

Colonel Ludington put down his axe and greeted Crosby with a warm handshake. "Enoch!"

Crosby smiled and returned the greeting, "Henry!"

Jacob and Joseph were surprised to see Enoch Crosby, the one they believed was a Loyalist, coming to see Colonel Henry Ludington. They did not like him and the side they thought he choose. Rather than have a confrontation at their friend's home they walked off to the side with a look of disapproval and wonder on their faces.

Crosby did not take notice of them, instead he tried to greet all the Ludington children by name. It was something he did each time he came. Each one smiled and did a curtsey or bow when he got their name right.

He looked at the two oldest girls and said "Hello Sybil! Hello Rebecca!"

He looked at the third daughter, hesitated for a moment and then said, "Mary!"

The girls smiled when he got all their names right.

Crosby then looked at Archibald and said, "Ummm, Henry?"

That was not his name. Archibald shook his head, *No!*

Henry, Jr. spoke up, "No! I am Henry!"

Archibald then said, "And I am Archibald!"

Sybil interjected a comment with a smile, "Mr. Crosby, you always mix up Archibald and Henry!"

Their father joined in the conversation, "Sybil, do you remember Mr. Crosby used to mix up you and Rebecca?"

Crosby smiled and said, "Well, sometimes, it is hard to tell such lovely girls apart."

That comment pleased Sybil and Rebecca. They smiled and gave him a curtsey.

Her father responded placing a hand on Sybil's shoulder. Then he looked at Sybil and spoke sarcastically, "I never have that problem, do I, Rebecca?"

Sybil shook her father's hand off her shoulder and looked at him in a reprimanding way, even though she knew he was kidding.

She then smiled and said, "Father!"

Their father's jest made them all laugh.

Sybil looked at Enoch and could tell he had a very serious look on his face. She realized he must have come with an important message for their father, something which was probably not intended for them to hear.

She also realized Jacob and Joseph thought Enoch was a Tory. They do not know Enoch was really a spy for the Rebels and she could see by the way they walked away from him, and the look on their faces, that they were upset Enoch was there.

She came up with an idea. She turned and spoke to Jacob, Joseph, and her siblings, "I think Mr. Crosby has some business to discuss with Father."

Crosby appreciated Sybil's perception. He nodded his

head, yet continued Henry's jest as he looked at Sybil and said, "Yes, Rebecca, I would like to speak with your father alone, if possible."

They all laughed knowing he was jesting when he called Sybil, Rebecca. Everyone laughed except for Jacob and Joseph. Nothing a Tory said could make them smile.

The Colonel spoke apologetically to Jacob and Joseph, "Jacob and Joseph, would you please excuse me? I have to complete an important transaction with Mr. Crosby"

Joseph held his axe in a threatening manner and spoke to Henry with concern while trying to intimidate Enoch, "Would you like me to stay close in case there is any trouble?"

The Colonel picked up his axe and held it firmly as he nodded his head and assured Joseph he was safe, "I am sure, I will be okay, but if I need you, I will call."

Sybil then called to the others, "Come along, everyone, let us get a drink of water."

She looked at them all and realized that may not be enough motivation. She knew they loved to make cartridges for the muskets, for the Militia, so she added, "And who wants to help me make some cartridges for the muskets?"

The children all responded, "I do! I do!"

Joseph replied with disgust directed at Enoch, "Yes, I would love to help make some cartridges, so I can use them on some Tories!"

Jacob was obviously upset Enoch was there but was confident Henry would do the right thing. "There will be a time and place for that, Joseph, "he said. "Yet this is not the time, nor the place."

They all headed off to the house together.

Enoch tried to hide a smile. He spoke with Henry while watching Jacob, Joseph and the children go inside, "I am glad to see that young man has no love for Tories."

Henry replied, "That is right, he has no love for Tories. He is very dedicated to the cause and is becoming a fine addition to my Militia."

Henry looked seriously at Enoch and said, "Just make sure you do not encounter him when he has a musket in his hands."

He smiled and continued in jest, "After all, you are a notorious Tory!

Enoch smiled and replied, "I will be careful!"

He then changed the subject and complimented Henry's family, "And by the way, you have a delightful family,

Henry smiled, "Yes I do, I am so blessed."

Crosby then complimented Sybil, "Sybil sure is growing up to be a fine young woman."

Henry shook his head in agreement then added an important fact, "She will be sixteen in just a few short weeks."

He paused and then said, "She is as good to me as having an eldest son."

Crosby said, "I know she has been a good messenger when you need to send messages to the Militia."

"Yes, she knows the roads and lanes very well," Henry replied.

He then looked at Crosby more seriously, "But, I am sure you are not here to talk about my wonderful family."

A very concerned look came across Crosby's face as he replied, "That is correct. I just met with Dr. Jonathan Prosser. You know who I mean?"

Henry shook his head yes, as he said, "Yes, the Committee of Safety has been keeping an eye on him."

Henry smiled and looked at Crosby with a feigned sinister look and teasingly said, "Of course, the Committee also told me to keep an eye on you."

Crosby smiled, then became very serious again, "As long as the right people know where my loyalties lie, and the wrong people do not, that is fine with me."

Henry patted Crosby on the shoulder and nodded his head in agreement, as a show of confidence.

Crosby continued and got back to the reason for his visit, "Dr. Prosser is one of those who thinks my loyalties are with the Crown."

Henry nodded in agreement.

Crosby then told him the important news he brought, "So he told me the British plan to attack our supply depot within the month!"

A very serious look of concern came over Henry's face. He walked around anxiously as he said, "We were expecting something like that."

He paused, then asked, "Did he say whether the raid will be against Fishkill or Danbury?"

Crosby shook his head, as he said, "No, he did not say."

Crosby paused and said, "I do not think he knows which

one, and I am not sure if they trust him enough to give him specific information like that."

He then stated something he observed which most Loyalists did not realize, "You know the British Regulars do not really trust their Tory sympathizers. I am sure they are thinking, if the Tories will turn against their own neighbors, maybe one day they will turn against them."

Henry shook his head in agreement.

Crosby continued, "Prosser said the Crown Forces will be here within the next month. He said he thinks the attack will be on Fishkill because that is the larger depot and it will be more demoralizing if they strike there."

Henry said. "Yes, that would be demoralizing."

Henry got a look of urgency on his face as he said, "We must get word to both Danbury and Fishkill, just to be safe!"

Crosby assured Henry he did that, "I already passed the word along to them."

Henry was pleased and relieved to hear that.

Crosby came closer to Henry to give him one more piece of troubling news, "There is one more thing."

Crosby hesitated. Henry saw the look of concern on Crosby's face and asked inquisitively, "Yes?"

Crosby shook his head with deep concern and continued, "Prosser said, he is gathering a group of men to go with him to join General Browne's Loyalist Regiment."

Henry smiled at that news then responded with some sarcasm, "That is good news. That will be a few less people I will have to watch out for."

Crosby smiled and shook his head again, then continued

with a very serious tone, "But, here is the troubling news."

Crosby hesitated again.

Henry asked inquisitively, "Yes?"

Crosby reluctantly continued. "Before they go, they plan to get a prize to take with them."

Henry acted like he did not know what Crosby was trying to say.

Crosby came out and said directly, "They plan to capture one Colonel Henry Ludington and take him as their prize to British headquarters, where they will collect the three hundred guineas bounty, which is on your head."

Henry smiled, took off his hat and acted like he was feeling for the money on his head. He then said, "I do not feel three hundred guineas on my head."

Crosby smiled and shook his head at Henry's humor. He said, "If I did not know you better Henry, I would think you are not taking this seriously. But I do know you!"

Henry put his hat back on and smiled, continuing with his sarcasm as he stared at Crosby and said, "And I know you too Enoch, and I am keeping my eyes on you, like the Committee of Safety said I should do."

Crosby smiled. He knew Henry realized the seriousness of the messages he delivered.

Crosby got back on his horse and then said one last thing, "Please take care Henry!"

Henry nodded, gave Crosby's horse a slap and sent him off, as he said, "God speed, my friend!"

As Crosby rode off, Henry picked up his axe and headed back to the house.

Chapter 8

Attempt to Capture Ludington
March 7, 1777 - Evening

It was March 7, 1777, another cold winter night in the Hudson Valley. Loyalist Dr. Jonathan Prosser and his associates, David Chase and Roger Cutler rounded up a mob of men to help with their insidious plot, promising them a profit from their loyalty to the Crown.

Prosser told them about the Crown Forces plan to attack one of the Rebel Supply Depots and bring a quick end to the war. He convinced the men to help him capture Colonel Henry Ludington and take him to British headquarters, where they would receive a huge reward. He said they would then join General Montfort Browne's Loyalist Regiment and bring a swift end to the war.

Prosser and his men believed if they were loyal to the Crown and carried out their unscrupulous plan they would not only get the bounty for Colonel Ludington but would also be given the lands of their rebel neighbors. They remembered how Beverly Robinson, an important Loyalist Colonel, took land away from people in their area a few years ago. They believed if they were on the same side as he, they too would be rewarded.

Chase and his men met Prosser in the Great Swamp, where Prosser hid muskets. With torches in hand they began to make their way down the road to apprehend Colonel Ludington. They were happy when they received word the Colonel was home without any Militia around.

As Prosser and his cohorts marched towards their destination, he knew they recruited some who did not have the best moral integrity. He was concerned one of them would shoot the colonel. He exhorted them, "Remember not to shoot anyone unless it is absolutely necessary."

One of the men was disappointed at that admonition and replied, "Aww! Dr. Prosser, I would really like to shoot that Rebel and get it over with!"

"Yes, let us shoot some Rebels!" another voice replied.

There was a murmur of approval from some of the other men, at the idea of shooting some Rebels.

Prosser spoke again, "Lord Howe, Commander of His Majesty's Forces prefers we capture Ludington alive."

He paused and then said, "And there is a nice large bounty we will all collect when we bring him in alive."

He paused, then spoke again, "You would like to collect that bounty, would you not?!"

Those who were there for ultraistic reasons, along with those strictly there so they could prosper financially, replied, with a hearty, "Huzzah!"

Some were upset with how their Rebel neighbors treated them and were looking forward to shooting someone. One of them said, "If I cannot shoot Colonel

Ludington, I hope there are some other Rebels I can shoot!"

Prosser assured him, "You will have plenty of opportunities to shoot as many Rebels as you want, after we bring Colonel Ludington to Lord Howe."

Prosser then added, "When we turn in Colonel Ludington, we will be rewarded, and become part of General Montfort Browne's Loyalist Regiment. Then you can shoot as many Rebels as you want!"

One of the men wearing an old frock coat asked, "Are they going to give us some nice red coats to wear?"

Prosser was surprised that man was there because he thought he might get a nice uniform. He thought about that for a moment and figured that was as good a motivation as whatever motivated others. He smiled and replied, "Unlike the Rebel Militia, who have to provide their own clothing and weapons, the Crown will give us nice green uniforms, with white facings. And they will also give us muskets!"

That response made a big smile appear on the face of the man who asked the question.

Prosser paused. He knew there had to be others there who were motivated by financial gain, one of the primary things which motivated him. He decided to verbalize that, and said, "And, when we defeat the Rebels, they will give us all the Rebel's land and houses!"

Some of them had their land seized by the Rebels. They liked the idea of taking away their Rebel neighbor's property. They enthusiastically shouted, "Huzzah!"

After a little while they saw some men approaching with torches. They stopped and waited to see who was approaching. They were hoping it was not the dreaded Rebel's Committee of Safety, which rounded up Loyalists.

Prosser was relieved when he saw the man leading the group was Roger Cutler. Cutler was thankful he found Prosser and the rest of the men.

Loyalists Seek to Apprehend Colonel Ludington

Image by Lyman Abbott, 1850
The Pictorial Field Book to the Revolution.

Cutler greeted Prosser, "Dr. Prosser, I gathered a few more men, loyal to the Crown."

A big smile came across Prosser's face as he greeted Cutler and said, "Good work, Roger."

Prosser looked at the group of men. He was glad to see Cutler rounded up more men than he expected.

Prosser then addressed all the men, "Now is the time for us to go get our prize! We will capture that annoying, obnoxious, Rebel, Henry Ludington and take him with us as our prisoner to New York. There he will see what it is like to be in prison for one's beliefs. Then we will receive our reward, join the Loyalist Regiment and help put an end to this cursed Rebellion once and for all!"

When he finished speaking he was surprised at how unusually silent the men were. He underestimated how nervous many of them were. If they were caught they knew it would surely mean prison for them.

He looked intently at them, then asked, "Are you with me?!"

Some hesitated but others responded to his question and enthusiastically shouted, "Yes!"

He was glad they finally showed some enthusiasm. But now they were passing a house and he realized there might be people in that home who might not like what they were saying. That made him nervous. He wondered, *perhaps they were a bit too loud?* He told the men, "Not so loud!"

When the men saw the nervous expression on Prosser's face they looked at each other and understood it probably was a good idea to be quieter. That made them nervous.

When Prosser saw their nervous looks. He made himself smile then spoke boldly but softly, "Long live the King!"

They responded with a subdued, "Long live the King!"

They continued down the road towards the Ludington House. After walking for a while one of the men with a loud, deep voice, and strong English accent said, "The Rebels are such an ungrateful lot! They should be grateful the King allows them to pay taxes!"

"That's right!" said another man, who did not seem to

have an accent at all. "It is an honor to be a subject of the King! And after all, Parliament has every right to tax anyone they want! How else do they expect the Crown to pay for the soldiers to protect us!"

Another man said, "And if it were not for those Crown Forces we would have been overrun by the French and all been forced to become Catholics!"

He was referring to the French and Indian War. The French, who were the enemy back then, were mainly Catholic. The British King and Parliament were Anglicans. To scare people, they said the Colonials would be forced to become Catholic if the French won that war.

After that everyone grew quiet again as they continued down the road.

It seemed like they had been walking for hours when Prosser had them stop. He then signaled for all of them to come close to him.

When they were all close enough to hear him, he said, "We are getting close to Colonel Ludington's, so every one of you put out those torches." He paused, then said, "We do not want them to see us coming."

He then laughed a sinister laugh and smugly said, "We will take them by surprise!"

"Yes, Sir!" many of them replied loudly.

Prosser quickly responded in a firm but restrained voice, "And be quiet! We do not want them to hear we are coming!"

As soon as the men put out the torches it became very dark.

Colonial Two-Story Home
Similar to the Ludington's home. Their home had a porch, stone chimneys on each end, an attic, and a side room.
Photograph by Larry A. Maxwell, 2018

Sybil was diligently keeping watch outside of her family home, hiding behind a tree with a loaded musket held firmly in her hands, looking, and listening for signs of anyone approaching.

She and Rebecca were trained by their father to load and shoot a musket accurately. They were both good shots. Any Tory who crossed their paths would be in big trouble.

Sybil heard a sound. She looked intently down the road. There in the darkness she saw something moving. She watched carefully. Finally, she could see the shape of men approaching. She knew men approaching at night, without lit torches, meant trouble. A serious look of concern came across her face. It was concern not fear. She knew exactly what to do. She quickly slipped out from behind the tree and quietly ran around to the back of the house where her sister Rebecca was keeping guard. Rebecca could tell something was wrong as soon as she saw Sybil.

Sybil quietly, yet firmly said, "Rebecca, quickly, inside,

there is a whole group of men coming!"

Prosser and his mob tried to quietly proceed down the road as they drew closer to the Ludington's home. They did not know they had been detected.

Sybil's mother, Abigail, was seated near the fireplace holding her baby daughter. Sybil's father, Colonel Henry Ludington was sitting in his chair reading.

As Sybil and Rebecca quickly entered the room, Henry abruptly stopped reading. He and Abigail instantly looked up with concern on their faces.

Sybil spoke quietly but with urgency, "Father, there is a group of men coming down the road toward the house."

Henry rose from his seat, grabbed his cartridge box, and put it on over his shoulder. He then grabbed his pistol and told Sybil and Rebecca, "Wake up your brothers and sisters. It is time for everyone to do as we practiced."

Henry carefully loaded his pistol as Sybil and Rebecca went upstairs. He adjusted his sword, which was on his side.

When Sybil and Rebecca reached the top of the stairs they saw the other children were all in bed. Sybil and Rebecca quickly and quietly woke up their sister Mary, and their brothers, Archibald and Henry, Jr. As they woke them, Rebecca indicated they needed to be quiet.

Sybil put a finger over her lips as she spoke to them, "Time to get up! Shhh!"

She then said, "Some bad people are coming, and Father needs our help to do what we practiced."

Mary, Archibald and Henry, Jr., rose quickly and quietly out of bed. The younger brothers, Derick and Tertullus did not stir, they stayed sound asleep.

Sybil gave instructions, "Mary, help Rebecca light the candles. Archibald and Henry, help me get the muskets and hats."

Prosser and his mob of Loyalists were getting very close to the house. He had them pause. Prosser was excited their task was going so smoothly. He smiled as he pictured easily capturing the Colonel and getting the big reward.

He gave orders, "Roger, take one group and go behind the house, that way. David, you take another group and go behind the house that way."

He smiled one of his sinister smiles and said, "We are not going to let our prize escape! We will surround the house and call for Colonel Ludington to surrender."

Just then, Rebecca and Mary set candles on top of the furniture, which was against the wall opposite from the windows. Then they lit the candles. The light from the candles created big shadows when they moved between the candles and the windows.

Sybil, Archibald and Henry, Jr., all came back in the room each holding a musket and wearing a man's hat. Sybil carried an extra musket and hat, which she gave to Rebecca. Rebecca put the hat on her head and put the musket against her left shoulder, just like the Militia did.

Sybil gave the command, "Now everyone, march back and forth, between the candles and the windows, while Mary makes sure the candles do not go out."

Sybil, Rebecca, Archibald and Henry, Jr., all put muskets on their left shoulders and marched back and forth in front of the windows. Even though the curtains were closed, their actions cast large shadows on the windows. The shadows were much larger than them. It made it look like there were quite a few men in the house, on guard.

Colonial Bedroom

Most bedrooms were open, with few furnishings. Lit candles on a dresser would cast large shadows on windows.

Just as Roger Cutler was about to lead his men to the back of the house, he looked up and saw movement in the windows. He froze in fear at what appeared to be soldiers marching upstairs in the house.

Cutler pointed at the windows and spoke with alarm, "Dr. Prosser! Look at the windows!"

Dr. Prosser and the others heard the alarm in Cutler's

voice and quickly looked up at the house with great concern. They were horrified when they saw what appeared to be many soldiers moving around upstairs in the house.

One of Prosser's men cried out in fear, "He has the Militia waiting in the house to attack us!"

The man with the deep voice and English accent was terrified as he shouted, "It is a trap!"

The look on Dr. Prosser's face changed from sinister glee to that of someone afraid for his life. He quickly turned and desperately yelled to the others, "Retreat! Retreat!"

Prosser's words were unnecessary because everyone was already running away as fast as they could.

Colonel Ludington was downstairs in the house, peeking out the window. He smiled as he watched Prosser and his men run away, down the road, looking like rats being chased by big invisible angry cats.

He turned and smiled as he looked at his wife, Abigail. She was relieved and smiled when she saw the smile on her husband's face.

The Colonel proudly called to his children, "You did it children! You did it!" He then shouted a loud, "Huzzah!"

Sybil, Rebecca, Archibald and Henry, Jr. were all excited. They yelled, "Huzzah!" As they did that they realized the other children were still sleeping.

All the noise woke up Derek and Tertullus. They rubbed their eyes, looking half-awake. Derek looked around and said, "Shhh! I am trying to sleep!"

The other children looked at each other, smiled, and then blew out the candles.

Chapter 9

Conflict at the Ganong's Home
March 8, 1777

John Ganong and Jesse his son were splitting wood outside of their home on this cold day. Neither one looked happy and they were not talking to each other.

Joseph Angevine, Jesse's friend who belonged to the Militia, rode up to the house with a sense of urgency. He had some very important news to share with them.

As he drew near, Joseph shouted, "Jesse! Mr. Ganong!"

Jesse and his father stopped splitting wood and looked up at Joseph. They saw the look of concern on his face and heard the urgency in his voice. Jesse could tell Joseph came with some important news.

Jesse's father, John Ganong, was a successful businessman. His business dealings kept him in close contact with people who had strong Loyalist leanings. Those Loyalists were at odds with the Rebels like Colonel Ludington who backed the Continental cause.

Though John was not an aristocrat he acquired many acres of land over the years and built a large home for his family, much larger than many others in the area.

Home of Loyalist Beverley Robinson
*Appletons' Cyclopaedia of American Bibliography, 1886.
Many Loyalists in New York were affluent.*

The Ganong's home was quite a distance away from the simple farm where Joseph lived. Joseph and his father's home was much closer to the Ludington's. He rode a long way that morning to get to the Ganong's house.

Joseph had important news he knew Jesse would want to hear. He could hardly contain himself. He learned how Dr. Prosser and the mob of Loyalists tried to capture Sybil's father and wanted to let Jesse know what happened.

Joseph quickly dismounted and tied his horse to one of the fence rails.

Jesse walked over to Joseph, shook his hand, and asked, "Joseph, what brings you out here?"

Joseph was very upset as he told what happened, "Jesse! Tories tried to capture Colonel Ludington last night!"

When Jesse's father heard Joseph say someone tried to capture Colonel Ludington he was filled with fear and became extremely upset. He was concerned something bad like this was going to happen and now it did! He tried to warn Colonel Ludington, but he would not listen to him!

John was so upset he wanted to make sure what he heard was correct. He asked, "Joseph, are you sure?"

Joseph could see John Ganong was distraught.

Joseph shook his head *yes* and explained slowly and carefully, "Yes, Mr. Ganong, it was Dr. Jonathan Prosser and a large group of Tories!"

John started shaking his head in dismay and spoke out in despair, "This is not good! Not good! I tried to warn Colonel Ludington!"

While Jesse's father was overcome with the idea of things getting worse for himself, Jesse was more concerned about the safety of Sybil and the Ludington family.

Jesse asked Joseph, "Did anyone get hurt?"

He saw Joseph perk up a little at that question and get a bit more optimistic.

Joseph was glad to report, "No! The wonderful thing is, no one was hurt."

That was great news to Jesse. He was thankful to hear no one was hurt. A look of relief came over his face. He said, "I am so glad to hear that."

As the news sank in Jesse's look quickly changed to a perplexed one. He asked Joseph, "How could someone try to capture Colonel Ludington, yet no one got hurt?"

Joseph smiled as he explained, "Sybil and her brothers and sisters helped scare them off."

That made Jesse smile, "Sybil and her brothers and

sisters helped scare them off?! Why am I not surprised?"

Jesse's father was greatly upset by this whole thing. He could barely think straight. He did not hear Joseph say, *no one was hurt.* All he could think about was how terrible this was and how much worse it could get.

He blamed it all on his stubborn friend, Henry Ludington. He was thinking to himself, *Why would Henry not be reasonable and give up his dangerous conflict with the Crown? Things will only get worse!*

Jesse and Joseph could see John shaking his head, pacing back and forth, fretting and muttering, "This is bad! This is so bad!"

Jesse walked over to his father, grabbed him by his shoulders, looked him in the eye and said, "Oh Father, can you not see!"

Since the Revolution started Jesse had many conflicts with his father. Jesse believed in the struggle for independence. His father believed the struggle was all a bad misunderstanding.

Jesse previously gave up discussing the struggle for independence with his father because it always became a heated argument. The Tories attempt to capture Colonel Ludington put his friend's family in danger and that was too much for him to take. Now, he could no longer contain himself. He had to say something.

Jesse looked straight into father's eyes and firmly said, "We must take a stand! You cannot be uncommitted!"

He felt this incident might be enough to make his father rethink things.

Hanging of Nathan Hale
*Harper's Weekly, November 24, 1860.
John Ganong knew the Crown hung Rebels.*

Jesse thought perhaps this would be a good time to ask his father for something very important to him, something his father refused in the past. This incident compelled him to ask again. He looked at his father and pleaded, "Please let me join the Militia!"

Jesse's father was very distraught. He was still shaking his head in disbelief at the news. He knew something bad just happened but feared much worse would follow if he gave Jesse permission to join the Militia.

He looked back at his son and emphatically said, "No! No! Absolutely not!"

That was not what Jesse wanted to hear. He became more upset with his father. He moaned in bitter disappointment, "Father!"

Jesse's father was extremely upset over what happened. He was afraid his whole world was going to fall apart.

He walked away from Jesse muttering, "This is so bad! What are we going to do?"

Joseph knew Jesse was upset and disappointed. He came closer to Jesse, put his hand on his shoulder and said, "I am so sorry Jesse, if I caused you any trouble."

Jesse stiffened up and responded with fierce resolve, "No, Joseph, You, did not cause any trouble!"

He paused a moment then continued, "I love my Father! But he is wrong! He thinks he can sit on the fence and wait this out! He still cannot accept the fact this is a war to the end. I cannot believe he will not open his eyes! Not even after this!"

Jesse's father was distraught as he went into the house shaking his head and muttering.

Jesse looked over to where his father was and said, "I fear this is all going to end badly for people like my father."

Joseph nodded his head in agreement then said, "Yes, I agree. It is time everyone chooses a side and takes a stand."

He walked over to Jesse as he continued to speak, I read that Benjamin Franklin said, *"We must all hang together or assuredly, we will hang separately."*

Jesse nodded his head in agreement and said, "I am sure the King would like to hang all of us, if he could."

He looked back at the house again as he said. "If only Father would realize that!"

Chapter 10

Sybil's Birthday Party
April 5, 1777

It was April 5, 1777, a beautiful unseasonably warm spring day in the Hudson Valley. Many friends and family gathered at the home of Colonel Henry Ludington to celebrate the sixteenth birthday of his daughter Sybil.

Sybil, Rebecca, and Mary Ludington were outside enjoying Sybil's party with their friends Joseph Angevine and Jesse Ganong.

Some of the younger children were playing *Graces*, a colonial game where the children toss a hoop in the air with two sticks while another child tries to catch it with a second set of two sticks.

During the festivities Colonel Ludington and Jacob Angevine were talking when two unexpected guests arrived. It was Rev. John Gano and Haym Salomon.

Colonel Ludington knew Gano. He smiled as he extended his hand, "Rev. John Gano, my favorite *Fighting Preacher*, I am always honored by your presence."

When the Continental Congress formed the Continental Army in 1775, Rev. Gano volunteered. Unlike some other clergy, who took a passive role, Gano brought his sword with him and fought alongside the men he served earning him the nickname *The Fighting Preacher*.

Rev. John Gano

Unknown Artist, 1780's.
New York Public Library

Gano responded politely to Colonel Ludington's comments, "Colonel Henry Ludington, the honor is always mine."

The Colonel introduced Jacob, "This is my friend Jacob Angevine. He earned his freedom from slavery for his service during the French and Indian War."

Gano shook Jacob's hand warmly as he smiled and said, "It is my pleasure to meet you Jacob."

A very serious look then came across his face as he said, "Slavery is an abomination and should be eradicated from the face of the earth!"

That made Jacob smile as he said, "I wish more men felt the same as you.

Haym could not contain himself. He interrupted, "I feel the same way! Slavery is indeed a despicable abomination!

Gano then introduced his friend, "Colonel Ludington, Jacob, I would like to introduce to you my friend, Haym Salomon."

As Haym, Henry and Jacob shook hands, Gano gave some background on Salomon, "Haym came to New York from Poland a few years ago. Soon, after his arrival he became a member of the first synagogue in New York City and a very active member of the Sons of Liberty. He has been a very good friend of the Revolution."

Haym Salomon Silver Medal

1973 Jewish Hall of Fame Medal.

Colonel Ludington smiled, "I am truly honored to meet you Mr. Salomon."

Salomon interrupted, "Please, call me Haym."

The Colonel continued, "Haym, I heard of your efforts

to help secure much needed funds to help us finance this war. That funding is so essential to our cause. And, I also heard, as a result of those efforts the Crown arrested you as a spy and let you be their *guest* in one of their jails."

Haym smiled and humbly replied, "Thank you for your kind words. I am glad to do whatever I can to help the cause of Liberty. And if that means being a *guest* in jail, then that is the price I am willing to pay."

The Colonel was very pleased with Haym's attitude. He patted him on the back and said, "I like you a lot!"

Haym smiled replied, "Colonel Ludington, I understand the Crown would also like to have you as a *guest* in their jail."

The Colonel smiled and said, "Haym, you may call me Henry. And Yes, I know they would like to have me as their *guest*. I hope I keep disappointing them."

"We love to disappoint the Crown," Haym interjected with a big smile.

Gano smiled, looked at Henry and explained the reason for their visit, "Haym and I were on our way to meet with the State Assembly at Kingston, when we heard you were having this birthday celebration for your daughter, and Haym asked if we could stop by and see you."

Haym said, "I always enjoy meeting someone who gives the British a hard time."

Henry expressed his gratitude, "And I am humbly grateful both of you have honored us with your presence."

Gano looked toward the children playing and asked Henry, "So, which one is your daughter?"

Henry smiled as he pointed out all four of his daughters and said, "That one, and that one, and that one, and that one."

Haym smiled when he saw Henry had so many daughters.

Gano smiled and interrupted Henry, "I meant, which one is the birthday girl?"

Henry smiled as he pointed to Sybil, "Oh yes, you mean Sybil. That is her, over there." They looked toward Sybil.

Sybil was playing with her friends.

Joseph Angevine said to Sybil, "So Sybil, you are now sixteen years old! You are finally a lady!" He bowed to her and she curtsied back to him.

Rebecca smiled and said in jest, "Yes, she is no longer a boy!"

That comment made them all laugh.

Jesse Ganong, who wanted to be more than just a friend to Sybil, said, "I am sure no one ever thought that!"

Rebecca smiled and said, "Father does!"

They looked towards their father and all laughed. Henry smiled back at them.

It was then another set of important guests arrived. Daniel and Abraham Nimham came down the road on their horses along with other members of the Wappinger Tribe.

The Ludington's home was located on the main military road between Boston and Philadelphia. Every traveler heading from New England southward would pass by their home on the way to the other states. It was not unusual for people to stop and visit the Ludington's.

The Nimhams were old friends with the Ludingtons. Daniel Nimham and Henry served together in the French & Indian War and opposed the British landlords in the Settler's Revolt.

Sketch of a Stockbridge/Wappinger Indian
*By Captain Johann Ewald, 1798.
Ewald was an officer in the Hessian Army.
He made this image during the Revolution after seeing
Daniel and Abraham Nimham and their men.*

One year after this party Daniel and his son Abraham, along with their Indian Corps, would return to the area and engage in an epic battle against the British.

Daniel and Abraham dismounted and greeted Henry with a warm handshake using both hands.

Daniel spoke first, "We could not pass through here

without stopping to visit our favorite Englishman."

Henry smiled and said, "Daniel, my old friend, I prefer the term *American* over *Englishman*."

Daniel was apologetic, "I did not mean any offense, my friend."

Henry immediately replied, "None was taken."

Henry then made the introductions, "Jacob, you already know these men, but Rev. John Gano, Haym Salomon, I would like to introduce you to my dear friend, Daniel Nimham, Sachem of the Wappinger Indians and his son Abraham."

Gano and Haym started to bow but Daniel and Abraham gave them the same type of warm handshake they gave Henry.

Haym asked Henry, "Does sachem mean chief?

Henry replied, "Yes, Haym, that is one meaning of the word."

Henry gave them more background of his friendship with Daniel Nimham, "Daniel, Jacob and I served together in the French and Indian War."

Gano spoke to Daniel, "I heard good things about what a great ally you have been in this war, and if I am not mistaken, was it not Beverley Robinson, who is now commander of one of the Loyalist Regiments, the one who used some forged deeds to take away your land, right after you faithfully served the Crown in the French and Indian War?"

Daniel shook his head in agreement, "Yes, and Colonel Ludington and many men in this area took up their muskets back then and stood with my people, while I took the fight to the courts and then all the way to England."

Henry said, "Many people do not know the British sent in regiments of Regulars from Poughkeepsie and New York to stop what they called, *The Settler's Revolt*. And it was here that British Regulars fired the first shots against American's. That was five years before the *Boston Massacre*. They tried to keep the whole affair quiet. But, it was that *Revolt* which ignited the spark that helped flame the fires of this Revolution. That *Revolt* caused Samuel Adams to call for the Sons of Liberty to unite!"

Abraham interjected, "And then, ten years after that, when we heard the English attacked Lexington and Concord. My father and I gathered many of our bravest warriors and went to Boston to join the fight. Hopefully this time we can drive our common enemy off our land!"

They all uttered in agreement, "Here! Here!"

Daniel placed his hand on his son Abraham's shoulder and made an announcement, "My son asked General Washington if he could gather all of us Indians into one regiment, to fight the Crown Forces together. And now, I am honored to tell all of you, General Washington granted Abraham's request and combined all Indians into one regiment under Abraham's command."

They all congratulated Abraham with a hearty handshake. Abraham smiled and humbly, but proudly responded, "My father is still the Great Sachem and he is a great and mighty warrior. He is the one who suggested I make the request to General Washington to create the

Indian Regiment. Now all Indians will be working together to defeat the British. I only command the regiment because it is my father's wish."

Henry responded looking at Abraham, "I am sure your father and General Washington made a good choice."

Daniel replied, "Yes, my friend, and now we are on our way to New Jersey to help General Washington."

Henry smiled and said, "I am so glad you stopped by today. It is excellent timing. Today is my daughter Sybil's sixteenth birthday."

Daniel smiled as he remembered Sybil, "I remember Sybil as the one who loves horses."

Jacob added, "She was born to ride."

Henry agreed, "She is one of the best riders I know. She is even better than me."

Daniel said, "My son Abraham reminded me about Sybil's birthday. He has a present for her from our family."

Henry smiled, "That is very kind of you."

Abraham asked, "Please excuse me, while I go give Sybil her present."

Abraham went over to Sybil. Sybil was with Rebecca and their friends. As Abraham approached them Sybil and Rebecca ran to greet him. Joseph and Jesse were intimidated at Abraham's warrior-like appearance and stood back a little.

Sybil smiled and warmly greeted him, "Abraham Nimham! It is so nice to see you again!"

Abraham smiled and said, "Happy Birthday!"

An even bigger smile came across Sybil's face, "That is

very kind of you Abraham!"

Abraham reached into his pouch and pulled out a beaded belt and gave it to Sybil. The Wappinger Tribe, like many other tribes in the Northeast, made belts with beads made from shells for special occasions. The beads were called wampum. This belt was called a wampum belt.

Sybil was very pleased with this special gift. She looked at the belt, "Thank you so much! It is beautiful!"

She noticed two red hearts on the belt. Abraham saw her trace them with her fingers.

He explained their significance, "Those hearts are the symbol of the Nimham family. My grandfather had them on the wampum belt he carried to important councils. The hearts remind us of the importance of approaching others with a true heart. If you do that others will respond with an open heart to you."

Sybil was deeply touched by the significance of this gift, "I am so honored."

Abraham smiled and continued speaking, "I understand turning sixteen is a special occasion for your people. If you were one of our people, at this age, this would be more of a wedding gift."

Sybil blushed, and Rebecca giggled at that suggestion.

Abraham looked at Joseph and Jesse with a smile and said, "Perhaps that belt will help you get a husband."

Sybil blushed even more.

Joseph and Jesse looked awkwardly at each other when they heard Abraham's words about Sybil finding a husband. They both inwardly liked that idea, but it made them blush and they tried to nonchalantly walk away.

As Abraham went back to his father another important guest arrived at the birthday celebration. Some were glad to see this guest arrive, many were not. It was Enoch Crosby. He arrived with an extra horse and dismounted off to the side, by himself.

When Sybil's father saw Crosby arrive he excused himself and went to greet Crosby.

When Joseph and Jesse noticed Crosby, they were disgusted.

Sybil ignored them and looked at the extra horse with interest.

Joseph spoke with repulsion, "Oh, no! That Tory, Enoch Crosby has come to ruin Sybil's party!"

Jesse joined in showing his contempt for Crosby, "He should know better than to turn up here."

Sybil interceded talking to them sternly, "Be civil!"

Jesse was angry and spoke sarcastically, "Alright! I will try to keep myself from spitting on him!"

Sybil looked at him with anger.

Joseph noticed Crosby had an extra horse, "Look at that extra horse he has with him, do you think he is going to try to capture the Colonel, so he can claim the bounty?"

Sybil gave Joseph a shove for what he said. Joseph fell and landed in the dirt on his back.

Enoch Crosby left Sybil's father and came toward Sybil, leading the extra horse.

Jesse helped Joseph up. The two of them stepped away to avoid Crosby.

Crosby came over to Sybil and said, "I have a gift for you Sybil."

He offered her the reins to the horse and said, "Happy Birthday!"

Sybil was so excited she could not contain herself. She wanted to make sure she understood what he said. She excitedly asked, "For me?!"

Crosby smiled as he continued to extend the reins of the horse to Sybil, "Yes, Sybil, it is my birthday gift for you."

The boys gave Crosby a disgusted look.

Jesse looked like he was about to spit at Enoch. Rebecca noticed that and punched Jesse in the chest so hard he ended up coughing. He then looked at Rebecca with a shocked look. She put up two fists threatening him.

Sybil quickly hugged Crosby, accepted the reins, and hugged the horse.

Rebecca glared at Jesse and Joseph letting them know she would not put up with any acts of disrespect from them toward Crosby. She then symbolically wiped off her hands and went over to Sybil and the horse.

Rebecca admired the horse and said, "Oh Sybil! What a pretty horse!"

Joseph and Jesse very reluctantly came closer.

Sybil was elated as she agreed with Rebecca, "Oh yes! He is the most beautiful horse in the world!"

Rebecca asked, "What are you going to call him?"

Joseph looked at Crosby with disgust and sarcastically suggested, "How about King George?"

Rebecca immediately put up her fists again, threatening

to hit Joseph, like she did Jesse. She glared at him menacingly and said one word, "Joseph!"

Joseph and Jesse wisely stepped back and did not say another word.

Sybil looked at her new horse thoughtfully and said, "He looks like a horse that will be good to ride both during the day and at night. At night, when I ride, I always look for the light from the stars to guide me."

She paused, then smiled and said, "I am going to call him Star!"

Rebecca liked that choice, "That sounds like a perfect name."

Sybil then turned to Crosby and said, "Oh thank you so much, Mr. Crosby!"

Jesse and Joseph were especially upset at how respectful Sybil was to Crosby but looked at Rebecca and knew it was best to be silent.

Sybil's parents, Henry and Abigail came over. Sybil excitedly showed them her new horse, "Oh Father! Mother! This is the best birthday present ever!"

Her parents smiled.

Sybil asked, "Can I take him for a ride?

Her father, nodded his head, "It is your horse!"

Sybil quickly jumped up on the horse and rode off.

As she rode off, Crosby pulled Henry aside.

Henry put his hand on Crosby's shoulder as they walked off a little way together. Henry said, "Thank you so much Enoch, I can see Sybil loves her gift."

Crosby smiled, "You are quite welcome. I think that

horse will be quite useful one day soon. And, I am so glad you are here to see it and not on some British prison ship."

Henry shook his head positively and responded without any sarcasm, "So am I, Enoch. It is a good thing Dr. Prosser's plan failed. Thank you for the warning."

Crosby then reminded Henry of another concern, "Henry, remember Dr. Prosser said the British would be coming within the month."

Henry nodded in agreement, "Yes, I hope he is wrong."

Crosby replied, "I do too, but I fear you will be involved in an armed conflict very soon."

"If it must be, we are ready and willing to do our part," Henry replied.

Joseph and Jesse walked by Crosby and Henry and kicked up some dirt.

Henry reprimanded them, "Lads! Show some respect!"

Jesse answered gruffly, "Sorry Colonel Ludington, but when he shows some respect for our country, then maybe we will show him some respect!"

Joseph and Jesse continued to walk off together.

Henry looked at Enoch and said, "Sorry Enoch, you know they mean well."

Crosby smiled and said, "Yes, I do appreciate their passion and dislike for Tories."

Henry also smiled and spoke in jest, "Yes, too bad you are one of those awful Tories."

Henry patted Crosby on the back.

Crosby smiled as he responded, "Yes, it is".

Chapter 11

British Fleet Embarks for Norwalk
New York City
April 22, 1777 – Tuesday 1 p.m.

It was April 22, 1777, a chilly and very windy afternoon. A fleet of twenty-six British ships sat docked at the south end of Manhattan Island. The fleet included war ships, transports, and a hospital ship.

An invasion force of about two thousand soldiers began to board the ships in preparation for their raid on the Rebel Supply Depot in Danbury, Connecticut. That force included red-coated British Marines, Regulars from seven different regiments, and mounted dragoons with their tall metallic caps emblazoned with a fearsome death skull and the words, *Or Glory*. They were joined by Loyalists from General Montfort Browne's Regiment wearing their green coats with white facings. Six three-pounder cannons along with artillerymen were also loaded on the ships.

The large force of soldiers tried to quietly board the ships hoping to avoid detection by Rebel spies. The success of this raid depended on the element of surprise.

A smaller diversionary fleet loaded earlier in the day and

sailed up the Hudson River. They went north toward Peekskill. There was a direct overland route from Peekskill to Fishkill where the main Rebel supply depot was located. It was hoped Rebel spies would see the first fleet embark and think the object of the raid was the Fishkill Supply Depot.

Captain Henry Duncan, commander of the fleet, was standing near the dock supervising the boarding of the fleet for the Danbury Raid.

Governor William Tryon, commander of the invasion force approached Captain Duncan. He was accompanied by General James Agnew, General William Erskine, and General Montfort Browne and their aides.

Tryon greeted Duncan with a tip of his hat, "Good afternoon Captain Duncan!"

Duncan dutifully returned the salute, "Thank you Governor Tryon."

Tryon introduced the rest of the senior officers participating in the raid., "General James Agnew, General William Erskine, General Montfort Browne, this is Captain Henry Duncan, He will be leading our invasion fleet of twenty-six ships."

Each officer replied with a nod of their head and grabbed the tip of their hats in salute

Erskine complimented Duncan, "Your reputation precedes you Captain Duncan."

Duncan replied, "Thank You, General Erskine."

Tryon signaled to his aides. One aide opened a map while another held the other side. As the other officers gathered around, Tryon pointed at the map, "Captain Duncan and his fleet will take us to this beach, on the east side of Norwalk, Connecticut. It is called Compo Beach. We will be joined there by more of General Browne's local Loyalists. We will then proceed to Danbury."

Erskine asked, "Do we expect much opposition along the way?"

Browne proudly interjected, "General Erskine, my Loyalists have informed me the Rebels expect some type of raid, but just as we hoped, they fortified their depot at Fishkill thinking that is the target and they have only left a token force at Danbury!"

Erskine asked another question with concern, "And what of Norwalk? Do we expect much resistance there?"

Tryon said, "It is my understanding they do not suspect a thing. When they see Captain Duncan's fleet arrive and see General Browne's Loyalists assemble. I am sure their hearts will turn cold and they will run rather than fight!"

Browne gloated, "My men and I do have that kind of effect!"

Tryon and Erskine looked at each other, reacting with visible dissatisfaction to Browne's pompous comment.

While they were talking, Duncan saw the last of the soldiers board the ships. With that important task completed he announced, "Gentlemen, your fleet awaits you!"

The generals boarded their respective ships. Sailors withdrew the boarding ramps while others untied the docking ropes.

The ships opened their uppermost sails. The blowing wind quickly filled the sails, allowing them to navigate and sail off.

They did not realize they were about to quickly encounter bad weather which would toss their ships around in the waters surrounding Manhattan for three days.

The Route the British Fleet Took to Compo Beach

Engraving by Covens and Mortier, 1780
The fleet left Lower Manhattan on Tuesday, April 22, 1777.
Bad Weather caused long delays.
One of the ships became stuck on rocks yet finally sailed through the narrow channel and into Long Island Sound.
They did not arrive at Compo Beach until Friday, April 25, 1777.

Chapter 12

Shooting Muskets
April 25, 1777 – Friday Morning

The morning of April 25, 1777 started out as a cold, dreary spring day in the Hudson Valley of New York and in neighboring Connecticut. The Rebels were expecting the Crown Forces to attack one of their supply depots within the month but were unaware a fleet of twenty-seven British ships, loaded with troops, was on its way to Norwalk, Connecticut, to launch a raid against the Rebel Supply Depot in Danbury. The British Commander General, The Lord William Howe, who organized this attack, believed this raid could bring an end to the Revolution.

It was a quiet morning, until the silence was broken by the loud sound of a blast from a musket. That blast was followed by the sound of footsteps, running through the woods. The sound of footsteps stopped briefly, and the silence was shattered again by another loud musket blast.

It was not one of the soldiers from the invading force who fired the musket, but seventeen-year old Joseph Angevine, a member of the Dutchess County Militia. He was not shooting at the enemy, he was practicing shooting a musket with his friend, Sybil Ludington.

A lot of musket practice was done shooting from a stationary position. Joseph knew that would not be enough to prepare him for the coming conflict, so he practiced running and shooting.

After he finished running through the woods and shooting the musket a second time, Sybil came towards him and complimented him, "Not bad, Joseph."

Joseph was tired and breathing heavily. He knew Sybil was very familiar with the Militia drill, and was good with a musket, so he was pleased with her compliment. He looked at Sybil and said, "Thank you."

Sybil gave him a big smile and said, "A bit more practice and you may almost be as good as me!"

Joseph was not sure if Sybil was teasing him. He looked back at her with a sneer on his face.

Suddenly, they heard someone on horseback coming their way and looked around cautiously. They were relieved when they saw it was their friend, Jesse Ganong.

Sybil called out, "Over here, Jesse!"

Jesse heard the musket blasts, as he was approaching, and had an idea it was Sybil and Joseph. His hunch was confirmed when he heard Sybil call his name. He headed directly over to them.

As Jesse came close, Joseph gave him a warm greeting, "Jesse, it is good to see you!"

Joseph shifted the musket to his left hand and reached up and heartily shook Jesse's hand with his right hand.

Jesse smiled as he replied, "Joseph!"

Jesse got off his horse and bowed his head to Sybil as he said, "Sybil!" She replied giving him a small curtsey.

Jesse looked at the musket Joseph was holding and asked, "Can I have a turn with that?"

Joseph looked at Jesse with surprise. He knew Jesse never fired a musket because his father would not let him join the Militia. Joseph asked him, "Are you sure?"

Jesse looked back at him and replied, "Very sure!"

Joseph and Sybil looked at each other and smiled. Joseph handed Sybil the musket to hold, while he took off the cartridge box and handed it to Jesse, who then put it on. Sybil then handed Jesse the musket.

Jesse looked at the musket, "So, how do I do this?"

As Joseph reached slowly for the musket to show him, Sybil grabbed it back out of Jesse's hands,

Joseph stepped back with a smile on his face and watched Sybil take charge.

Sybil then reached into the cartridge box, which Jesse was wearing, and removed a cartridge. She then went through the loading sequence, explaining it and demonstrating it effortlessly, step by step.

Sybil held the musket in her left hand with the lock facing towards Jesse, "First, you open the pan like this."

She opened the pan on the musket with her right hand, "Then, you prime the pan."

Sybil bite off the end of the cartridge, spit out the end and put some powder in the pan.

"Then, you close the pan, cast about and load the charge." Sybil cast the musket about properly and inserted the cartridge in the end of the barrel.

"Then, you ram the charge." She withdrew the rammer and rammed the charge down the barrel in one swoop.

"You then, return the rammer." Sybil withdrew the ramrod from the barrel and put it back in the channel.

"Then, you come to the poise." She placed the musket in the poise position in front of her face.

"You then, make ready." Sybil said, as she cocked the musket, while in the *poise* position.

"Then, Present." She then pointed her musket into the woods.

"And then, Fire!" Sybil pulled the trigger and the musket shot with a blast! The bullet flew into the woods and hit something.

Joseph smiled as he saw how smoothly Sybil did the whole procedure. Jesse was watching and concentrating intently on what was happening.

Sybil handed Jesse the musket, "Now Jesse, you do it."

Jesse accepted the musket, then looked at Joseph, indicating he needed help, but did not want to say that. Joseph smiled, nodded, and pointed toward Sybil.

Jesse then looked at Sybil, looking like he needed help, but only asking with his expression. Sybil smiled, nodded her head, and then gave the commands.

First, she said, "Prime and load!"

Jesse looked baffled. Joseph explained, "That means to grab a cartridge and follow the loading and firing commands."

Jesse awkwardly grabbed a cartridge from the cartridge

box.

Sybil continued with the orders, "Open, pan!"

Jesse opened the pan.

Sybil gave the next command, "Prime the pan!"

Jesse bite off the end of the cartridge, spit it out and slowly poured some powder in the pan.

Sybil interrupted him. She did not want him to put in too much powder, "That is enough!"

Jesse stopped. Then Sybil continued the orders, "Close pan, cast about, and charge the barrel."

Jesse almost hit himself in the head as he cast the musket about.

Joseph smiled and put his hand over his mouth trying not to laugh. Sybil smiled.

Jesse recovered and put the cartridge down the barrel.

Sybil continued the orders, "Ram the charge!"

Jesse withdrew the rammer wildly, almost hitting himself. Joseph laughed. Sybil tried to act serious but could not help but smile.

Jesse rammed the charge down the barrel.

Sybil continued the orders, "Return, rammer!"

Jesse fumbled to return the ramrod. He eventually got it back in the channel.

Sybil spoke, "Come to the poise!"

Jesse looked baffled at that command. Joseph motioned to Jesse to put the musket in front of his face.

Jesse raised the musket in front of his face, but not correctly.

Sybil helped him get the musket in the proper position.

Then she said, "Make ready!"

Jesse cocked the musket in the *Poise* position.

Sybil gave the command, "Present!"

Jesse pointed the musket into the woods.

Sybil stopped and gave Jesse one last word of advice, "Make sure you exhale as you pull the trigger."

Jesse nodded his head then Sybil gave the last command, "Fire!"

Jesse closed his eyes and fired. The recoil threw him a little off balance.

Sybil yelled at him, "Next time, plant your feet better. And never close your eyes when you shoot!"

Joseph was watching and smiling the whole time.

Jesse gathered himself, smiled and responded sarcastically, "Yes! Sergeant!"

Sybil looked at him very seriously, "Wipe that smile off your face, soldier!"

She then started to laugh and then they all laughed.

Then Sybil got very serious and said, "Try that again. And this time, imagine you are shooting a Tory!"

Jesse nodded his head. Something seemed to click. His whole demeanor changed to a very determined serious look. He replied, "Yes! Sergeant!"

This time, as Sybil gave the commands, Jesse did it all smoothly.

Sybil gave the first command, "Prime and load!"

Jesse put the musket in the position to load. He quickly grabbed a cartridge from the cartridge box.

She gave the next command, "Open, pan!"

Jesse smoothly opened the pan.

Sybil continued, "Prime the pan!"

Jesse bit off the end of the cartridge, spit it out and put the right amount of powder in the pan.

Sybil gave the next command, "Close the pan, cast about and charge the barrel!"

Jesse closed the pan, cast the musket about and put the cartridge down the barrel.

Sybil continued, "Ram the charge!"

Jesse withdrew the rammer in one swift motion and rammed the charge down the barrel.

Sybil gave the next order, "Return, rammer!

Jesse quickly returned the ramrod back in the channel.

Sybil said, "Come to the poise!"

Jesse raised the musket in front of his face in the proper position. He looked like a seasoned veteran.

Sybil continued, "Make ready!"

Jesse cocked back the hammer on the musket.

Sybil said, "Present!"

Jesse pointed the musket into the woods.

Sybil gave the final command, "Fire!"

Jesse fired the musket smoothly. There was a blast and a brief controlled kickback from the musket.

Joseph was impressed. He came over, patted Jesse on the back and said, "Well done, Jesse!"

Sybil came close and congratulated Jesse, giving him a kiss on the cheek as she said, "Well done!"

Jesse blushed at the kiss, Joseph looked startled.

Just as they finished, it then started to rain.

Loading a Musket

Franklyn Maxwell, 4th New York Regiment of the Continental Line, loading a Musket in Patterson (Fredericksburg), New York.
Photograph by Larry A. Maxwell

Chapter 13

Crown Forces Land at Norwalk
April 25, 1777 – Friday 5 p.m.

The British invasion force of some two thousand men landed at Compo Beach, near Norwalk, Connecticut about five o'clock on the rainy afternoon of Friday, April 25, 1777. They planned to march to Danbury and destroy the Rebel Supply Depot, hoping to bring a swift end to the Rebellion.

They left New York City three days before, on the afternoon of Tuesday April 22, hoping to arrive at Compo Beach that evening undetected.

Things did not go as planned. It took them three days longer to get to Compo Beach than they expected. When they attempted to leave New York City they encountered unexpected strong winds which kept changing directions and even trapped one of the ships at one point.

Those winds, which preceded two days of rain, kept blowing the fleet in the opposite direction. It took Captain Henry Duncan's experience and excellent navigational skills to get the fleet out of the East River, into Long Island Sound, and over to Norwalk.

Compo Beach at Low Tide

Late Afternoon – The time of day the Crown Forces landed.
Photograph by Larry A. Maxwell, 2017

Compo Beach at Sunset

Crown Forces unloaded until 10 o'clock at night.
Photograph by Larry A. Maxwell, 2017

Compo Beach was not a harbor with docks for war ships so the generals and their army all had to disembark from their respective ships on landing craft.

When they landed, as the rest of the troops began the long process of unloading and coming ashore the generals gathered together to discuss their plans.

Governor Tryon addressed Captain Duncan, "Captain Duncan, I must commend you. I never expected such contrary winds when we set out. Yet you handled the fleet quite well."

Duncan nodded his head in thanks for the compliment, "Thank you Governor Tryon. I never had such a challenge as I did in those waters. I apologize for the delay."

Tyron replied, "I am not happy about the delay but there is no apology necessary Captain. You have no control over the weather. You did your job very well and gave us a safe voyage the rest of the way."

Erskine changed the subject. He was eager to begin the attack, "It is time to teach the Rebels a lesson!"

As the rest of the troops were disembarking a company of Loyalists arrived from the surrounding area. They were part of General Montfort Browne's Prince of Wales Loyalist Regiment. They brought along some new recruits who were emboldened to join when they heard there was a chance this action would help bring a swift end to the Rebellion.

The sight of the British fleet and the company of armed Loyalists along the shore helped stifle resistance from the local town folk in Norwalk.

The leader of the local Loyalist Company approached

the group of officers. He was looking for General Browne, his commander.

He took off his hat and bowed his head in in salute, "General Browne, we are at your service."

Crown Forces Landing at Compo Beach
By Robert Lynn Lambdin.
Westport Schools Permanent Art Collection
On Display at Westport Town Hall

Browne smiled as he saw the company of Loyalists in their green uniforms along with the group of new recruits.

He returned the salute with a nod of his hat and addressed the leader of the Loyalist Company, "Thank you son. Have your company join the rest of the regiment!"

The Loyalist officer nodded his head in compliance, "Yes, Sir!"

He rejoined his company and had them march off to join

the rest of General Montfort Browne's Regiment.

Browne looked at the others and spoke, with boisterous pride, "With my Loyal Regiment, I am sure we will have the victory."

Tryon and Erskine grimaced at each other, obviously weary with Browne's pompous attitude.

Tryon spoke sarcastically, "Perhaps General Agnew, General Erskine and I should wait here with our regiments while you and your Loyalists take care of the Rebels?"

Browne did not catch the fact Tryon was being sarcastic. At first he responded like he thought it was a good suggestion but then realized that probably was not the best idea.

He spoke in a condescending manner to Tryon, "I would hate to have you come all this way and not get a chance to see my men and I in action."

Tryon was not pleased with Browne's response.

Erskine was annoyed and could not contain himself. He boldly spoke up, "Governor Browne (he said *Governor* instead of using *General*, Browne's preferred title) you egotistical, pompous bag of wind! Perhaps I should remind you, Governor Tryon is the one in charge!"

Browne was shocked at Erskine's words.

Erskine continued his rebuke, "And never forget, your *Loyalists* never did enlist in a Regular unit, but waited to see how things would turn out before they joined us."

Browne did not like Erskine's comments.

Erskine said more, "And we are not even sure if we can really trust them, so we gave them those green regimentals instead of red ones, so we can easily distinguish them from the faithful Regular troops!"

Browne was greatly insulted. He replied with indignation, "Well, I never!"

Tryon interceded, "Gentlemen! Gentlemen! Let us remember who the real enemy is!"

Browne turned away in a huff and headed over to his troops.

Tryon smiled at Erskine, nodded his head, and said, "And, General Erskine."

Erskine looked at Tryon questioningly.

Tryon smiled, leaned closer to Erskine, and said, somewhat quieter, "Well said."

Erskine smiled, then headed to join his troops.

It was getting late in the day. It took four hours to get all the men off the boats. There was no time to set up camp and rest. They needed to march the entire way to Danbury, in the rain, so they could catch the Rebels unaware.

To mislead the Rebels from their ultimate destination they choose to first march east towards Fairfield instead of marching directly north to Danbury.

Chapter 14

Conflict Between Father and Son
April 25, 1777 – Late Friday Afternoon

It was late in the afternoon on Friday, April 25, 1777. John Ganong was seated comfortably in his home reading while his wife Mary was doing some needlework. They had no idea the Crown Forces were landing at Compo Beach.

John was a successful businessman. Though he did not consider himself a Loyalist he had many business associates with strong Loyalist ties. Those connections helped his business succeed and the success of his business allowed him to build a home which was larger and more comfortable than most of his neighbors.

The silence was disturbed as the door opened and John's son Jesse entered. He was wet from riding in the rain, which started when he finished his musket practice with his friends Sybil Ludington and Joseph Angevine. He entered the house and started to walk right past his father. He was angry with his father and it showed on his face.

John looked up at his son and asked inquisitively, "Jesse, where have you been?"

Jesse planned to walk right past his father. When his

father addressed him, he stopped and stood still looking ahead, not making eye contact. He replied curtly, "I have been with Sybil and Joseph."

Jesse's father knew Sybil was Colonel Henry Ludington's daughter and that Joseph was in the Militia. He feared it would only bring more trouble to his family if Joseph continued to associate with them.

John looked closely at his son Jesse. He thought he noticed something on his face. He stood up and went over to Jesse to get a closer look. He saw the residue of black powder from shooting a musket on Jesse's face. He also recognized a familiar odor. Having served in the French and Indian War he knew the smell of the black powder left upon a person after firing a musket.

He was upset at what he saw and smelled. In an angry tone he said, "You smell like black powder!"

Jesse responded with a shrug and started to walk away. After the Loyalists attempted to capture Colonel Ludington, and his father adamantly refused to allow him to join the militia, Jesse no longer cared what his father thought.

As Jesse walked away John spoke out more with concern than passion. Jesse stopped and listened with his back to his father. "Son, you must realize this Rebellion is a lost cause. It is going to end soon."

His father tried to add something he thought was optimistic, "We will have peace again. The King and Parliament mean good for us. They will not harm us if we just leave them alone!"

Jesse turned around and looked angrily at his father. He

disagreed with everything his father just said. He responded with passion in his voice, "Father! They will not leave us alone! The King and Parliament would rather have us all hanged, than have peace!"

Jesse looked his father directly in the eye and said, "When will you realize we are at war! If we do not fight for our liberty what are we worth?"

After speaking so abruptly, Jesse stormed off.

John was cut to the heart by his son's words. He shook his head in despair and put his head in his hands.

His wife sat by silently during this conflict. She did not like seeing her husband and son at odds with each other. She feared nothing good would come of this.

Tory Tax Collector

*Nicolas Ponce and Francois Godefroy, engraving circa 1784.
Some Loyalists were abused by Rebel mobs.*

Chapter 15

Confrontation at Bethel
April 26, 1777 – Saturday Afternoon

It was Saturday afternoon, April 26, 1777. The Crown Forces left Compo Beach about ten o'clock last night. The steady rain made the roads very muddy which made it extremely difficult moving their six cannons. They were also slowed down by some small resistance along the way. They were glad when they reached Redding about eleven o'clock in the morning and took a two-hour break for breakfast.

Before the Crown Forces arrived many people sympathetic with the Rebel cause fearfully loaded wagons and headed out of town. The Rebels who remained saw no hope in offering resistance. The Loyalists enjoyed rounding up their annoying Rebel neighbors and taking prisoners.

About one o'clock in the afternoon General William Erskine led the advance out of town as the Crown Forces resumed their march, continuing north toward Bethel. Their destination was the supply depot at Danbury.

When they came to Hoyt's Hill in Bethel, a parish of Danbury, a rider appeared on the crest of the hill in front of them. He ascended the hill on a horse waving a sword over his head like a confident general in command of an army.

General Erskine, who was leading the advancing army, was alarmed when he saw the menacing figure waving his sword. It looked like a general preparing his men for an attack. He was not going to allow his men to fall into a trap.

He yelled the command, "Come to the halt." The whole army abruptly stopped their advance.

Erskine watched and listened as the figure on the hill turned to look back over his shoulder and yelled, "Halt! The whole universe! Break off by nations!"

Erskine was puzzled, He never heard such commands before. It sounded like there must be a very large force waiting to oppose them over the crest of that hill.

General William Tryon rode to the front to see why the advance stopped. General Agnew and General Browne stayed back with their troops. General Erskine updated Tryon, who then took command.

Rather than change head-on into an unknown force Tryon decided to make a stand. He pulled out his sword and yelled the command, "Advance the cannons to the front!"

His command was echoed by other officers down the line, "Advance the cannons to the front!"

The two long columns of soldiers moved to each side of the road to allow the artillery crews to trudge ahead. They struggled to move the cannons up the muddy road. Each cannon created ruts in the road, which grew deeper and made it more difficult to maneuver each successive cannon.

Finally, all six cannons were in front of the army spread out in a wide row ready to repel the enemy attack.

The officer on the hill ahead of them rode back and forth holding his sword straight up in the air as he looked at the Crown Forces with a menacing glare.

When the cannons were in place Governor Tryon called the infantry into position, "From column into line!"

Crown Forces Wait for the Enemy to Attack

Crown Forces reenactors waiting for orders to attack.
Photograph by Gary Vorwald

Officers echoed his command, "From column into line."

With impressive precision the Crown Forces formed neat orderly rows between and behind the artillery with their muskets on their left shoulders.

As the troops were forming into rows, Governor Tryon yelled, "Load cannons!"

Each of the artillery captains gave the orders to their crews to prepare and load each cannon.

As the cannons were loading, Tryon yelled orders to the

soldiers lined up in rows, "Prime and Load!"

The officers echoed his command, "Prime and Load!"

Like a well-oiled machine every man went through the proper loading sequence and finished with their muskets held in the *ready* position in front of their face.

All eyes were looking at the summit. They watched apprehensively as the officer on the hill rode back over the summit and out of sight. They had no idea how great a force opposed them and what carnage lay ahead.

Everyone waited apprehensively for the front line of the Rebel Army to advance over the hill.

They waited and waited, and then waited some more.

General Erskine stood firmly on his horse, next to Governor Tryon, with his sword draw.

Tryon noticed the prolonged anticipation made some of his men started to move nervously. He yelled, "Steady!"

The other officers echoed his command, "Steady!"

After what seemed a long while Erskine looked at Tryon and asked, "Do you think they are waiting for us to advance on them?"

"They must think me a fool if they think I will charge blindly over a hill!" Tryon replied adamantly.

"Neither would I," Erskine agreed.

Tryon said, "We shall wait for them to advance and then we will crush them!"

Erskine agreed that was the best strategy, "Well said!"

As they waited anxiously for the Rebel advance General Browne wondered what was delaying the action. He finally came riding up to join Tryon and Erskine.

Condescendingly he asked, "What are we waiting for?"

Erskine was impatient with Browne. He replied with indignation, "We are waiting for them to attack us! We are not foolish enough to ride over the hill into an ambush!"

Browne did not like Erskine's attitude. He looked at Tryon and said, "Perhaps I should send some of my scouts around their flank to assess the size of their army?"

Tryon was tired of waiting. He liked that idea and replied, "Excellent idea General Browne! Send out your scouts!"

Browne gave Erskine a pompous look as he replied to Tryon, "Yes! Sir!" He then rode back to his men.

In a few moments three scouts on horseback headed to the left of the summit and three headed to the right.

Tryon, Erskine, and the rest of the army watched and waited apprehensively.

The scouts came riding back over the hill much sooner than expected. That baffled everyone. They rode back close to where the Generals thought the enemy was waiting.

The first scout back yelled, "There is no one there!"

Tryon and Erskine sat in disbelief on their horses as the other scouts reported the same thing.

General Browne rode back to the front to hear the report.

Erskine smiled, "They must have run away like scared rabbits when they saw the size of our force!"

Tryon asked the scouts, "Could you tell how many of them there were as they retreated?"

The scouts all responded, "One."

Erskine asked, "One regiment?"

One of the scouts reluctantly replied, "No, Sir." He hesitantly said, "All we saw was one rider riding away as fast as he could."

What the scouts saw was twenty-five-year-old Luther Holcomb riding off by himself. Holcomb smiled a big smile as he rode off knowing his ruse worked. He single-handedly delayed the entire army of the Crown Forces.

General Browne could not contain himself. He laughed and said sarcastically said to Erskine, "No, we are not foolish!"

1796 German Map of Connecticut

*Printed by Sotzsen, Hamburg, Germany.
Bethel is Northeast of Danbury.*

Chapter 16

Danbury Attacked

April 26, 1777 – Late Saturday Afternoon

After marching all day and night through the rain for almost thirty miles the Crown Forces finally reached Danbury late in the afternoon on Saturday, April 26, 1777. They only had two hours of rest at Redding and survived an encounter at Bethel with Luther Holcomb and his invisible army. They were tired but invigorated at the thought of destroying the Rebel supplies and ending the Rebellion.

Governor William Tryon, General James Agnew and General William Erskine gathered just outside of Danbury.

Governor Tryon spoke with confidence, "Gentlemen, we made it to Danbury without much opposition."

General Montfort Browne sent his scouts ahead to see what type of resistance they would encounter in Danbury. He was very pleased with the word he received back from them. He joined the other officers and greeted Tryon and Agnew. He purposefully did not greet Erskine.

Tryon asked, "General Browne! What news do you bring?"

He gave his report with pompous conceit and an *I told you so* attitude. He was proud he was correct that they would make it to Danbury without much *real* opposition.

Browne could not forget Erskine's negative comments and was gloating over the fiasco in Bethel. He sneered at Erskine as he gave his report. "It is exactly as I said! The Rebels thought we planned to attack Fishkill. So, all they left here is a small token force defending Danbury."

Erskine jeered back at Browne. He was glad to hear the good report but did not like Browne's attitude.

Tryon looked at his officers and said, "Gentlemen, you have your orders. It is time to teach the Rebels a lesson which they will not forget. Let us see how well their little Rebellion goes without their supplies!"

He then said, "Take what you can and burn the rest!"

Tryon looked at Browne, "Make sure your Loyalists tie a ribbon on their doors, so their homes will be protected!"

Browne shook his head in agreement and responded, "We shall protect our Loyalists and destroy the Rebels!"

Tryon exhorted them, "Long live the King!"

The others responded, "Long live the King!"

They then rode to join their respective brigades.

This was the second day a cold spring rain fell. It was heavy at times. Everything and everyone was soaked. Battles were not usually fought in the rain, mainly because muskets will not fire if the black powder gets wet. That is why soldiers were exhorted to *keep their powder dry.* Despite the rain the generals leading the raid knew they had to follow through with the attack. If the muskets would not fire they knew they could use their bayonets.

General Erskine led the first Brigade into town at about 5 p.m. As he did the rain started to subside.

Colonel Joseph Platt Cooke
Portrait by William Jennys, 1790-1795

Colonel Joseph Platt Cooke was Commander of the Rebel Supply Depot at Danbury. Earlier in the day he received a desperate appeal from General Silliman to send troops to the coast to help repel an invasion by the Crown Forces. General Silliman did not know the supply depot at Danbury was the Crown Forces destination. Colonel Cooke responded by sending some Militia along with most of the men from the 1st Connecticut Regiment under the command of Colonel Jedediah Huntington. That left only one hundred men with Colonel Cooke to defend Danbury.

Now Colonel Cooke stood with his men on the main street with sword drawn waiting for the Crown Forces.

Thomas Starr stood next to him bravely holding the Liberty flag. The Liberty flag was used as a battle flag throughout the Revolution. It's thirteen-alternating red and white stripes waved boldly in the wind.

From the time the Crown Forces landed at Compo Beach until they reached Danbury they wanted to maintain an element of surprise, so they tried to be as quiet as possible. Now there was no need to be quiet, so they marched into town with drummers and fifers playing.

As the powerful intimidating sound of the music drew closer, Colonel Cooke yelled to his men, "Form a line here!"

Cooke's men responded promptly and formed a line with two rows. They were apprehensive but ready to do whatever they could to stop the advance of the enemy.

Cooke then yelled to his men, "Prime and load!"

Cooke's men bravely followed his orders and did the complete loading sequence then stood nervously waiting for the imminent arrival of the Crown Forces.

Soon two Continental soldiers came running down the road as fast as they could. One of them cried out, "Colonel Cooke they are almost here!"

The Crown Forces appeared with an overwhelming number of soldiers coming down the street in a slow determined march. General Erskine was leading the advance on horseback as the musicians played.

As more and more Crown Forces arrived the situation began to look more desperate to Cooke and his men.

Musicians Play as Crown Forces Enter Town
Gary Vorwald and musicians lead troops into battle.
Photo by Kenneth Grant

Erskine was startled when he saw Cooke's men standing in the street. The thing that startled him was the fact Cooke's men were wearing red regimental coats faced in white and were led by an officer dressed the same. In the British Army only royal regiments wore red coats faced in white. It appeared to him they were facing British Regulars.

Erskine was an officer and a gentleman and would never shoot someone unless he was positive they were the enemy. He ordered his men to stop, yelling out, "Come to the halt!"

The Crown Forces came to an abrupt halt. Erskine lowered his sword while his men stood in line with their muskets on their left shoulders.

Colonel Cooke was pleased to see the Crown Forces stop their advance. He wondered how long that would last.

Erskine was perplexed. He did not know he was facing the local Militia and some men from the 1st Connecticut Regiment of the Continental Line. The men in the 1st Connecticut Regiment wore red coats faced in white, which was their traditional uniform from before the Revolution. Colonel Cooke also wore a red coat faced white.

Erskine was puzzled when he saw the Liberty flag, Thomas Star was carrying. Erskine saw those flags in battle and knew it was the symbol of the Rebellion.

General Browne rode up to Erskine. He wanted to attack and wondered why the advance stopped. He asked Erskine, "Why have we stopped?"

Erskine explained, "It looks like there are some of our Regulars standing over there in the street!" He pointed down the street and added, "But they are flying the accursed Liberty flag, the battle flag of the Rebels!"

Browne was surprised to see some Militia along with men wearing red coats. He had never seen the Liberty flag but realized if those men were holding a symbol of the Rebellion then this was not good. He spoke firmly, "If that flag is the Rebel's battle flag I do not care what they are wearing they are traitors."

Erskine replied, "Seeing those red coats with white facings made me stop. As you know those white facings usually indicate royal regiments from England or Wales and I do not want to fire on our own men."

He paused and then continued speaking with firm resolve, "But I agree, that flag is clearly an unacceptable symbol and cannot be tolerated."

Erskine turned to Browne. "Go back and get your men ready for action."

Browne smiled and replied, "My men and I are always ready to take action against the Rebel scum."

Erskine raised his sword and yelled the commands to his men, "First Company! Make Ready! Present! Fire!"

They pointed their muskets down the street at the Rebels and fired. It felt like the ground shook as the sound of a massive volley of muskets filled the air. The musket balls stuck some Rebels. They fell helplessly to the ground.

Colonel Cooke quickly replied yelled the firing sequence to his men, "Make Ready! Present! Fire!"

As Cooke's men fired two of the soldiers next to General Erskine were struck and killed. Erskine was shaken and immediately shouted to his men, "Prime and Load!"

Like a well-oiled machine the Crown Forces loaded their muskets again.

As the Crown Forces reloaded Cooke yelled to his men, "Fire at will!"

Cooke's men, though greatly outnumbered, stood bravely. They reloaded and continued sporadic firing. As soon as each man shot his musket he loaded it, fired it again, and then reloaded and fired again.

When the Crown Forces completed their loading sequence, Erskine yelled, "Fix! Bayonets!"

The soldiers fixed their bayonets over the end of their muskets. That allowed them to either fire or use the bayonets in a dreaded bayonet charge. That struck fear in the heart of Cooke's men.

Cooke realized his men could not withstand a British bayonet charge. He yelled to his men, "Retreat! Retreat!"

Cooke and his men withdrew. Those who were loaded, shot at the Crown Forces, then turned and ran.

Erskine yelled, "Bayonet Charge! Advance!"

The Crown Forces yelled a long-protracted *Huzzah* and advanced forward in a smooth, powerful, aggressive line.

The Regulars were followed by Loyalists who went into buildings looking for Rebel supplies. When they approached a house, they looked to see if there was a ribbon tied to the door. If there was a ribbon they turned away.

Muskets continued to fire sporadically. People were yelling and screaming in fear. Loyalists continued looting, taking supplies out of shops and homes.

Some Loyalists came out of one building rolling crates of rum out into the street. They yelled *"Huzzah!"* as they opened some of the crates and loudly laughed with glee as they filled mugs with rum and passed them around.

Some of the Regulars looked around to make sure an officer was not watching, then joined in the libation.

Carts were seized and loaded with the confiscated supplies. When a building was emptied, it was set aflame. Once the carts were filled, the extra supplies were piled in the street and set on fire.

Colonel Cooke stopped behind a building and spoke with messengers mounting their horses. He said, "Go to the colonels of the local Militias and tell them the Regulars and Tories have attacked and are burning Danbury!"

As the messengers rode away on their mission the

Crown Forces pressed towards Cooke and his men. Cooke's' men fired their muskets back at the Crown Forces.

Cooke yelled, "Retreat!" They turned and followed him heading away from the Crown Forces.

Musket fire continued. People could be heard screaming all around Danbury. The Crown Forces took some people away at gunpoint as the looting and burning continued.

The rain that subsided earlier started to fall again.

Danbury Raid Monument

Plaque on a Boulder on Main Street, Danbury, Connecticut. Remembering the Danbury Raid. It reads: *The Revolutionary Village Which Centered About This Green With Its Store Of Supplies For The Army Was Sacked And Burned By A Force Of Two Thousand British April 26, 1777 Warned Of The Gathering Militia The Raiders Departed Next Morning In Haste But Were Attacked And Harassed By The Rising Colonials And Driven To The Refuge Of Their Boats On The Sound They Kindled A Fire That Blazed At Saratoga*
Photograph by Larry A. Maxwell, 2018

Larry A. Maxwell

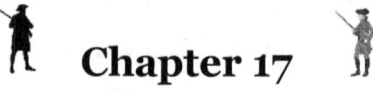

Chapter 17

American Officers Meet at Redding

April 26, 1777 – Late Saturday Afternoon

It was late afternoon on Saturday, April 26, 1777. General Silliman and almost four hundred Militia were approaching Redding, Connecticut. Rain fell for the past two days soaking everyone. The Crown Forces left Redding a few hours ago, reached Danbury and began their raid.

If things went as planned the raid on Danbury would have been over but bad weather kept delaying the expedition. It had been four days since the Crown Forces boarded their ships in New York and almost twenty-four hours since they landed at Compo Beach. They wanted the raid to be a secret, so they could attack the Rebels unaware.

Last month Brigadier General Gold Selleck Silliman, Commander of the Connecticut Militia, suspected the Crown Forces were going to launch an attack against Connecticut and appealed to General George Washington for additional regiments to help with its defense. Washington did not have any intelligence to confirm a possible attack and denied the request.

General Silliman lived in Fairfield, Connecticut, not far

from where the Crown Forces landed. He received word of the landing early Saturday before sunrise and immediately sent word to the Militia in Connecticut. and as far away as Massachusetts, calling for help to repel the invasion.

He sent a message to Colonel Joseph Platt Cooke at Danbury to send as many men as possible to help him. Colonel Cooke responded by sending most of his force. Silliman did not yet know Danbury was the Crown Forces ultimate destination or he would not have given that order.

To mislead the Rebels and disguise their destination, the Crown Forces marched east toward Fairfield instead of directly north toward Danbury.

Some four hundred men responded to General Silliman's call. They rallied with him and began to pursue the Crown Forces. His scouts reported Governor Tryon and his army turned north and were heading toward Redding. Silliman sent messengers to inform others then led his men toward Redding to try to stop the Crown Forces.

When Silliman was about two miles south of Redding there was a break in the rain. Another general approached on horseback leading a small group of men.

Silliman was pleased when he recognized this general as one whom many people respected because of how he distinguished himself in battle. Silliman knew that officer's battlefield experience could be a big help in this crisis.

When that general drew near to Silliman he grabbed the edge of his hat and nodded to Silliman. That was the kind of salute given to one of equal or lower status.

That general said, "General Silliman, I was visiting

family and came as soon as I received the news about the Crown Forces invasion and your request to meet you at Redding."

Silliman greeted him with greater respect than that general offered to him. Instead of touching the brim of his hat, Silliman took off his hat which was much more respectful and nodded his head in salute as he said, "General Benedict Arnold it is a pleasure to see you again."

Portrait of General Benedict Arnold

A miniature by Pierre Eugene Du Simitiere, October 3, 1780
This is considered the only authentic portrait of Benedict Arnold.

At that time General Benedict Arnold was a well-respected general and considered a hero of the Revolution.

Later his heroism would be forgotten by most when he becomes America's most notorious traitor.

Silliman continued his very respectful greeting acknowledging the value of Arnold's experience, "General Arnold, I am honored by your presence and can most assuredly use your assistance."

Arnold smiled in appreciation of the gracious greeting and replied, "I appreciate those kind words. I understand this engagement falls under the authority of the State of Connecticut. Seeing your commission comes from the State of Connecticut and mine from the Continental Congress, I humbly submit myself to you. I will have my men fall in with yours and we can head to Redding together."

Arnold loved to be in charge but always tried to follow proper military protocol. If the response to this engagement had been initiated by the Continental Congress then he would have been the ranking officer. He understood this engagement was under the authority of Connecticut. That meant General Silliman outranked him and was the proper person to be in change. That is the only reason he offered to have his men fall in under General Silliman.

Silliman and Arnold rode together to Redding. Their combined force of soldiers followed them.

When they arrived in town they were directed to the home of a member of the Militia who escaped being captured by the Crown Forces. He told them the Crown Forces arrived with around two thousand men and six cannons, that they stopped for lunch, took some prisoners, and left only a few hours before the Rebels arrived.

Shortly after Silliman and Arnold arrived Major General David Wooster entered town. He came with another hundred men. He was directed to the home where Silliman and Arnold were located.

General David Wooster

This portrait is attributed to J. B. Longacre, published in 1835. This bears a strong resemblance to the fictitious Thomas Hart portraits of 1776. It also looks very similar to Richard Purcell's portrait of Lord William Howe. Most of Longacre's portraits are considered accurate. This portrait is often incorrectly identified as done in 1750. Wooster was not in Quebec until 1754.

Wooster was older than Arnold. They had a conflict at the beginning of the Revolution. Wooster later became Arnold's commanding officer and gained respect for him. When Wooster arrived, Arnold immediately greeted him with proper respect. He removed his hat and make a small bow as he respectfully said, "General David Wooster."

Instead of returning the salute Wooster extended his hand and gave Arnold a handshake and said, "General Benedict Arnold, I am so glad you are here. I am sure your experience will be a great help to us!"

Wooster then turned to Silliman, took off his hat and nodded his head in salute as he said, "General Silliman it is an honor to fall in with you."

Silliman returned the same hat-off salute and replied, "General Wooster, I am honored to have you here and humbly turn command over to you."

According to military protocol General Wooster, whose commission also came from the State of Connecticut, was of a higher rank than General Silliman. Silliman knew that and so did Arnold. Arnold was a stickler for proper protocol, so he accepted Wooster's command.

Arnold quickly acknowledged Wooster's command. He said, "General Wooster, how may I best serve?"

Silliman gave an update to Wooster, "Our host informed us the Crown Forces left here marching north to Bethel. They have a force of close to two thousand men along with six cannons.

Wooster spoke up, "Then it appears their destination is our supply depot in Danbury."

Silliman was distraught to acknowledge that. He interjected, "I deeply regret to inform you, I did not know Danbury was the Crown Forces destination. When they landed at Norwalk they headed east towards my hometown of Fairfield, so I sent a message earlier today to Danbury requesting Colonel Cooke to send me as many soldiers as possible to help repel the invasion. He sent me most of the 1st Connecticut Regiment which were on duty with him."

Silliman now realized his decision backfired and left Danbury vulnerable. He gave a disparaging detail, "I regret to report Colonel Cooke has only about one hundred men with him to defend the depot."

"That is most unfortunate," Wooster said.

Wooster realized how discouraged Silliman was because of the decision he made to take troops away from Danbury. Wooster did not criticize Silliman, instead he put his hand on Silliman's shoulder and said, "You meant well and did the right thing with the information you had."

Wooster was known for his kindness and respect for others. It made him well loved by many.

Arnold could see these circumstances made it important to reach Danbury as soon as possible. He tried to turn the discouraging news into an opportunity to thwart the Crown Forces. He said, "Then we shall follow General Wooster to Danbury forthwith and stop the Crown Forces!"

Wooster agreed with Arnold's suggestion but added some bad news, "General Arnold, I believe that is our best course of action, but the rain has started to come down again and quite intensely, and the wind has picked up making it almost impossible to proceed."

Arnold said, "I am sure our men are willing to follow you, through rain and wind."

Wooster replied, "I appreciate your confidence in our men, but they are already soaked and tired from marching all day. And making matters worse, two days of rain have made the road extremely muddy and barely passable."

On a more somber note he said, "Reports say Governor Tryon is leading the invasion and that his invasion force includes men from two regiments which were at Lexington and Concord, and at Bunker Hill. They suffered great loses there. I understand they are looking for revenge."

Arnold added, "It is dangerous to face someone who desires revenge, it makes them fight more passionately."

Silliman concurred with Arnold, "Speaking of revenge, the invasion force also includes a regiment with hundreds of Tories mostly from right here in Fairfield County. They look at us as traitors and would love to see all of us in British prison ships!"

At that time Arnold saw Loyalists as notorious and dangerous. He spoke passionately, "They are the traitors!"

Wooster spoke again, "You are both correct. The truth is we have only about five hundred men. They have almost two thousand. We are outnumbered about four-to-one."

Wooster showed his understanding of the situation and his consideration for his men as he said, "It would be good for our men to have some rest before we go into battle. I believe we can afford to wait for a reprieve in the rain. That will probably take only an hour or two at most."

He smiled as he said, "You know how quickly the weather changes here in Connecticut."

Silliman also smiled as he said, "That is true. I think it has already changed about four times today."

Wooster replied, "I am sure the weather is just as bad around Danbury and will slow down Tryon and his forces. Hopefully we will arrive before they attack Danbury."

Wooster did not know the Crown Forces were already in Danbury and their intense attack already began.

Take Notice Recruitment Poster

Printed by B. Jones, Philadelphia, 1798-1815.
This poster is often shown in books as a Revolutionary War recruitment poster. This was not printed until after the war. The officers listed in this poster were members of the 11th Infantry Regiment, which was not formed until 1798.

Chapter 18

Messenger Arrives at Ludington's
April 26, 1777 – Saturday 9 p.m.

It was now Saturday April 26, 1777, a cold night in the Hudson Valley. Though some neighboring towns had some reprieve from the rain it rained steadily in Dutchess County for two days and it was still raining. The roads were muddy and the rivers were high.

It was about nine o'clock in the evening. Colonel Henry Ludington and his wife Abigail were sitting around the fireplace. He was reading and she was mending clothes. Their children were upstairs sleeping except for Sybil and Rebecca, who were still awake talking with each other.

The peaceful silence of the evening was suddenly disturbed by someone pounding on the door.

The Colonel stood up and grabbed his sword. Abigail stopped her work and looked up. She was very concerned, "Henry, who do you think that is?"

Henry cautiously replied, "I am not sure."

The Ludingtons lived on the main road so it was not unusual for people to visit them, but it was unusual for someone to call that late, especially on a rainy night.

Henry looked out the window to see if he could tell who was at the door. It was too dark to see who it was. All he could make out was the shape of a man and a horse tied to the post near the door.

With his sword drawn he went to the door and opened it. As he did the man at the door stumbled into Henry's arms and weakly asked, "Colonel Ludington!"

He was soaking wet and obviously exhausted. He did not appear to be a threat. Henry led him to a chair and said, "Abigail, please get a dry blanket for this lad."

Abigail quickly got a blanket and put it on the messenger. Sybil and Rebecca heard the commotion and came downstairs looking concerned.

Abigail looked at the man shivering and said, "Let me get you something warm to drink."

She went to the fireplace, got a cup, and filled it from a kettle near the fireplace and brought it back to him.

Henry knelt near the messenger and reassuringly said, "You are safe now."

The messenger was exhausted. He struggled to speak, "Colonel Cooke from Danbury sent me. I rode as fast as I could, but the rain and muddy roads made it difficult."

Sybil and Rebecca stayed back a little. With great concern Sybil asked, "Father, what is happening?"

The messenger spoke in despair, "The Regulars and Tories attacked and are burning Danbury! It is terrible!"

His words made everyone respond with concern.

Abigail exclaimed, "Oh, Henry!"

Alarmed, Sybil and Rebecca each cried, "Father!"

Henry asked the messenger for more information. "When did this happen? How many were there?"

The messenger was holding the mug with both hands which Abigail gave him. It was his first drink he had since he set out from Danbury, hours ago.

He replied to Henry, "They came after ...." He paused for a moment trying to gather his thoughts. Then he continued, "After noon, Yes, it was late afternoon."

"I think it was the whole British Army. Colonel Cooke tried to stop them but there were too many!"

Henry asked more questions, "Is Colonel Cooke alright? What about the supplies?"

The messenger took another drink from the mug and said, "Last I saw him, Colonel Cooke and a group of our men were still alive."

He spoke with more concern, "But the Tories and Regulars were taking everything! They were looting and burning piles of things in the street!"

Henry shook his head in concern and looked at his family and said, "We must call out the Militia!"

He paced around, then with great disappointment he said, "We thought they would have attacked the main depot at Fishkill."

Abigail came over to Henry. She was distraught. He put his arms around her. All she could say was, "Oh, Henry!"

The alarming news made Sybil and Rebecca hold tightly to each other.

Henry put his arms out for his daughters. They came over and he put his arms around them and hugged them.

After a few moments he released them and got down to business, "I must stay here and assemble the troops."

He looked at Abigail and Rebecca and said, "Abigail, Rebecca, while we wait for the men to arrive I need you to help make as many cartridges for the muskets as we can."

Rebecca responded affirmatively, "Yes, Father!" Then she and her mother began to gather the supplies for making cartridges.

Henry placed his hands on Sybil's shoulders, looked at her intently and said, "Sybil, you have been my faithful messenger before. Now I need you to ride again, to call out the Militia, under much more difficult conditions."

As he said that, Abigail stopped what she was doing and looked at Henry. She said, "But Henry! It is raining, and it is so dark! And who knows how many thieves and Tories are waiting to ambush any messenger they see."

She started to say, "What about …?" She was going to suggest the messenger from Danbury but turned and saw he was sound asleep in the chair.

Henry looked at Abigail and then at Sybil and said, "He is exhausted. There is no other way. It needs to be Sybil."

Abigail was disappointed but knew he was right.

He said, "I know Sybil can do this."

Sybil realized the immense responsibility and did not hesitate. Very enthusiastically she said, "Oh, Yes, Father! I know the way and I will do my best!"

Sybil was clearly excited at this opportunity. She wanted to do something meaningful for the cause of liberty ever since she heard of the ride of Paul Revere, William Dawes, and Samuel Prescott.

"And I can use my wonderful new horse which Mr. Crosby brought me on my birthday!" she said.

Once Rebecca realized Sybil was going to make the ride she went and got Sybil's riding boots and brought them to Sybil and helped her put them on.

Sybil's mother brought her a cloak, put it on her and said, "You are going to need this! It is a dreadful rainy night out there."

Abigail then hugged Sybil tightly.

Sybil looked intently at her father.

He looked back at her and said, "You know the route is forty-miles long but in the dark and rain it will seem like much more than forty miles. Make sure you pace yourself."

Sybil listened intently as her father gave her more instructions, "And as your mother said, you know it is not unusual to find Tories or thieves waiting to ambush anyone who passes by on the road. Perhaps this rain is a good thing, even those type of people usually know enough not to go out on a night like this!"

Abigail grew more concerned, especially when she heard Henry say, *on a night like this*. She ran to Sybil and hugged her again and said, "Please, be careful!"

Sybil hugged her mother and said, "Yes, Mother! I will!"

Sybil started to walk towards her Father, then stopped, looked back at her mother with longing and said, "Please pray for me!"

Her mother reassured her, "We will Sybil, we will!

Henry spoke to Abigail as he and Sybil headed to the

door, "I know Sybil can do this. This is something God has prepared her for."

Henry and Sybil went outside into the rainy night. They headed to the barn to get her horse ready.

As they were saddling her horse, Henry gave her more instructions, "I am so proud of you Sybil. I know you have always wanted to do your part to help our struggle for liberty. Now the time has come. It is your turn to do what Paul Revere and the others did."

A more serious look came across his face, "But you will be doing so much more. You will be riding alone in the rain and in the dark for a much longer distance."

Sybil replied, "Mehitable Prendergast rode eighty miles to appeal to the Governor and save her husband. I know I can ride forty miles to save our country!"

She smiled and said, "I will do my best, Father! I know the way! I could almost do it blindfolded!"

Henry said, "I think blindfolded might be a better condition than this rain and darkness."

He admonished her, "Remember to ride as swiftly as you can! You must be careful. All the snow we had this winter and these spring rains will make some of the streams extra high."

As he double-checked her saddle he strongly warned her, "Make sure you avoid as many dark places as you can, it is too dark to see. Do not stop for anyone along the way!"

He then added a word of comfort, "We will pray the rain will stop so you will be able to see better."

He helped Sybil up onto the saddle.

He then gave Sybil her mission, "Sybil, there will not be enough time for you to dismount and knock on each door."

He handed Sybil a stick and said, "Use this stick to wake people up by pounding on the shutters and doors. When they come to their door you will not have time to engage in a conversation. Just tell them, *Call to arms! The Regulars and Tories are burning Danbury! The Militia is needed! Call to arms!*"

He paused and said, "No other explanation is needed they will know what to do. As soon as you deliver that message, go on to the next house, and then on to every other house as fast as you can."

He then gave Sybil one more very important piece of fatherly advice, "And, then, come back home, safe!"

Sybil repeated her father's instructions, "Yes, Father! I will say, Call to arms! The Regulars and Tories are burning Danbury! The Militia is needed! Call to arms!"

Henry smiled, shook his head in affirmation and said, "Yes, that is right! You have a long hard ride ahead of you!"

Henry looked up toward Heaven and said a quick prayer, "God, please give Sybil safety as she rides."

Sybil responded with a quick, "Amen!"

Henry gave her horse a swat and said, "God speed!"

Sybil rode off into the rain and began her historic forty-mile ride, to call out the Militia.

Chapter 19

Sybil Arrives at the First House
April 26, 1777 – Almost 10 p.m. Saturday

It was almost ten o'clock at night on Saturday, April 26, 1777. Rain had been falling for two days making it a cold wet night for anyone outside. The roads were wet and muddy which made it much more difficult to travel.

Sybil left her home a little while ago to call out the Militia. It did not take long for her to get wet and muddy. It also did not take long to reach the first house.

The first house Sybil came to was a simple country home. The lights were off. Everyone inside was asleep.

As Sybil rode up to the front door she pulled back on her horse's reins and came to a stop. She took the stick her father gave her and banged on the front door of the house and yelled, "Call to arms! Call to arms!"

She waited a few moments and then the door to the house opened slowly. A light from a lantern illuminated a musket barrel which appeared through the door, pointing outside. Sybil did not expect that. She quickly moved back.

It was Samuel, the owner of the house who opened the door. He was asleep when Sybil knocked on the door. Her knocking woke him out of a sound sleep. He quickly jumped out of bed quite alarmed. No one ever came to Samuel's house that late at night. He was concerned because he did not know what to expect so he grabbed his musket, and a lantern, and came to the door.

Simple Colonial Home
Hand Sketch.

He stood there at the door holding the lantern in his left hand which was also supporting his musket, which was in his right hand. He was only wearing his night shirt which hung down to his knees.

Samuel took a step forward extending the lantern a little further out the door and pointed his musket outside as he spoke gruffly, "Who is it? And what do you want?"

Sybil moved around on her horse as she spoke, "It is I, Sybil Ludington, Colonel Henry Ludington's daughter."

Samuel held the lantern further outside, so he could get a closer look at the rider. The light shone out into the darkness and illuminated Sybil. He recognized it truly was her. He then lowered his musket and said, "Sybil? What are you doing here this late at night and in the rain?!"

Sybil remembered what her father said. Though she

wanted to explain what she was doing she knew there was no time to engage in a conversation. She did as she was told and gave the message as her father instructed her, "Call to arms! The Regulars and Tories are burning Danbury! The Militia is needed! Call to arms!"

Samuel was alarmed at the serious message. He replied the way Sybil hoped he would. He said, "Oh No! I will get my son and we will tell the others to come at once!"

Sybil turned and rode off to the next home.

Samuel went back inside and woke Jedediah his son. They both quickly dressed, grabbed their muskets, and headed to Colonel Ludington's.

Militiaman Prepares to Respond to the Call

*By Benson John Lossing, 1850.
Pictorial Field Book of the Revolution.*

Chapter 20

The Looting and Burning Continue
April 26, 1777 – Very Late Saturday Night

It was very late Saturday night, April 26, 1777. While Sybil was on her ride calling out the Militia the Loyalists continued to loot and burn Danbury. They enjoyed taking vengeance on the frightened disloyal Rebels. The rain did not deter them.

Residents of Danbury later reported things got much worse after the soldiers became drunk on the stolen rum.

A family huddled together in fear, inside their home, trying to avoid the terror taking place around them. They lived close to the main street with no yard in front of their house putting them dangerously close to the passing groups of looting Loyalists.

They heard the screaming and gunshots which started in the afternoon and continued into the evening. They saw people dragged out of their homes by Loyalists who took whatever they wanted and then burned down the houses.

They watched the soldiers go up to some homes and then walk away doing no harm. The father noticed there was a ribbon on the door of those homes. He knew some of those houses were the homes of people he suspected had Loyalist leanings. He correctly assumed the ribbons were a signal to protect the Loyalist homes.

The family cowered in a corner in fear for their lives, as shadows of angry men danced across their front windows, as the looting Loyalists with torches perilously passed by their home. They hoped and prayed the looters would pass by and leave their home unmolested.

They were terrified when three Loyalists walking down the road stopped in front of their house. In the dim light they could see one had a torch in one hand and a bottle of rum in the other. The other two men with him were each holding muskets. They looked like they were laughing.

The one with the bottle raised it to his mouth and took a long drink. When he finished drinking, the bottle was empty. He wiped his mouth, threw it to the ground and laughed as it smashed in pieces. He then turned toward the house and stared at the window.

As he peered closer at the house the wife gasped. Her husband quickly put his hand over her mouth emphasizing the need for them to be as quiet as possible, so they would not be detected.

Suddenly they heard a loud boom. It sounded like a musket was fired close by. That made the men in front of the house duck. Then the one who smashed the bottle pointed down the street and said something to the others.

They looked down the street where he pointed. Then raised their muskets, pointed them in the direction he pointed and fired.

The family held each other closer as the percussion from the musket blast made their front window rattle.

After firing their muskets, the three men moved down the street. The family breathed a great sigh of relief.

That family did not get much of a reprieve. Shortly after the three Loyalists left they watched as two more soldiers stopped in front of their window.

Like the first three men, one of these had a torch in one hand and a bottle in the other. The other man had a bottle in one hand and a sack filled with spoil slung over his shoulder.

The soldier with the torch in his hand turned towards the house and held it close to the window moving it back and forth, trying to see if anyone was inside. The family cowered in fear. They covered their mouths, so they would not scream out in fear.

The soldier thought he saw something inside. He put his face closer to the window. The family trembled in despair as they thought this would surely be the end for them.

Suddenly they heard another musket blast. The men in front of the window quickly turned, looking for the source of the musket blast,. Then the two men quickly moved away.

The family was greatly relieved. The father held them close and said a prayer of thanks.

Chapter 21

Sybil and The Bandits
April 26, 1777 – Very Late Saturday Night

It was cold, rainy, and very late at night on Saturday, April 26, 1777. That was not a very good night for traveler's or for bandits as Sybil rode through the cold and rain.

One of the dangers of travelling around that area, even before the Revolution, was the fact that sometimes there were thieves who waited along the side of the road to rob unsuspecting travelers. Those thieves were usually called *highwaymen* but during the Revolution they became known as either *cowboys* or *skinners*.

Even though it was late at night and the weather was awful, two desperate bandits waited next to the road that evening hoping some helpless unsuspecting traveler would come their way.

They positioned themselves on opposite sides of the road at a place where the road grew narrow. That was the same road Sybil was riding on to call out the Militia. They were waiting for unsuspecting travelers to pass by, so they could pounce on them and rob them of anything valuable.

The leader of the two bandits was older than the other. He was wearing a dark heavy wool work shirt and had an oil cloth draped over his head and shoulders, to help keep him dry. He held a crude wooden club in his hands.

He had a not so bright accomplice who was wearing dark heavy clothing and a wool blanket over his head and shoulders. That blanket was warm but not as effective at repelling the rain as the oil cloth the leader wore. He also carried a wooden club to use on his unsuspecting victims.

They were outside waiting in the cold and rain for hours. The accomplice finally complained, "I am so wet and cold! I wish I was someplace with a nice warm fire."

The bandit leader did not like the cold and rain and was also very uncomfortable, but he believed if they waited long enough their discomfort would be rewarded. He replied indignantly to his companion, "Stop your complaining, just think about how rich we are going to be when we catch some unsuspecting traveler."

His accomplice liked that idea. He shook his head in agreement and smiled, "I sure would like to be rich!"

The bandit leader spoke firmly, "Keep thinking about that and be quiet! We do not want anyone to know we are here!"

After a few more minutes of misery the accomplice asked, "Are you sure someone will be out on a night like this?"

The leader knew it was a bad night to travel but he thought surely someone would have to travel their way that night. He responded affirmatively, "Of course they will! This is a main road. People pass by here all the time."

He paused for a moment and said, "And look at it this

way, no one will ever suspect we would be out on a night like this and that will make them easy prey."

His accomplice liked that idea. That made him forget about being wet and cold for a little while.

It was not long after that conversation the bandit leader heard the sound of someone approaching. He said, "Quiet! I think I hear someone coming! Get ready!"

Both bandits stepped out into the middle of the road. It was dark. They knew no one would see them. They planted their feet firmly and got their clubs ready to attack their unsuspecting prey. This was what they were waiting for and why they put up with this miserable weather, or was it?

As they stood there looking forward to their prize, Sybil came riding up fast in the dark and rain. She did not see them, and they barely saw her.

As she came upon them her horse galloped through a big murky puddle. A big splash of muddy water flew out of the puddle in all directions, soaking both bandits.

To make matters worse, one of the hooves of Sybil's horse unsuspectingly hit the bandit leader in the head and sent him falling backwards on the cold, wet, muddy ground.

Both bandits were covered with soaking wet mud as Sybil continued to ride on past them. Though they surely noticed her, she never noticed them.

The accomplice was bewildered. He wiped some of the mud off his face and said, "What was that?"

The bandit leader shook his head and reluctantly said, "That was the signal for us to go find that warm fire you were talking about."

Chapter 22

Americans Arrive in Bethel
April 26, 1777 – Almost Midnight Saturday

It was almost midnight on Saturday, April 26, 1777. The exhausted American Rebel Force led by General David Wooster, General Benedict Arnold, and General Gold Selleck Silliman just arrived in Bethel, Connecticut only a few miles away from the Rebel's supply depot.

They left Redding about six-thirty in the evening after waiting an hour-and-a-half for a break in the rain. That rest helped refresh the men and the break in the rain allowed them to continue their pursuit of the Crown Forces.

When they left Redding they soon discovered it was a good thing they had that rest because they did not realize just how difficult a struggle the journey was that lay ahead. If it had been during daylight they would have seen the road was almost impassable, not just because of two days of rain but because of the deep ruts caused by the advance of the Crown Forces and their heavy artillery.

The journey was harder because the sun set before they left Redding and the clouds obscured the light of the moon and stars. It was further compounded because shortly after they left Redding the rain started again further reducing visibility and making the journey even more uncomfortable.

When they arrived in Bethel they were all wet, muddy, and exhausted. They were frustrated because it took much longer to reach Bethel than they expected.

The thing which discouraged them most was when they saw smoke and flames rise from Danbury revealing the Crown Forces already launched their atrocious attack.

Crown Forces Raid and Burn

Reenactors from the Brigade of the American Revolution.
Photograph by Gary Vorwald

General Arnold spoke with some who fled Danbury. They told him how the invaders went beyond taking the supplies and started looting and setting on fire the homes of those not loyal to the Crown. They saw people violently dragged from their homes and others brutally killed.

General Arnold found General Wooster and gave his report. He expressed extreme displeasure as he reported the actions of the Crown Forces in Danbury, "General Wooster, as you know, the Crown Forces attacked Danbury. I learned Colonel Cooke put up a valiant defense, but the opposing force was too great. And, the Crown Forces not only stole our supplies but got into a drunken rage and burned homes and murdered people!"

Silliman also spoke with refuges and confirmed what Arnold said. "Yes, General Arnold, people told me the same things and said, the Tories were the worst of the lot!" He paused, then angrily said, "If I had my way all traitors would be hung!"

Arnold and Wooster shook their heads in agreement and both firmly said, "Yes!"

Arnold was intensely angry, he passionately exclaimed, "We need to go and stop them!"

Wooster was obviously shaken by the news yet responded with reluctant resolve, "I would like to do that, but our men are exhausted, and our powder is wet. You know wet powder renders our muskets useless. We would not stand a chance against them without our muskets."

Silliman wanted to attack but saw wisdom in Wooster's words, "No matter how much I would like to stop this atrocity, I believe we have to wait until morning to attack."

Arnold wanted to attack but reluctantly agreed it was the best decision to wait for the morning. He responded with impassioned determination, "In the morning when they are hung over and confident we will strike them hard and if we cannot defeat them we will drive them back into the sea."

Wooster was pleased with the others response and said, "We will show them our resolve and our love for liberty!"

"For liberty!" echoed Arnold and Silliman.

Chapter 23

Sybil Arrives at Another Home
April 27, 1777 – Long Before Sunrise Sunday

It was Sunday, April 27, 1777, long before sunrise. The rain was still falling but not as hard. The Crown Forces were still looting and burning Danbury. The Rebels were resting in Bethel planning to attack in the morning and Sybil was still riding.

She was soaking wet from riding in the rain and along muddy roads for many hours. She was terribly tired but faithfully pressed on.

Sybil stopped at many houses sounding the call to arms. At each stop men responded to her call and headed to Colonel Ludington's, some on horseback, some in wagons and others on foot.

She now rode up to another simple country house and pounded on the door with her stick as she did at the other houses.

She yelled, "Call to arms!" and waited for a response.

When no one responded she pounded again and yelled, "Call to arms!"

Finally, a man cautiously opened the door. He was

unexpectedly shaken out of a nice deep sleep by Sybil's call and pounding. He was barely awake as he jumped out of bed, grabbed a lantern, and headed to the door.

As he opened the door he poked the lantern outside to illuminate the darkness while he held the door securely with his other hand. Sybil noticed he looked like he had been sleeping very hard.

He was surprised when the lantern revealed a soaking wet girl on a horse with a stick in her hands. He thought he recognized her but was not quite sure if he was awake or dreaming.

Sybil looked at him and gave her call with passion, "Call to arms! The Regulars and Tories are burning Danbury! The Militia is needed! Call to arms!"

The man stood there dumfounded. This was not at all what he expected to find at his door in the middle of the night.

As soon as Sybil finished giving her call she turned and rapidly rode off to the next house.

The man stood in the doorway of his house for a few

moments. He was in a daze. He wondered if he was dreaming.

He thought he recognized the girl on the horse as Sybil Ludington, Colonel Henry Ludington's daughter. He wondered why he was dreaming Sybil would come to his house in the middle of the night.

As he stood there for a few more moments, mulling those thoughts over in his mind, suddenly he realized this was not a dream, he was indeed awake.

The seriousness of Sybil's message finally took hold of him. He was in the Militia and realized he needed to respond to the call right away.

He left the door open as he quickly headed back into his house to get the rest of his clothes on. He grabbed his musket and headed out the door to go to Colonel Ludington's. He did not think about the danger only that he was needed to respond to help defend freedom.

Colonial Militia Respond to the Call
By Felix Octavius Car Darley, 1877.

Chapter 24

Making Ammunition

April 27, 1777 – Sunday Long Before Sunrise

It was the wee hours of the morning on Sunday, April 26, 1777. If it had been a normal night. Everyone in Colonel Henry Ludington's family would have been asleep for many hours, but that was not a normal night.

A British force of close to two thousand men were looting and burning Danbury, Connecticut. A messenger from Colonel Joseph Platt Cooke, arrived hours ago asking for help. Colonel Ludington's oldest daughter, sixteen-year old Sybil Ludington was riding through the dark rainy night to call out the Militia.

Sybil's family were all awake helping prepare for the Militia to arrive. Colonel Ludington's wife Abigail, their daughter Rebecca, and son Archibald were making cartridges, which are the ammunition used in muskets. Mary and Henry, Jr., were helping by playing with their younger brother Tertullus and watching their baby sister.

To make cartridges for the muskets one person cut out pieces of old newspaper to the proper size.

The next person used a wood dowel, with a musket ball at the end, and rolled the paper around the dowel and ball.

They then twisted the end near the musket ball closed. Sometimes they tied a piece of string around the outside above the musket ball, but they did not do that this time.

The next person poured the right amount of black powder into each cartridge, and folded the last end closed.

Making the musket balls, which went into the cartridges, was Colonel Ludington's job. He melted lead in a small cast iron pot over coals at the edge of the fireplace. He then poured the melted lead into a mold which formed a small round musket ball. He then trimmed off the edge which was left on the musket ball by the mold. Then he put the completed ones in a small bowl on the table for those assembling the cartridges.

As they completed each cartridge they placed them in big wooden bowls. When the Militia arrived later they would grab handfuls of the ammunition and fill their cartridge pouches. Most pouches held nineteen rounds in a wood block. Additional cartridges were placed in their pouch under the wood block.

Rebecca was glad her sister Sybil was helping by riding to call out the Militia, she was thankful she too could help.

Rebecca said, "Father, I am glad we can help make these cartridges for the soldiers."

Henry smiled and spoke, reinforcing the importance of what they were doing, "Your help is greatly appreciated. Every man will come with some cartridges, but we need to make as many as we can."

He paused and then said, "I fear we will be engaged in a fierce battle and we will need many more cartridges than the men will have with them."

Abigail looked up from her task and spoke with motherly concern, "I pray Sybil is alright!"

Henry spoke to reassure her, "I am sure the Lord is watching out for her."

Suddenly their conversation was interrupted by someone banging on their front door. The family immediately stopped what they were doing. They looked at each other with a look of concern on their faces.

Henry picked up his sword and headed to the door. He cautiously opened the door with his sword drawn.

There were two soaking wet people standing at the door. It was Samuel, the man from the first home Sybil came to, along with his son Jedediah.

They held muskets in their hands while water dripped off their hats and off the wet wool blankets draped over their shoulders. They were soaked from making their way through the pouring rain to the Ludington's.

When they saw Colonel Ludington standing there with his sword in his hand, they took a step back.

Samuel quickly said, "No need for that Colonel! It is me Samuel and my son Jedediah!"

Henry smiled, lowered his sword and invited them into the house, "Samuel, Jedediah! Come inside out of the rain!"

Samuel and Jedediah entered the house. They were so wet, water continued to drip off them.

Samuel said, "We got the message from Sybil that the Regulars and Tories are burning Danbury."

Inside a Typical Colonial Home
*H.W. Pearce, 1876 Engraving.
Very typical image of items found in a colonial home.
Cooking was done in the fireplace.*

He paused for a moment held up his musket and said, "We are here to help drive them back to the sea."

Jedediah his son got an angry look on his face and said, "I would like to drive them all the way back across the ocean to their King George!"

Henry smiled and responded, "That sounds like a good idea."

Abigail Ludington poured a cup of coffee for each of them and brought it to them. Before handing them the cups she said, "Take off those wet things and have a cup of coffee to warm you up."

They took off their hats and wool blankets and gladly received the warm cups from Abigail.

As they started to drink their coffee there was another knock at the door.

This time when Colonel Ludington opened the door three men stood there. It was a father accompanied by his two sons who were in their teens. Just like Samuel and Jedediah all three of them were carrying muskets and were soaking wet.

Colonel Ludington recognized them as men in his Militia. He smiled as he said, "Come in!"

The younger of the two sons walked over to where the Colonel's family were making cartridges.

He looked at Rebecca Ludington and smiled. He knew who she was and was very pleased to see her. She smiled back at him and seemed very pleased to see him too.

He asked, "Can we help?"

Rebecca smiled and moved over a little to make some room for him. "Oh yes! We can use all the help we can get."

The younger son smiled and signaled for his older brother to come over to the table and help make cartridges.

There was another knock on the door.

Colonel Ludington headed to answer the door.

Men from Colonel Ludington's Dutchess County Militia continued to arrive. They all responded to Sybil's call and came to fight for liberty and to help drive the Crown Forces back into the sea.

Chapter 25

Sybil Faces an Obstacle
April 27, 1777 – Sunday Long Before Sunrise

It was a long time before the sun would rise on Sunday, April 27, 1777. It was a welcomed relief when the rain finally stopped in that part of Dutchess County, but the roads were wet and muddy from two days of steady rain which made them much harder to travel on. The two days of rain also caused the rivers and streams to overflow, making them very difficult to pass in many places. This was a bad time for someone to be traveling.

One person travelling at that difficult time was Sybil Ludington. She was riding to call out the men in her Father's Militia. The roads she travelled on passed through many streams. Many of those streams were high and overflowing their banks.

Sybil came galloping down the road and approached one of the overflowing streams. Throughout the night she jumped over some other brooks on her horse but this one presented a more serious obstacle. This stream was overflowing to the point where its banks were completely covered with raging water. It looked like there was no way to safely cross that stream.

Sybil rode up along the stream looking for a safe way to cross. It might have been possible to find a safe place to cross if it were not so dark out. She turned her horse around and rode in the other direction. To complete her mission, she had to cross that stream. She was extremely frustrated because she unable to find a safe place to cross.

She rode back to the road where she first faced the obstacle of this swollen stream. This was a very difficult discouraging situation. Though she could not find a safe place to cross she decided she was not going to allow that to stop her. She was determined to complete her mission.

Sybil spoke to her horse, "There is no easy way around this one Star, but we have to cross this stream."

She looked up toward Heaven and said a quick prayer, "Lord, I need your help on this one!"

With a disregard for the danger and with firm resolve, Sybil urged her horse forward and headed boldly into the dangerously overflowing stream.

The rapidly rushing water pressed hard and strong against them, making it very difficult to go forward, but they continued to press on. It was an extremely hard struggle to find sure footing, but she and her horse, continued to slowly move forward with fierce determination,

Suddenly her horse lost his footing and started to slip. Sybil was afraid he would fall and break a leg, ending their ride and maybe his life. She was very thankful when he quickly regained his footing. They continued to press on through and finally came out safe on the other side.

Once they were safely across the stream, Sybil looked back for a moment, then looked up and said, "Thank you!"

She then tightened up on the reigns, and with fierce determination, rode on with her mission.

She would face more streams on her ride but that was the most difficult one. She was thankful she faced that obstacle and overcame it.

Overflowing Stream in Putnam County
This is one of the swollen streams Sybil crossed on her forty-mile ride, to call out the Militia.
Photograph by Larry A. Maxwell, Spring 2018

Chapter 26

Militia March off to Battle
April 27, 1777 – Before Sunrise Sunday Morning

It was about an hour before sunrise on Sunday, April 27, 1777. Sybil Ludington was still riding throughout lower Dutchess County calling out the Militia. After she arrived at each house and gave the call to arms the men left their homes and headed to the Militia Training Ground next to Colonel Henry Ludington's home in Fredericksburg.

All through the night the Militia arrived. By about an hour before sunrise there were about two hundred men, standing in clusters in the field across from the Colonel's home. Colonel Ludington, Lieutenant Colonel Reuben Ferris and Captain Edmund Baker stood together talking.

Jabez and Judah Chase came up to Colonel Ludington. Jabez said, "Colonel, we got the message from Sybil and came right away."

His brother Judah wanted the Colonel to know they, and the other men, were coming because of Sybil, "The whole countryside is responding thanks to your daughter."

Henry replied with a big smile and nod of his head.

When Colonel Ludington saw many of his men arrived, he turned to Ferris and Baker and said, "It is time to call the men together."

Captain Baker yelled, "Fall in!" That was the command to call the troops into formation.

The men who were scattered around the field came together and formed two rows with their muskets in their left hand, resting on their left shoulder.

Baker then yelled the next order, "Order, arms!"

As soon as that command was given each man grabbed his musket with his right hand and put the butt of his musket near his right foot. Their right hand then held their musket near the end of the barrel as they put their left arm by their side.

Colonel Ludington came forward to address the troops. Captain Baker was on one side and Lieutenant Colonel Ferris on his other side.

The Colonel stopped and gave the command, "Take your ease."

Captain Baker echoed his command, "Take your ease!"

The men responded by taking a more relaxed position.

Colonel Ludington began to address his troops with respect, urgency, and passion, "All of you heard the alarm sounded by my daughter Sybil."

One of the men interrupted shouting, "Three Huzzahs for Sybil!"

In response to his call all the men grabbed their hats with their left hand and waved them in the air as they shouted, "Huzzah! Huzzah! Huzzah!"

Colonel Ludington was obviously pleased by the men's cheer for his daughter. After they were done he nodded his head in gratitude and then continued speaking, "I want to thank every one of you for responding to the call. I know these are not the ideal circumstances to be given a call, but you still came, and I am deeply grateful."

The Colonel then gave more details of why they were called, "As most of you know by now, the British Regulars and a large Tory Regiment have attacked our supply depot at Danbury. They stole our supplies of food, clothing, guns, and power. Those supplies were important to help our struggle for independence."

He paused as a more somber look came across his face. He then continued, "They set many building on fire and have taken prisoners!"

One of the men yelled out with great concern, "I have family in Danbury!"

A few others had the same concern and spoke up saying, "Me too!"

Colonel Ludington did not rebuke the interruptions. He knew how an attack on nearby Danbury affected many of them. He paused, then continued to speak, "I know many of you have family and friends in Danbury and I know you are concerned for their safety."

He continued his exhortation with an important update, "I received word from another messenger, that General Wooster, General Silliman and General Benedict Arnold are at Bethel and plan to attack the Crown Forces in Danbury in the morning."

The Colonel, looked at the men, and spoke with greater intensity, "They plan to drive them back to the sea and want our help!"

He paused, then looked at his men and asked, "Are you with me?!"

All the men took off their hats, waved them in the air, and responded enthusiastically yelling, "Huzzah! Huzzah! Huzzah!"

The entire time Colonel Ludington was talking more men continued to arrive.

After the rousing cheer of affirmation from his men the Colonel continued to speak. "I will take those of you who are here now, and we will head to Danbury."

He looked at Lieutenant Colonel Ferris and said, "Lieutenant Colonel Ferris will stay here and wait for the rest of the men and will follow us forthwith."

Ferris nodded his head affirmatively and said, "Yes, Colonel!"

Colonel Ludington looked at the troops again and passionately yelled, "Are you ready to do your part for liberty lads?!"

The men again took off their hats and waved them in the air as they enthusiastically shouted, "Huzzah! Huzzah! Huzzah!"

The Continental Army normally marched from place to place by foot. These men were not the Continental Army they were the Militia. Militia from larger towns often marched from place to place on foot like the Continental Army. Dutchess County was a rural agricultural area. Most of the men lived quite a distance from one another and had horses and wagons. It was common for most of the men in Colonel Ludington's Regiment to respond on horseback or to come in a horse drawn wagon rather than on foot.

The Colonel spoke again adding some important information, "For us to arrive in time to be of any help we need to have every man on a horse or in a wagon. If any of you responded to the call on foot I want you to ride with those who came with their wagons. Those of you who came with your wagons take as many men, who came by foot, with you in your wagons. If there is not enough room in the wagons then some of you may need to take another man with you on your horse."

He paused then gave the command, "You are dismissed to form up on your horses and in the wagons!"

Captain Baker echoed Colonel Ludington's command, "Dismissed to form up on your horses and in the wagons!"

Colonel Ludington had one group on horseback ride in the front with him. He had another group ride with the wagons and another group ride in the back as a rear guard.

He watched to make sure all the men were on horseback or in a wagon. He then rode to the font of the line and yelled, "Forward to Danbury! We shall drive the enemy back to the sea!"

All the men shouted another round of "Huzzah!"

They rode off into the night, determined to help make a difference.

Lieutenant Colonel Ferris stayed behind waiting for the rest of the men to arrive.

Chapter 27

Sybil at the Ganong's
April 27, 1777 – Before Sunrise Sunday Morning

It was Sunday, April 27, 1777, before sunrise. The Crown Forces were still looting and burning Danbury. Sybil Ludington was riding all night to call out the Militia. She now approached another home. When she realized, it was the Ganong's home she stopped and hesitated.

Sybil Rides on Through the Night

Ericka Rose portrays Sybil at Sybil Rides 240th Event.
Living History Guild Photograph

Jesse Ganong, her friend, lived there. He wanted to join the Militia but his father, John Ganong, would not allow him to join. His father was a successful businessman who had dealings with people with strong Loyalist leanings. He believed the Revolution was a bad misunderstanding which would end soon if people stopped aggravating the Crown. He wanted to stay as neutral as possible.

After hesitating Sybil decided she should ride up to the house and give the call. She rode up and banged on the front door with her stick, just as she did at all the other houses. She then yelled, "Call to arms! Call to arms!"

In a few moments, the front door opened slightly, revealing Jesse's father, John Ganong, standing there in his nightshirt holding a small lantern.

John tried to see who would be calling at this time of night. As he looked out the door he saw a soaking wet person on a horse. He thought it looked like Sybil Ludington. He was confused, why would Sybil be at their home at such a strange hour?

He called to the rider, "Sybil? Is that you?"

Sybil responded, "Yes, Sir!"

Perplexed, John asked, "What are you doing here?!"

She hesitated for a moment, knowing John Ganong was uncommitted and opposed to his son Jesse being in the Militia, but she decided she must give the call.

She said, "Call to arms! The Regulars and Tories are burning Danbury! The Militia is needed! Call to arms!"

That news was not something John was expecting. He was hoping things would get better. He did not expect there would be an attack especially one as close as Danbury. He never thought something like this would happen. He was greatly alarmed.

He stepped back a little and with greatly dismay said, "This cannot be! They would not attack Danbury!"

Jesse came to the door and pushed past his father. He came out of the house putting on his frock coat and hat.

Jesse looked at Sybil and said, "Sybil, I heard your call! I do not have a musket, but I want to help!"

Sybil smiled, she was very glad to hear that. She replied, "Father will give you one."

She turned and rode off, on to the next house.

Jesse went and got his horse ready. He then started to head in the direction from which Sybil rode up to the house.

His father stood there in disbelief. He was hoping it was a bad dream, but he knew it really was happening as he saw Jesse riding off.

He yelled to his son, "Jesse! Do not go!"

Jesse yelled back to his Father, "Father, I must go!"

The last thing his father heard Jesse say, as he rode off into the night was, "I must fight for liberty!".

John Ganong stood in the door of his house for a moment shaking his head in disbelief. He muttered, "This is terrible!"

In despair John put his head in his hands and slowly walked back into the house. In desperation over his future, he said, "Oh no! What are we going to do?"

Chapter 28

Crown Forces Leave Danbury
April 27, 1777 – Early Sunday Morning

It was early in the morning on Sunday, April 27, 1777. The town of Danbury was burning as the Crown Forces started to withdraw from the city. Some soldiers were leading groups of prisoners taken during the raid. Confiscated wagons were loaded with Rebel supplies. Some Loyalists pushed or pulled two-wheeled carts overflowing with goods they plundered from Rebel homes. Others carried their booty in sacks slung over their shoulders.

Crown Forces Leaving Town
Photograph by Gary Vorwald

Governor William Tryon, General James Agnew, General William Erskine, and General Montfort Browne were standing together at the edge of town. They were in a joyous mood talking about their victory, everyone except Erskine.

Browne spoke loudly with his pompous attitude, "That will teach the Rebel scum what happens when they are disloyal to their king!"

Tryon responded with some sarcasm, "General Browne, I see your men enjoyed the rum they found!"

Browne smiled with a smug look on his face, "They do deserve to celebrate a job well done!"

Erskine was so upset he could not contain himself any longer. He was a career military man who believed strongly in military protocol. Looting and burning the homes of civilians was not acceptable to him. He had to say something. He spoke out with disparaging passion, "That was not proper military protocol!"

His comment startled everyone and instantly stifled the celebratory mood. Tryon agreed with Erskine, but he was glad the raid was a success. He sought to counterbalance a tense moment, "You are right General Erskine, but I cannot argue with success."

Erskine appreciated a military victory, but he believed this military victory was compromised by the improper actions of Browne's Loyalists. He felt he must express his displeasure or further "successes" could be marred by such unacceptable actions.

He spoke out again expressing his disapproval, "I am

not sure I call it a success when our soldiers are supposed to gather supplies and burn what we cannot carry away, yet instead they get drunk and burn down a city!"

Browne was self-righteous and acted like he was not phased at all by Erskine's comments. He was gloating in his success and the feigned support from Tryon. He would not accept Erskine's rebuke because he felt entirely justified with the actions of his men.

Browne boisterously replied to Erskine's rebuke, "They should burn every Rebel home and hang them all by the neck!"

Erskine felt disgust for Browne and responded with a dire warning, "I am sure this is going to cause them to retaliate against us with extreme vengeance."

Browne was very smug. He laughed and sarcastically said, "While they run away from us!"

Tryon felt it best to ignore the conversation between Erskine and Browne. He immediately changed the subject, signaling one of his junior officers who was holding a map to come close. Tryon had him hold one end of the map while he called another aide over to hold the other end open.

Tryon then pointed to the map and spoke, "They will expect us to go back the same way we came."

He pointed to the map and said to the other officers, "Look here."

The others came close and looked where Tryon pointed on the map. Erskine still had an angry look on his face.

As he pointed at the map, Tryon said, "We will go back along a different route, here through Ridgefield."

Erskine liked that idea. He was glad he was finally able to express his approval of something. "Excellent plan Governor!"

Tryon closed the map and said, "We will be back safe in our ships and on our way back to New York before the Rebels know what hit them!"

Erskine expressed his pessimism, "I hope you are right!"

Browne responded with arrogant confidence, "Trust me, the Rebels have run away and are hiding from us. We have seen all the resistance we are going to see!"

Erskine scowled at Browne.

1777 Map of Tryon's Raid on Danbury

By John Montresor
Montressor was the Chief British Engineer in North America.
The Library of Congress, Washington, D.C.

Chapter 29

Sybil Rides as the Sun Rises
April 27, 1777 – Sunrise Sunday

It was the morning of Sunday, April 27, 1777. After a cold rainy night, the sun finally rose and peaked over the hills in Dutchess County, New York.

The Crown Forces finished their raid on Danbury, Connecticut and were on their way back to their ships in Norwalk, on an alternate route through Ridgefield. They were encouraged they only encountered some unorganized resistance from some small groups of Militia along the way.

Unbeknownst to them, all night long Militia in lower Dutchess County New York, responded to the call from sixteen-year old Sybil Ludington and began to assemble on the training ground across from the home of Colonel Henry Ludington. The first group of two hundred men left with the Colonel a few hours ago. Lieutenant Colonel Reuben Ferris waited behind for the rest of the men to arrive before he would leave with them.

Sybil rode all night long on cold wet muddy roads, going from house to house, calling out the Militia through the cold, dark and rain. She faced obstacles along the way but kept going on.

When the rain stopped in Dutchess County a few hours ago, that was a real blessing, but the rest of the night was still cold and dark, and Sybil was very wet. Her cold wet clothing was draining her strength and she was extremely tired but there was no time to rest because there were many more homes she had to reach, and they still laid many miles ahead of her.

As the sun started to rise its rays not only drove away the darkness but also began to spread their warmth. That warmth not only spread over the wet chilly earth but also began to warm anyone outside under its rays.

As the sun broke through the trees and shone upon Sybil, it started to warm her wet rain-soaked clothing. The warmth slowly spread from her clothing to her body. The higher the sun rose the brighter it became.

The sun's rays became warmer and warmer and started to dry Sybil's wet clothing and warmed her spirit. That was a welcome relief which brought a smile to her face.

When Sybil came to a clearing where the sun was shining bright, she stopped for a moment, spread her arms wide and soaked in the warm rays of the sun.

She then looked up and said, "Thank you!"

Sybil was still tired but those few moments in the sun gave her an additional spark of energy.

She put her head back down, tightened up her horse's reins and rode on to call out the rest of the Militia.

Chapter 30

American Officers Plan Response
April 27, 1777 – Early Sunday Morning

It was early in the morning on Sunday, April 27, 1777. A light rain continued on and off throughout the night but finally stopped. The Crown Forces, which plundered Danbury throughout the night, left not long after sunrise. They were heading back to their ships by a different route, one that would take them through Ridgefield, Connecticut.

Sunrise saw the American Rebel Force under General David Wooster, General Benedict Arnold, and General Gold Selleck Silliman prepare to depart from Bethel and head to Danbury. They intended to launch an attack and repel the ravaging invaders.

Right before they set out, scouts whom General Wooster sent out earlier, reported back that the Crown Forces left Danbury and were on their way to Ridgefield.

Wooster immediately called Arnold and Silliman together to update them. When they reached him, he was looking intently over a map of the area with his aides.

Wooster pointed at the map and said, "General Arnold,

General Silliman, I was looking at this map which shows the area between Danbury and Norwalk."

Colonial Fairfield County Connecticut
Map by Thomas Kitchen, 1758.

He told them, "Our scouts reported Tryon and his men have left Danbury and are heading back along a different route than the way they came. They are heading back to Norwalk by way of Ridgefield."

General Arnold looked with interest at the map and the projected route of the Crown Forces. Earlier that day he wrote a letter to Brigadier General Alexander McDougall stating he thought the Crown Forces were marching on to Fishkill and then Peekskill. He did not expect them to go back to Norwalk.

Arnold was pondering what to do when Wooster looked at each of the generals and said, "Gentlemen now it is our time to show them how we respond to injustice!"

Arnold and Silliman wholeheartedly agreed with what Wooster said and responded with a look of determination as they nodded in agreement.

Arnold spoke up and with intense passion, said, "We must show them our resolve!"

Wooster appreciated their support, "It is important to show the Crown Forces we will not just sit by and let them get away with such horrendous actions."

He paused then said, "I know we are greatly outnumbered but we must respond as the Militia did two years ago in response to the attack on Lexington and Concord."

He said, "Remember how those brave, dedicated men inflicted significant damage to the retreating British Regulars. I hope we too can inflict such damage to the retreating Regulars and their Tory allies."

He pointed again at the map as he said, "General Silliman, General Arnold, I need the two of you to take four hundred men and proceed to Ridgefield, to cut them off."

He then looked up and said, "I sent messengers to have Colonel Bradley and the 5th Connecticut Regiment go to Ridgefield. I also sent messengers to the Yorkers under Colonel Drake and Colonel Ludington to join you there."

Arnold and Silliman both thought that was an excellent idea. They nodded in agreement with the details.

Wooster continued, "I will take the remaining men, along with Colonel Jedediah Huntington and the 1st Connecticut Regiment, and we will launch a rear attack."

Colonel Jedediah Huntington
He commanded the 1st Connecticut Regiment.
Engraving by A.H. Richie from a painting by Col. Trumbull.

Arnold agreed that sounded like a good plan and again replied enthusiastically, "Excellent plan General Wooster! We will have them trapped!"

Wooster appreciated the compliment but then expressed cautious optimism, "We may not be able to stop them, but we will make them pay!"

The others agreed enthusiastically.

Wooster then said his last words emphatically, "With God's help we will indeed show them our resolve!"

Chapter 31

Opposition South of Danbury
April 27, 1777 – About 9 a.m. Sunday

It was Sunday morning April 27, 1777. Shortly after sunrise the rain stopped. The Crown Forces were marching down the road heading west and then and south from Danbury towards Ridgefield, back to their fleet which was waiting for them at Compo Beach, near Norwalk.

The soldiers were tired from a long day and night but were in good spirits, especially since the rain stopped.

Some of the men were carrying sacks of confiscated goods over their shoulders, followed by wagons filled with more goods. The wagons were manned and protected by Loyalists who were talking and laughing.

Two Loyalist friends talked with each other as their regiment headed down the road. They each had a musket in one hand and a sack slung over one shoulder, filled with things they plundered from a Rebel home.

The older looking one smiled as he said to the younger, "I am so glad it stopped raining."

His friend smiled and agreed, "So am I."

The older looking one reflected on their time raiding

and plundering the Rebels in Danbury. He had a smile on his face as he said, "That was fun!"

His friend smiled and enthusiastically agreed with him, "Yes it was!" He paused as he shifted his sack of loot and then said, "The Rebel scum never knew what hit them!"

Some Rebel Militia moved through the woods quietly approaching the line of Crown Forces. They moved undetected, close to the road, near the two Loyalist friends.

The Militia officer quietly commanded his men, "Spread out along the wall and behind the trees, quietly!"

The Crown Forces continued marching along cheerfully, with a false sense of security. A Militiaman pointed his musket at one of the Loyalists. He slowly but firmly pulled the trigger. Two others did the same. As the muskets fired they made a very loud *Boom!*

The older looking Loyalist, and a man behind him, were each hit by a musket ball. They fell lifeless to the ground. Fear gripped the hearts of their companions.

A Loyalist officer ran to the edge of the road and sought to take control of the situation. He quickly called his men to action. He yelled the command, "Form a line!"

The friend of the older Loyalist dropped his sack and responded to the command. He quickly put his musket up to his left shoulder and formed a line along with the other Loyalists facing the woods. They stood in fear as they saw the smoke from the muskets wafting through the woods.

The Loyalist officer yelled, "Prime and load!"

As soon as he gave that command, and while his men started to follow his command, another Rebel fired his musket. The bullet from that musket hit the officer. He grabbed his chest and fell helpless to the ground.

The soldiers standing near him were filled with fear as they watched him drop. They looked nervously at the woods as they continued to load their muskets. More musket shots were heard. Another soldier in the line was hit and fell backwards.

A second Loyalist officer quickly came forward and apprehensively took the first officer's place. He continued to yell out the orders for loading and firing. He paused briefly between each order giving his men time to complete the order, "Make Ready! Present! Fire!"

The Loyalists all fired their muskets at the same time, unleashing a volley of muskets fire. Smoke filled the air. The Militia quickly and quietly moved away.

Loyalists Return Fire

Reenactors from the Brigade of the American Revolution.
Photograph by Gary Vorwald, 2014

Chapter 32

Sybil at the Last Home
April 27, 1777 – 9 a.m. Sunday

It was Sunday morning, April 27, 1777. The sun rose a few hours earlier and helped dry off Sybil Ludington's wet clothing. She was exhausted from riding all night. By this time, she rode almost forty miles on a loop calling out the Militia throughout lower Dutchess County, New York. Her task was almost complete.

An older couple was seated inside their modest country home that Sunday morning, eating a simple breakfast, before going to church.

Their meal was interrupted by a pounding sound on their door. They both rose from their seats and went to the door to see who was there. As soon as the man opened the door he saw Sybil Ludington slumped down on her horse.

Sybil looked up and tried to shout. Her voice was almost gone. She gave it all she had and with a hoarse, weak voice said, "Call to arms! The Regulars and Tories are burning Danbury! The Militia is needed! Call to arms!"

The woman thought she recognized Sybil. She asked, "Sybil Ludington? Is that you?"

Kitchen in a Typical Colonial Home
*1940's postcard of a colonial home.
The fireplace was the center of the home.*

Sybil replied wearily, "Yes, Ma'am."

The woman was very concerned when she saw how exhausted Sybil looked. She wanted to help her. She said, "Oh, my dear! You look exhausted! Please come inside and warm yourself up by the fire and have something to eat!"

Under other circumstances, Sybil would have accepted that invitation. She responded politely but with urgency, "Thank you very much, but there is no time for that."

The woman realized Sybil must have been riding for a long time. She asked, "How long have you been riding?"

Sybil was very tried. She knew she had to leave and head towards home, but she knew it was important to be polite.

She responded, "Since about nine o'clock last night, Ma'am."

When the woman first saw Sybil, she thought maybe Sybil rose early in the morning and then rode to their home. She was surprised to learn how long Sybil was riding.

She said. "My dear it is nine o'clock in the morning. You have been riding all night!"

Sybil responded as she turned to ride away, "God gives me the strength I need! I must go on!"

The woman yelled to her, "We will be praying for you!"

The man grabbed his musket, kissed wife, and headed out the door and on to Colonel Ludington's to join the rest of the Militia to go fight for liberty.

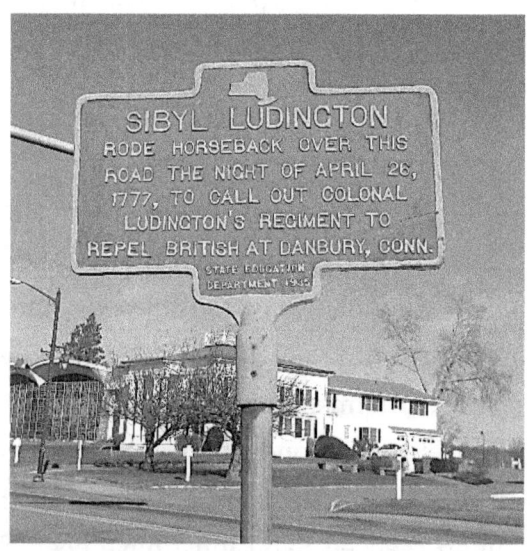

Historical Marker for Sybil's Ride
One of the numerous historical markers placed by the New York State Department of Education in 1935, to identify the route of Sybil's ride. This one is on Route 52, next to Lake Gleneida (previously Shaw's Pond).
Photograph by Larry A. Maxwell, 2017

Chapter 33

Wooster Attacks the Crown Forces
April 27, 1777 – Late Sunday Morning

It was late morning on Sunday, April 27, 1777. The Crown Forces were marching down the road towards Ridgefield for a few hours. They encountered only a little resistance on the way but that was about to change.

An artillery crew, toward the rear of the Crown Forces, heard some occasional musket fire along the way but had not been fired upon. They were thankful for that.

What they heard was the sound of General David Wooster with the 1st Connecticut Regiment, attacking the very far end of the Crown Forces' line.

It was not long before the thankful thoughts of the artillery crew, who had not been fired upon, were suddenly disrupted. They saw General William Erskine rapidly approaching on his horse waving his sword over his head.

The General yelled, "The Rebels are behind us lads!"

Those words sent shivers down the spine of the men on the artillery crew.

Erskine yelled urgently, "Get that gun turned around and show them what happens when they oppose the King's

Army!"

The artillery crew stopped, turned their cannon around and struggled to move their cannon to the rear to face the approaching enemy. The muddy road made that difficult, but they finally managed to get in position.

One of the British officers yelled the command, "Load the cannon."

He then yelled, "Infantry form a line on each side of the cannon!"

The Regulars formed two rows on each side of the cannon.

The cannon crew went through their loading sequence. They ran the worm down the barrel, then the sponge. A charge was advanced, put in the barrel, and then rammed in place. One of the artillery men inserted a pick into the touchhole, piercing the charge. He then inserted a metal tube, loaded with powder which served as the fuse, into the touchhole. Now the cannon was ready to fire.

While the cannon crew were loading, the officer ordered the infantry to do the loading sequence for their muskets. He yelled, "Prime and load!"

When the soldiers finished the loading sequence they came to the *Ready* position. Now both the cannon and the infantry were loaded and ready to fire.

The officer then yelled another command to the infantry, "Front row, take a knee."

In one swift movement the front row of soldiers went down on one knee with their muskets pointed ahead and waited for the Rebels to appear.

For the past few hours Major General David Wooster, along with men from the 1st Connecticut Regiment of the Continental Army and some local Militiamen, marched hard and fast towards Ridgefield. They attacked the Crown Forces in a small skirmish. Now they came back to strike another blow. This time there was a cannon facing them.

As the Crown Forces saw Wooster and his men draw close one of their officers yelled, "Fire!"

The cannon and infantry fired simultaneously.

A cannon ball plowed across the field and a massive volley of musket balls flew past Wooster and his men.

Wooster yelled with intense determination, "Come on my boys, never mind such random shots!"

His men were spread out in open order advancing in two wide rows with their muskets on their left shoulders. Wooster yelled to his men, "Halt!"

His men quickly came to a halt.

Wooster swiftly gave orders which his men immediately followed. They were already loaded so he gave the firing sequence. He paused briefly after each command, "Make Ready! Present! Fire!"

Wooster's troops followed the sequence, pointed their muskets at their enemy and fired a volley in unison.

He then quickly yelled to his men, "Fire at will!"

Wooster's troops reloaded, then each man started to shoot individually as fast as he could at the Crown Forces.

Both the Crown Forces infantry and cannon returned another round of simultaneous fire. The thundering boom from the cannon, and the smaller booms from the muskets, shook the ground. Smoke from the cannon and muskets clouded the view and made it hard to see.

When the smoke started to clear a little it revealed Wooster was hit and knocked off his horse.

One of Wooster's men rushed up to help him.

He yelled, "General Wooster! You have been hit!" He stayed close by his side.

The Crown Forces reloaded. After the smoke cleared, the British officer again yelled, "Fire!"

The soldiers fired again.

As soon as they fired the officer yelled another set of commands, "Front Row! Stand! Prime and Load!"

The soldiers stood, loaded their muskets and were ready to fire again.

Wooster's troops returned fire. A couple of soldiers fell.

The officer yelled a different command, "Fix, bayonets!"

The dreadful sound of soldiers fixing their bayonets filled the air.

The officer then extended his sword towards the Rebels and yelled, "Charge!"

He led them boldly forward against the enemy. They all yelled a very loud and long "Huzzah!"

Major General Wooster was taken off the field by the soldier who first came to his side. He did not know Wooster's back had been broken and that Wooster's wound was mortal. General Wooster, the man who bravely led the charge against the Crown Forces, now lay unconscious and near death on the field of battle.

Those around Wooster reloaded and fired at the Crown

Forces as long as they could. When they saw the advancing bayonet charge drawing near many of them reluctantly withdrew. Some stopped every few yards to fire at the advancing force.

Wooster was taken to Danbury. A few days after the battle his family saw him one last time. He died from his wounds at the Dibble House in Danbury.

Wooster's last words were, "I am dying but with a strong hope and persuasion that my country will gain her independence."

Monument to General Daniel Wooster

*The tallest monument in the cemetery.
Wooster Cemetery, Danbury, Connecticut.
Photograph by Larry A. Maxwell, 2018*

Larry A. Maxwell

Monument to General Daniel Wooster

One side of monument depicts Wooster shot in battle.

Other Side of Monument to General Daniel Wooster

*Narrative about Battle of Ridgefield on one side of monument.
Wooster Cemetery, Danbury, Connecticut.*
Photographs by Larry A. Maxwell, 2017

Chapter 34

Sybil Returns Home
April 27, 1777 – About 10 a.m. Sunday

It was about ten o'clock Sunday morning on April 27, 1777. Colonel Henry Ludington left Fredericksburg a few hours earlier with about two hundred men, headed for Danbury, Connecticut, to help drive back the Crown Forces. On the way they received word the Crown Forces departed for Ridgefield and were ordered to proceed there.

After the Colonel left with the first group men continued to come to the training ground near his home, throughout the night and all morning long. They came in response to Sybil's call on her all-night ride.

Lieutenant Colonel Reuben Ferris and Captain John Crane stayed behind waiting for the rest of the men to arrive, before they marched off to join the others.

About two hundred more men arrived over the next few hours. As the men arrived they gathered together in small clusters on the training ground. They started some small campfires along the edge of the training ground to warm themselves.

Jesse Ganong, Sybil's friend, was one of the men who

responded to the call and arrived as part of the second group. His father did not want him to respond to the call, but he still came.

Jesse was outside the Ludington's house talking with Rebecca Ludington, Sybil's younger sister. As they were talking they looked up and saw Sybil approaching.

Sybil came slowly riding up the road toward the house. She was slumped over her horse, looking totally exhausted.

She raised her head as she saw the house. She did not know where she was. She weakly said, "To arms! To arms!" Then slumped over.

Jesse and Rebecca ran quickly to Sybil. Rebecca held the bridle as Jesse started to help Sybil off her horse.

Rebecca was alarmed to see how exhausted Sybil looked. As Jesse reached for Sybil, Rebecca was so concerned all she could say was, "Sybil!"

Sybil was delirious. She raised her head and attempted to yell one more time, "To arms! To arms!"

She then collapsed in Jesse's arms.

Sybil's mother, Abigail, was waiting anxiously for Sybil. When she saw Sybil ride up she ran as fast as she could to Jesse, who was now holding her daughter.

Abigail was so alarmed at the way Sybil looked. She cried out, "Sybil!"

Sybil muttered softly one more time, "To arms!"

Jesse safely held Sybil and spoke to her proudly, "You did it Sybil! You did it!"

Abigail was saddened to see Sybil so exhausted but was relieved to see her daughter home safe. With motherly love,

Abigail said, "Oh, Sybil! My dear child!"

She then told Jesse, "Jesse please take her in the house!"

Jesse was already taking Sybil to the house, yet politely replied, "Yes, Ma'am!"

Jesse, Abigail, and Rebecca went into the house together and took Sybil up to her bed.

Back outside Captain John Crane approached Lieutenant Colonel Reuben Ferris. He took off his hat in salute and respectfully said, "Lieutenant Colonel Ferris."

Ferris tipped the brim of his hat in respect and said, "Yes, Captain Crane?"

Crane gave Ferris the word that the men were ready. He said, "Sir, I believe most of the men are here now."

This was the moment they were waiting for. Ferris gave the official word for Crane to have the men assemble, "Have them fall in!"

Crane turned towards the men and yelled out the order, "Fall in!"

The men quickly formed orderly rows of companies with their muskets on their left shoulders.

When they were lined up Captain Crane yelled, "Order arms!"

The men came to the *Order Arms* position with the butt of their muskets resting on the ground next to their right foot with their right hands near the end of the barrel.

Ferris then walked up and down the line and addressed the troops.

Larry A. Maxwell

The Minute-Men of the Revolution

Lithograph by Currier & Ives, 1876
Correctly shows Militia wore civilian clothing.
Picture omits the neck stock or cravat which all men wore.

Militia at the 225th Anniversary of Sybil's Ride

Reenactors in historically accurate uniforms.
[Left to Right] George Warnecke in Continental Uniform. Others as Militia: Larry A. Maxwell, Nicholas Finelli, Jack Klix, Fred Lambert, Phillip Weaver, and George Bock.
Photograph Carmel, New York, April 2002

As Ferris was speaking Jesse came back outside, carrying a musket Sybil's mother gave him. He did not have one of his own. He ran and joined the other soldiers in line.

"I am thankful all of you came in response to Sybil's call," Ferris said.

One of the men shouted out, "Three cheers for Sybil!"

All the men simultaneously took off their hats and waved them in the air as they shouted three *Huzzahs*!

"Huzzah! Huzzah! Huzzah!"

After the cheer Ferris continued to address the men, "As you know by now the British Regulars and their despicable Tory allies raided and burned Danbury last night."

The men responded to that news shouting *Boos* of disapproval.

One of the men man yelled, "Cowards!"

Ferris then updated his men. He said, "Another messenger arrived and said General Benedict Arnold, General Wooster and General Silliman are at Bethel and plan to attack the Crown Forces this morning and drive them back to the sea."

He did not know the Crown Forces left Danbury a few hours ago and were on their way to Ridgefield. A messenger would bring him that news later.

Ferris continued, "I am sure all of you know Colonel Ludington and the first group of men left a few hours ago. We knew many of you had quite a distance to come so Captain Crane and I waited here for the rest of you to arrive."

He knew everyone was tired and was glad they all came.

He continued, "I know you have come a long way, but it is now our time to go join the fight and drive the Redcoats and those blasted Tories into the sea!"

He paused and then asked the men, "Are you ready to go join the fight!"

All the men took off their hats and responded wildly shouting, "Huzzah! Huzzah! Huzzah!"

Ferris shouted out enthusiastically, "For liberty!"

The men raised their hats again and yelled in response, "For liberty!"

Ferris then ordered them to mount their horses and wagons and head off to join the fight.

Colonial Militia Assemble

Reenactors from the B.A.R. portraying Colonial Militia.
Living History Guild Archival Photograph

Chapter 35

Barricades in Ridgefield
April 27, 1777 – Late Sunday Morning

It was late Sunday morning on April 27, 1777. The people in Ridgefield knew the Crown Forces invaded Danbury. When they heard of the looting and burning they were glad the invaders went to Danbury through Redding instead of through their town. They hoped and prayed the Crown Forces would return to their ships the same way they came.

Their hopes were dashed when a few hours earlier a messenger arrived in Ridgefield and informed them the force of close to two thousand Crown Forces were on their way back to Norwalk, right through their town.

Captain Ebenezer Jones assembled the 1st Ridgefield Militia. He knew a well-placed barricade could be a very useful deterrent against a marching army. He picked a spot in town where there were buildings on the west side of the road and a steep drop-off on the east side. A barricade at the spot would provide a good defensive position and would surely slow down the Crown Forces.

He then called upon everyone in town to come help. Men, women, and children, from all over town, young and old, responded. They brought carts and barrels and chairs and whatever else they could find and started to build the barricade.

When Captain Samuel Lawrence arrived with his men from the nearby 3rd Westchester County Militia they wholeheartedly joined in the task of building the barricade.

While the people were building the barricade in Ridgefield, Major General David Wooster launched a series of unexpected attacks north of town, on the Crown Forces.

Those attacks by Wooster and his men slowed down the advance of the Crown Forces. That gained additional time for those in Ridgefield to prepare.

About an hour-and-a-half-ago Colonel Philip Burr Bradley and some fifty men from the 5th Connecticut Regiment of the Continental Line arrived in town. Many of the men in the 5th Connecticut Regiment were from Ridgefield.

Captain Jones, who was the leader of the Local Militia, had every right to retain control of the operation yet graciously turned command of the operation over to Colonel Bradley, who was a senior officer in the Continental Army. That one decision changed the direction for the rest of the operation.

The first thing Bradley did was send sentries north to keep watch on the main road leading into town.

He told them, "Go north of town and keep watch for the Crown Forces. As soon as you see them come back and let me know."

The sentries ran up the road with haste.

Bradley had the rest of his men help fortify the barricade. He walked up and down and carefully inspected the barricade to make sure it was strong.

Fight at Ridgefield

Barricades erected to block the Crown Forces advance.
Connecticut Historical Society Collection

When he discovered a weak point in the barricade he yelled, "Fill in this gap over here!"

People responded and found more things to help make that part of the barricade stronger.

Everyone was encouraged when close to noon more help arrived. It was General Benedict Arnold and General Silliman on horseback accompanied by a few hundred Militia.

Colonel Bradley was very glad to see the new arrivals. He stopped to greet them with a very respectful hats-off salute, "General Arnold! General Silliman! It is so good to see you!"

Arnold and Silliman remained on their horses and returned the salute with a proper tip of their hats.

Arnold praised Bradley and his men, "Colonel Bradley, I see you and your boys from the 5th Connecticut have been busy!"

Bradley showed them the barricade, "Yes, we have."

Bradley gave credit where credit was due. "Captain Ebenezer Jones of the 1st Ridgefield Militia came up with the idea of building this barricade and picked this advantageous spot."

General Arnold looked around as Bradley spoke and saw it was indeed a very good location for the barricade.

Bradley continued, "Captain Samuel Lawrence and the 3rd Westchester County Militia arrived next and helped. When I arrived with my men we joined them."

He paused, then with passionate resolve he proclaimed, "We plan to stop the Crown Forces right here in Ridgefield! They will get no further!"

Arnold was inspired by Bradley's words and dedication as well as his work and the work of his men. He respectfully said, "Colonel Bradley it will be an honor for us to stand with you!"

Bradley appreciated Arnold's compliment and said, "General Arnold, General Silliman, the honor is all ours!"

General Silliman was a general in the Connecticut State Militia but Colonel Bradley, like General Arnold, was an officer in the Continental Line. The fact that a Continental Line officer was in charge meant General Arnold was now the highest-ranking officer present.

Colonel Bradley took off his hat and bowed his head as he said, "General Arnold, you being the senior officer, I respectfully yield command to you and am your humble servant."

Anyone who knew Arnold, knew he liked being in charge. Up until this point he did not have a problem yielding control to the Connecticut Militia Generals because that was proper military protocol. Yet now that his opportunity to lead arrived he gladly seized the moment.

Trying not to look too overjoyed. He replied to Bradley, "Colonel Bradley I am honored."

Arnold's countenance changed. He got a look of bold determination on his face. He immediately pulled out his sword, turned his horse around to face the men, and yelled emphasizing each word so all could hear him, "When the Crown Forces come, we will give them lead!"

His words were few but inspired everyone.

All the soldiers, along with General Bradley and General Silliman responded enthusiastically. They took off their hats and yelled three *Huzzahs*, as Arnold kept his sword raised.

North of town the Crown Forces regathered after what they viewed as an annoying encounter with General Wooster. They managed to pull their cannon back in line on the muddy road and continued their march south toward Ridgefield.

Feeling optimistic and almost invincible, General Tryon instructed his musicians to play as they advanced.

Chapter 36

Battle in Ridgefield
April 27, 1777 – Early Sunday Afternoon

It was early afternoon on Sunday, April 27, 1777. The Militia and Continental soldiers were working all morning erecting a barricade in Ridgefield, hoping to stop the advance of the Crown Forces. When the barricade was finished it was filled with two rows of men who would alternate shooting when the attack began.

Suddenly the sound of drums and fifes playing military music was heard. Everyone in town became apprehensive.

The sentries, sent out earlier, ran down the street in advance of the Crown Forces. It became very clear the dreaded enemy was coming down the road toward them and would be there shortly.

The sentries scurried over the barricade. Colonel Philip Burr Bradley stood bravely, staring intently up the road.

General Arnold and General Silliman were on horseback about thirty yards behind the barricade. Their men were positioned to protect the flanks. They would reinforce the barricade or stop the Crown Forces if they broke through or bypassed the barricade.

When Colonel Bradley finally saw the Crown Forces approaching he yelled, "Here they come!"

Battle of Ridgefield Historic Marker
This marker is located on the main street in Ridgefield, Connecticut, where the main battle started.
Photograph by Larry A. Maxwell, 2017

He shouted the command, "Make ready!"

There was a long pause as he waited for the Crown Forces to get closer. Then he shouted, "Present!"

The men pointed their muskets through the barricade. The Colonel waited until the Crown Forces came within musket range. Then he yelled as loud as he could, "Fire!"

On the *Fire* command the soldiers fired their muskets in one simultaneous volley. It sounded like roaring thunder and made the ground shake. Some of the soldiers in the front row of the Crown Forces line fell to the ground as they were hit by the assault of musket balls.

As soon as the men in the first row behind the barricade fired, they stepped back and let the second row of men step forward to take their place.

The Crown Forces stopped their advance about fifty yards from the barricade. Their officers had them form a line and quickly return fire with a massive volley. Musket balls ripped through the barricades striking some of Bradley's men with deadly force.

The first row of men who dropped back, reloaded. Bradley gave orders to the second row, who were now at the front of the barricade. This time he gave the commands more rapidly, "Make Ready! Present! Fire!"

Bradley's men fired. As soon as they fired, the Crown Forces returned fire with another volley.

Cannon Crew Fires

*Franklyn Maxwell and Xavier Ojeda,
Living History Guild members fire cannon.*
Living History Photograph

Musket fire went back and forth between the Rebels and the Crown Forces. This continued until three British cannon crews advanced their guns to the front line.

Companies of British Regulars and companies of Loyalists formed lines on each side of the cannons.

While the cannon crews were loading the Regulars fired a volley. A few moments later the Loyalists fired.

Bradley yelled to his men, "Fire at will!"

Bradley's men each reloaded and returned fire, independently shooting their muskets one after another.

Suddenly all three cannons fired. A section of the barricade was violently blown away, throwing debris and men in different directions.

Bradley called to his men, "Retreat!" He quickly led his men back from the barricade. As Bradley and his forces retreated, some stopped, turned around, shot back at the enemy, then quickly rejoined the retreat.

The Crown Forces advanced down the street like a massive wave and poured through the barricade. When they came through they formed rows and fired mercilessly at the Rebels. Governor William Tryon and General William Erskine followed their men through the barricade.

Tryon shouted out, sounding more desperate than victorious, "We have broken through and have them on the run! We must advance to the ships!"

General Erskine was concerned at the strength of the resistance they faced. He asked Tryon, "What about the goods we captured in Danbury? They are slowing us down."

Tryon yelled, "We must advance swiftly. Have the men

take what they can but leave the rest behind! We struck a major blow against these Rebels!"

Erskine yelled to his men, "Take what you can and leave behind whatever slows you down!"

Some soldiers, who were pulling heavy loaded carts, threw aside some of the supplies and then moved more quickly through the barricade.

The cannons advanced and fired upon the retreating Rebels. One cannon ball stuck the Keeler Tavern where some of the Rebels took a stand.

Erskine waved his sword and urged his men forward. He yelled, "It is time to return to New York in victory!"

Bradley's men were slowly doing a fighting retreat. As they retreated they stopped, turned and shot, then retreated a little further and repeated the process of shoot and retreat.

General Arnold rode forward leading a large company of men. As he waved his sword he boldly yelled, "Lads! Listen here! We must hold this line! Right here! Right now! For liberty!"

The men who were retreating stopped and fell in with the men who were with Arnold. They formed a line and fired their muskets back at the Crown Forces.

A British officer at the head of the Crown Forces advanced closer yelling the command, "Form a Line!"

The Crown Forces stopped and formed two rows a little more ragged than usual. The officer yelled pausing briefly between each command, "Make Ready! Present! Fire!"

The Crown Forces fired. This time Arnold and his horse were both hit. His horse was struck by nine musket balls. It fell and pinned him to the ground.

A Connecticut soldier saw Arnold fall and yelled in despair, "They killed General Arnold!"

The Rebel troops scattered and the Crown Forces boldly advanced.

Exploit of Benedict Arnold
Engraving by Kendrick and P. Neeber.
The Youths' History of the United States, 1887.

Arnold was pinned under his horse and struggled to free himself. A Loyalist in a green coat approached him with a bayonet fixed to his musket. He looked at Arnold and yelled victoriously, "Surrender! You are my prisoner!"

Arnold managed to pull his revolver out from his saddle holster and shouted back at the Loyalist, "Not yet!" He then pulled the trigger.

The Loyalist's plan to capture Arnold was thwarted as the bullet from Arnold's musket struck him at close range. He fell backwards, and his musket flew out of his hand.

Arnold struggled and freed himself. He picked up his sword and stumbled off to the side. When he saw men retreating he gathered his strength and hobbled quickly back to the street and called for the men to make a stand. He bravely held his sword up and yelled, "Rally men! Rally!"

The soldier who previously cried, *Arnold is dead*, recognized Arnold's voice. He turned around and yelled, "General Arnold is alive!"

Arnold cried out louder, "Rally around me!"

The men were inspired when they saw and heard General Arnold, who they thought was dead, standing defiantly against the enemy. They came running to where he stood and boldly fell in around him. They relentlessly fired against the mighty sea of Crown Forces advancing toward them.

Soon, General Silliman and his men came forward and reinforced General Arnold and his men. They firmly stood refusing to give up the ground to the Crown Forces.

The Crown Forces realized the best thing to do was to go around the Rebels, rather than continue a deadly head-to-head confrontation. That decision saved many lives.

Chapter 37

Crown Forces South of Ridgefield
April 27, 1777 – Sunday Sunset

It was late Sunday afternoon on April 27, 1777. The sun was about to set. The Crown Forces retreat from Ridgefield was hampered by Rebel Forces pursuing them all.

Rebel Militia from surrounding areas poured in all day joining the attack on the Crown Forces with vengence.

This brought back bad memories to the men in the Crown Forces from the 4th Regiment of Foot and 23rd Regiment of Foot. It reminded them of how many of their companions were picked off, two years ago, on their return to Boston after they attacked Lexington and Concord.

The Crown Forces were now south of Ridgefield near the border of the Parish of Wilton. It was two days since they disembarked. Most of them had not slept for two days. Soon it was going to be dark. They were exhausted and had little strength to go any further.

General William Erskine and his men were near the back of the line of the Crown Forces covering their retreat. All along the way they were pursued by Rebels who fired upon them and then ran.

As it grew darker the attacks grew more sporadic.

Just when they thought the fighting was done for the day, suddenly they heard the blast of a musket come from the woods. One of the men in line was struck and fell.

Erskine and his men came to an abrupt stop, firmly held their muskets, and looked in the direction of the sound.

Continentals Attack from Woods

*John and Kyle Esposito,
Reenactors from 4th N.Y. Regiment.*
Living History Guild Photograph

A sergeant quickly called to the others near him, "Form two rows, on me!"

They quickly formed two rows, facing the woods.

The sergeant then yelled, "Front row, take a knee!"

The men in the front got down on one knee. The others stood behind them. Both rows pointed their muskets towards the woods.

The sergeant shouted the command, "Make ready!"

They all fully cocked their muskets.

He then yelled, "Front row! Fire!"

The men in the front fired. Smoke from their muskets filled the air. As soon as they fired they quickly reloaded.

As they were reloading another musket blast came from the woods. The ball from that blast struck the sergeant, who fell to the ground mortally wounded.

The other men who were standing next to him were shaken. They immediately fired back then quickly reloaded.

Now both rows were loaded. A corporal took charge. He anxiously waited looking for any movement in the woods.

Erskine and his aide watched carefully.

They waited and then waited some more. Everything was quiet. Nothing happened.

Finally, when it seemed like it was safe, Erskine gave the command, "Take your ease Lads!"

The men breathed a sigh of relief as they lowered their muskets. Those who were kneeling stood.

Erskine then said, "Fall back in line and keep a watch as we move forward."

They started to move forward again, all the while looking carefully to their left and right as they proceeded. Every few steps the men in the back stopped, turned around and looked, keeping an eye out for a rear attack.

As they proceeded, one of Governor Tryon's aides rode up to Erskine. The aide took off his hat in salute and nodded his head as he said, "General Erskine?"

Erskine returned the salute grabbing the tip of his hat

and nodding slightly.

Tryon's aide said, "Governor Tryon requests you to join him."

Erskine turned to his own aide, who was on a horse besides him, and said, "Take over."

Erskine's aide nodded his head and replied, "Yes, Sir!"

Erskine then rode off with Tryon's aide.

When Erskine reached Tyron at the front. He gave an informal salute by nodding his head to Governor Tryon as he said, "Governor Tryon your aide said you wanted to see me?"

Tryon replied, "Yes, General Erskine. The scouts tell me it is still about ten miles to the ships. That is almost half a day's march without any unforeseen delays."

Erskine was very disappointed to hear that. He was hoping they were closer than that. He said, "I did not realize we still had that far to go."

Tryon was frustrated by all the delays and resistance they encountered. Angrily he said, "We should have reached the ships by now!"

Erskine replied in frustration, "Those blasted Rebels have relentlessly been coming up behind us and shooting mercilessly at our men!"

Erskine shook his head, "They fight like dogs! And that has slowed us down significantly. We had no choice but to stop and take a stand every few hundred yards to repel them."

Tryon agreed with Erskine, "That is a good analogy, General Erskine! Those Rebels are like a pack of dogs!"

Though he was greatly disappointed at the way things unfolded, Tryon appreciated how valiantly Erskine and his men fought. Amid all the discouragement he spoke words of encouragement. "You and your men have done quite well and fought with honor."

Erskine nodded his head in appreciation of the compliment, "Thank you Governor."

Tryon then explained, "I believe ten more miles is too far for our men to go. They have not slept in two days and though many have fought valiantly and would march on, if we commanded them. I believe we must stop here, and rest for the night."

Erskine agreed and used a biblical parallel, "I greatly desire to continue on to the ships, but I agree with you, though the spirit is willing, the flesh is indeed weak."

Tryon asked, "Do you think those blasted Rebels will stop pursuing us and take a rest, if we stop?"

Erskine gave that question some thought. Back then very few battles took place in the dark. He then responded, "Though they are a bunch of dogs, even dogs get tired and need to rest."

Tryon smiled at that reply. He said, "Then set out sentries and tell the men to stop and rest for the night."

Erskine replied, "I am sure they will appreciate that."

The Crown Forces gratefully stopped their retreat and welcomed a chance to get some much-needed rest.

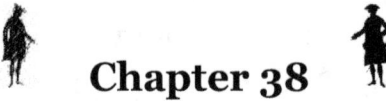

Chapter 38

Ludington Meets Arnold
April 27, 1777 – Late Sunday Evening

Right after the sun set on Sunday, April 27, 1777, General Benedict Arnold was pleased when he learned the Crown Forces stopped to rest for the night south of Ridgefield near the Wilton border. He knew his men were tired and could not fight effectively in the dark, so he ordered them to rest.

While his men rested Arnold, who was always looking for an advantage, rode south around the Crown Forces to find a good place where his army could take a stand in the morning and inflict the most damage.

Meanwhile Colonel John Lamb and his Continental Artillery, who responded to Silliman's call, arrived earlier near Norwalk. General Arnold was able to rendezvous with Lamb. They found an ideal place to position their troops and artillery to launch an attack. It was overlooking the bridge over the Saugatuck River, not far from where the Crown Forces docked their ships.

Lamb situated his regiment then returned with Arnold. Arnold then gathered his fellow officers to discuss plans for the next day.

Continental Artillery Fire Cannon
*Artillery attached to the 4th N.Y. Regiment.
Charlie Arbor, Sharon Ojeda and 1776 Venture Crew.*
Living History Guild Photograph

A couple of hours earlier Colonel Henry Ludington and his men arrived in Ridgefield after the battle. They were saddened when they saw the shattered barricade and the dead and wounded scattered around the town.

They were inspired when they learned of General Arnold's brave stand and how the other Militia and Continentals were fiercely pursuing the retreating Crown Forces.

Colonel Ludington and his men did not linger in Ridgefield. They were given some food by the townsfolk then proceeded south to join the others and help drive the Crown Forces back to the sea.

It was after nightfall when Colonel Ludington and his men arrived at the place where the Continentals and Militia stopped to rest for the night.

They looked around and saw men huddled around small

campfires warming themselves. Many of those men's faces were partially blackened from the blast of their muskets. Many were sleeping after a long hard day.

After their long journey the idea of getting some rest was very appealing to the Colonel and his men.

Off in the distance they could see the campfires from the Crown Forces. That gave them an eerie feeling knowing the enemy was resting so close to them.

Colonel Ludington found a place for his men to rest. They were ready and eager to fight but it looked like the fighting was done for the day and they would be resting for the night. Most of them were extremely tired after traveling all night and day and welcomed the opportunity to get some much-needed rest.

The Colonel asked a sentry, "Where are the officers?"

The sentry pointed him in the right direction. The officers were meeting not far away from where he arrived.

One of the aides standing guard greeted the Colonel as he approached, "Sir, may I be of assistance to you?"

Colonel Ludington responded, "Yes, you may young man. I am Colonel Henry Ludington of the 7th Regiment of the Dutchess County Militia. I just arrived from Fredericksburg, New York and am reporting for duty with two hundred men and expect another two hundred men to arrive in a few hours."

When the aide learned Ludington was a colonel he respectfully took off his hat, nodded his head in a salute and said, "It is an honor to meet you Colonel Ludington."

He then introduced himself, "My name is Edmond

Ogden with the 5th Connecticut Regiment."

Ogden realized the Colonel and his men travelled quite a distance. He said, "I believe Fredericksburg is more than thirty miles away from here. Is that correct?"

"Yes, it is," Colonel Ludington replied. "I received a message about nine o'clock last night that the Crown Forces invaded and burned Danbury. I sent out my daughter Sybil to ride some forty miles to call out the Militia. When the first two hundred men responded I left my second in command behind to wait for the rest of the men and we came as quickly as we could. We stopped briefly at Ridgefield then proceeded here. The whole trip was about thirty-five miles"

Ogden was amazed at what he just heard. "Let me see if I understand you correctly. You received the message from Danbury about nine o'clock, last night."

"Yes," Colonel Ludington replied.

Ogden asked, "Then you sent out your daughter Cecil to ride some forty miles to call out the Militia?"

"Yes, my daughter rode some forty miles to call out the Militia, but her name is Sybil," he replied.

"Why did you send your daughter, Sybil?" Ogden asked.

Colonel Ludington replied, "Because she is my oldest and she is the best rider I know."

Ogden remembered last night's bad weather. He asked, "And she did that last night when it was raining and cold and dark?"

"That is correct," the Colonel replied.

All of this seemed quite extraordinary. Ogden wanted to make sure he understood correctly, "If I understand you correctly, your daughter rode forty miles to call out the Militia. That means some of your men had to travel many miles from their homes to your assembly point and then travelled an additional thirty miles with you to get here?"

"Correct again," Colonel Ludington said.

Ogden smiled, "Your daughter must be quite a special young lady. I would love to meet her one day."

He added insightfully, "You and your men must be very dedicated, and extremely tired after coming all that distance."

"We are tired, that is true. But we are ready to help drive the Crown Forces back into the sea," Colonel Ludington replied anxiously, wanting to see the other officers.

Ogden realized he should stop asking questions and introduce the Colonel to the other officers, "Let me introduce you to the other officers. I am sure they will be glad to meet you."

Ogden led Colonel Ludington to the other officers. "Begging you pardon, General Arnold," Ogden said. "I have someone to introduce."

The other officers were talking. They stopped and looked at Ogden and Colonel Ludington.

General Arnold responded, "You may proceed."

Ogden began to introduce the Colonel, "General Benedict Arnold, may I introduce Colonel Henry Ludington of the 7th Regiment of the Dutchess County Militia. He just arrived from Fredericksburg, New York with two hundred reinforcements."

He paused and then said, "He anticipates an additional

two hundred more men arriving in a few hours."

General Arnold greeted Colonel Ludington enthusiastically, "Colonel Ludington it is a pleasure to meet you. Your arrival is well timed. We desperately need more men to strike another blow at the Crown Forces."

Ludington took off his hat and respectfully bowed his head in a salute. "Thank you General Arnold, your reputation precedes you. It is an honor to meet you. I am your humble servant."

General Arnold made the rest of the introductions. Each officer nodded his head as he was introduced. "This is General Gold Selleck Silliman of the Connecticut State Militia, Colonel John Burr Bradly of the 5th Connecticut Regiment. And this is Colonel John Lamb of the Continental Artillery. He and his men going to help us teach the Crown Forces a lesson."

Colonel Lamb smiled, reached out his hand and shook Colonel Ludington's hand. Colonel Lamb was one of the leaders of the Sons of Liberty in New York. When the revolution started he formed an artillery regiment.

Colonel Lamb asked inquisitively, "Did that soldier say you were from Fredericksburg, New York?"

Ludington replied, "Yes Sir, Colonel Lamb."

Colonel Lamb was familiar with the area. He realized Colonel Ludington and his men came quite a distance. He asked, "Colonel that is a long distance away. How did you and your men arrive as quickly as you did?"

Larry A. Maxwell

Portrait of Colonel John Lamb

*By Benson John Lossing, 1850
Pictorial Field Book of the Revolution.
Lamb's face was disfigured from a wound he received at the Battle of Quebec. This picture has Lamb's alleged personal signature.*

Ludington replied with a brief summary, "When a messenger arrived from Danbury, my daughter Sybil set out on horseback riding some forty miles to issue the call to arms. As soon as half of our men arrived, I took that first group and we came on horseback and in wagons, so we could get here as quickly as we could."

Lamb complimented him, "Coming on horseback and wagons was a wise move to get here sooner."

Lamb then asked for clarification of something he thought he may have misunderstood. "Did you say your daughter rode some forty miles to summon the troops?"

Ludington replied proudly, "Yes Sir! She did!"

Arnold was impressed. He complimented Sybil, "Colonel Ludington you have quite a remarkable daughter."

Edmond Ogden spoke up, "Begging the General's pardon, may I add something?"

Arnold replied, "Yes?"

Ogden added, "I thought the General might like to know that after Colonel Ludington's men travelled many miles to the Colonel's house, they went another thirty-five miles all day and night to arrive here, only stopping briefly in Ridgefield."

Arnold was amazed and pleased, He said, "I can see you and your people are very dedicated to the cause."

Ludington humbly replied, "We try to do our best."

Arnold was pleased with that response. He replied, "Your best is all we can ask for."

Arnold then motioned to Colonel Ludington and said., "Come look at what we have planned."

He showed the Colonel the plans for the next day's battle.

Chapter 39

Back at the Ludington's Home
April 28, 1777 – Monday Morning

It was the morning of Monday, April 28, 1777, at the home of Colonel Ludington in Fredericksburg, New York. While the Crown Forces and Rebels were about to enter battle in Norwalk, Sybil Ludington was about forty miles away sleeping safely in her bed.

Abigail Ludington, Sybil's mother, entered her room. She came close to Sybil and gently spoke her name, "Sybil."

Sybil was deep in sleep. She was dreaming she was riding to call out the Militia. Suddenly, she sat up yelling, "Call to arms! Call to arms!"

Her Mother reached over and hugged her and said, "It is okay Sybil."

Sybil was startled at first. She looked around and realized she was only dreaming and was safe at home in her own bed.

When she saw her mother, she said, "I was dreaming."

An excited look came across Sybil's face and she smiled as she said, "I dreamed Father had me ride all night in the cold and rain to call out the Militia."

She looked at her mother and said, "It seemed so real Mother!"

Abigail smiled and put her arm around Sybil and reassured her, "It was not a dream. It was real Sybil. You did it!"

The look on Sybil's face changed to one of wonder.

Her mother looked at her and said, "Sybil, I am so proud of you. You rode all night through the rain and through all the dangers and you called out the Militia."

Her mother paused then told her something Sybil did not know. She said, "And they came! Hundreds of them! And they marched off with your father to drive back the Crown Forces!"

Sybil was excited to realize she really did ride and that it made a difference. She was so excited, she exclaimed, "Oh Mother!"

Sybil had no idea how long she slept. Her mother decided to let Sybil know, "My dear you slept all day and all through the next night! It is Monday and time to rise and shine and come to breakfast."

Sybil was still in a daze. So many thoughts were going through her mind as she sat on the edge of her bed and shook her head trying to get oriented.

Her mother smiled as she went downstairs.

Sybil rose from her bed and started to head downstairs. She stopped for a moment and looked at herself in the mirror. The girl looking back at her clearly slept very hard.

She said to her image in the mirror, "I am such a mess!"

She quickly brushed her hair then went down the stairs.

When she reached the bottom of the stairs, her sister Rebecca ran over to Sybil and escorted her to the table as she said, "You did a wonderful job, Sybil!"

Archibald looked up from his place at the table and said, "I wish I could have done the ride!"

Sybil looked at him with a smile and said, "Perhaps one day you will, Archibald."

Their mother, Abigail shook her head and smiled.

Henry, Jr. looked at Sybil and said, "So do we call her Sybil Revere now?"

They all laughed.

Abigail then took charge of the conversation. "Let us pray for this meal and especially for safety for Father and the others."

Colonial Dining Area
Old Postcard of 1752 Colonial Kitchen.
This is similar to the place where Sybil and her family ate.

Chapter 40

British Officers Before Last Battle
April 28, 1777 – Monday Morning

It was early in the morning on Monday, April 28, 1777. The Crown Forces rested overnight south of Ridgefield, near the border of Wilton Parish on their way back to Norwalk.

The Crown Forces did not have any tents because when they started this expedition, their commanders thought that after they marched to Danbury and captured the Rebel supplies they would have slept one night in homes in Danbury and then would be back in their ships by the following night. So now they had to sleep on the ground. Some slept against trees, some against walls.

That was the first rest many of them had since they landed in at Norwalk more than two days ago.

After rising in the morning, the army marched into Wilton, where some local Loyalists brought them food for breakfast. They made it a short stop and did not do any looting because they expected the Rebels, who were pursuing them last night, to be upon them at any time.

They did not know the entire Rebel army left early in the morning, led by General Benedict Arnold, marched around the Crown Forces, and were now positioned between them and their ships at Compo Beach.

Continental Army and Militia on the March
Soldiers from the Brigade of the American Revolution.
Living History Guild Archival Photograph

Governor William Tryon, General James Agnew, General William Erskine, and General Montfort Browne had a quick breakfast in one of the Loyalist's homes.

Erskine spoke up. "Governor Tryon, thank you for allowing the men to rest last night. I am sure they could not have gone any further without a night's rest."

Browne responded with his pompous brashness, "If it was not for those blasted Rebels we would have been in our ships and on our way back to New York by now!"

Erskine could not contain the disgust he felt for Browne and his Loyalists. Erskine and his men were all professional soldiers. In his mind Browne's men were not professionals and were almost lower than the Rebel Militia. He questioned their loyalty and viewed them as undisciplined opportunists. He believed his view was reinforced by their unacceptable conduct which he witnessed on this expedition.

Erskine spoke up with unrestrained indignation in his voice, "Were it not for your undisciplined Loyalists getting drunk and acting so improperly in Danbury, and stirring up such an impassioned resistance, we would have been safe back in New York City by now!"

Erskine's previous insulting comments about Browne and his men annoyed Browne but this time he had enough.

Browne responded indignantly, "General Erskine, I have had enough of your disrespect and complaining!"

He stood up and continued speaking with unbridled passion, "I would think twice, if I were you, before you speak ill of me or my brave Loyalists! Were it not for those Loyalists fighting faithfully for our King you and your men would have been defeated and would be back in England, long before this!"

Erskine sneered as Browne spoke.

Browne continued, "My men are loyal subjects of King George and they want to stop this Rebellion which was started by their traitorous neighbors who disregard and dishonor our King! My Loyalists have every right to celebrate when they have a victory because of their loyalty to their Crown and country!"

He recounted the abuse his men experienced at the

hands of their Rebel neighbors, "They had their houses and lands taken away by those infernal Rebels! Many of them have been spit at, mocked, abused, and even imprisoned by those God forsaken Rebels! All because of their loyalty to the Crown!"

As Erskine contemplated what Browne was saying, the sneer disappeared from his face.

Browne continued, speaking with even greater passion. "Do not criticize them! Let them plunder those who have stolen from them! Let them burn down every Rebel home! And let them do whatever it takes to demoralize and destroy those who would do anything to prolong this Rebellion!"

He reminded the others how well his men just fought, "Look how well my Loyalists fought at Ridgefield! They marched defiantly into Rebel musket fire and drove them back!"

Browne stopped, squared his shoulders and said, "I am proud of my Loyalists! And you should be too!"

His response gave a very important insight into how some of the Loyalists thought and explained why they acted the way they did. That was something Erskine did not take into consideration.

Erskine humbly realized he misjudged Browne and his men. They were now properly vindicated in his mind. Erskine was a man of character. He took off his hat and bowed apologetically to Browne.

Tryon responded, "That was well put General Browne. I had not considered that before."

Browne was pleased he and his men were vindicated.

Tryon then changed the subject to one of utmost importance. He said, "It is a good thing Rebels get tired too. It was a fairly quiet night."

Browne added a somber note, "My scouts told me Rebel reinforcements and cannon arrived during the night."

Erskine then brought up a sore point, "Governor Tryon, I heard your adversary, Colonel Ludington and his Militia arrived during the night."

Tryon responded, showing his disgust for Ludington, "Yes! That blasted Ludington is determined to make my life miserable. I shall have to raise the bounty on his head!"

Browne smiled as he replied, "Or perhaps you shall have his head today!"

Tryon shook his head in agreement with that idea.

He then changed the subject back to the day's plan. "General Erskine, as I lead the troops to the ships I need you to reinforce the rear lines. I am sure the Rebels will try to hit us with all they have."

Erskine nodded in agreement showing his resolve as he said, "Then we will hit them back!"

Erskine paused and looked at Browne, proving his change of heart, as he said, "And I am sure General Browne and his men will make those Rebels think twice before they oppose those loyal to the King!"

Browne smiled and said, "That we will!"

Browne then gave the exhortation, "Long live the King!"

Tryon and Erskine replied, "Long live the King!"

Larry A. Maxwell

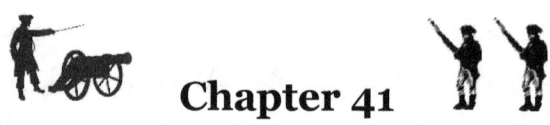

Chapter 41

Battle in Norwalk
April 28, 1777 – Monday Morning

Early in the morning on Monday, April 28, 1777, before the Crown Forces rose and marched into Wilton, General Benedict Arnold roused the American Forces and led them undetected around the Crown Forces, to Norwalk.

Arnold positioned Colonel John Lamb and his artillery and the Fairfield County Artillery, near the Saugatuck Bridge. They were in a field across from the road which led to Compo Beach, where the Crown Forces fleet was docked.

He placed Colonel Henry Ludington, Captain Edmund Baker, and their men from the 7th Regiment of the Dutchess County Militia along a stone wall, not far from the artillery.

Not long before the Crown Forces arrived, General Arnold sent Edmond Ogden bearing an important message, to Colonel Ludington.

When he arrived he said, "Colonel Henry Ludington, I have a message for you from General Arnold."

The Colonel was waiting anxiously to receive his orders. He remembered Ogden. He smiled and said, "Greetings Edmond Ogden, what word do you have for me?"

Ogden relayed the orders he was given, "The Crown Forces are drawing near. Colonel Lamb and the artillery will begin the engagement then you are to launch your attack as soon as Colonel Lamb finishes his artillery barrage."

Ludington acknowledged the order, "Thank you, Edmond, you may return and tell General Arnold I received his orders and will comply."

Ogden replied, "General Arnold said I am to stay with you and report back to him after the action."

The Colonel smiled and patted Ogden on the shoulder, as he said, "Then stay you shall!"

Ogden smiled and heartily replied, "Yes, Colonel!"

While Ludington and Ogden were talking, Lieutenant Colonel Reuben Ferris, Captain John Crane, and the rest of Colonel Ludington's Militia arrived. They dismounted from their horses and wagons. Sybil's friend, Jesse Ganong, was among the men who arrived.

Ferris had his men stretch their legs. He left Captain Crane in charge as he went to see Colonel Ludington.

He took his hat off in salute, "Colonel Ludington, Captain John Crane and I, and the rest of the 7th Regiment of the Dutchess County Militia are reporting for duty."

Colonel Ludington was very happy to see them. He enthusiastically extended his hand, exchanged a hearty handshake, and said, "Reuben, it is so good to see you!"

Ferris said, "Thanks to your daughter Sybil's courageous ride, the rest of the men arrived in the morning some hours after you left. We then set out on our horses and wagons. We stopped very briefly in Ridgefield and then came here as fast as we could."

He paused and reluctantly said, "It was a very long march and I must admit we are tried."

Then, with a gleam in his eye he added, "But we are ready to fight!"

The Colonel asked the question, which was weighing on his mind ever since he left home, "How is Sybil?"

Ferris smiled and gladly said, "She made it back before we left. She looked exhausted, but she is safe."

Colonel Ludington gave a big sigh of relief, "Thanks be to God!"

The cannons were firing before Ferris arrived. While they were talking the Colonel noticed the firing stopped.

He realized the time for the attack was upon them. He gave Ferris orders, "You arrived just in time. The artillery barrage has stopped. It is time to attack. Bring your men over here and fall in behind my men."

Ferris ran back to his men and had them fall in. Though they were all very tired they eagerly grabbed their muskets and marched with Ferris over to the Colonel.

Colonel Ludington bypassed pleasantries and addressed his men, "This is Edmond Ogden from the 5th Connecticut Regiment. General Arnold sent our orders through him. Our orders are to attack when the cannon barrage stops."

Colonel Ludington continued, "As you can hear the cannon barrage has stopped."

He then spoke with intense passion, "It is time for us to show the Crown Forces we will not sit idly by and allow them to take away our freedom! We will not put up with injustice! We will make them pay! Follow me and we will drive the Crown Forces into the sea!"

The men responded enthusiastically yelling, "Huzzah! Huzzah! Huzzah!"

Colonel Ludington called out, "Prime and load!"

The command was echoed down the line.

As soon as the men finished loading the Colonel yelled the command, "First company, advance!"

The soldiers yelled out a loud, "Huzzah!" as the Colonel led the first group over the wall. Sybil's friend Joseph Angevine was in that group.

When that first group advanced a few yards away from the wall the Colonel yelled, "Take Care!" Then immediately after that he said, "Halt!"

His men stopped their advance and formed a line.

Continental Soldiers Maneuvering in Battle

Men of the 2nd N.Y. and 4th N.Y. Regiments.
Living History Guild Archival Photograph

He yelled, "Make Ready!" And the men responded by cocking their muskets.

He then said, "Present!" They responded by pointing their muskets at the enemy across the field.

He paused, then forcefully yelled, "Fire!"

The whole line of men shot their muskets. The sound echoed across the field and a cloud of smoke filled the air.

The Crown Forces, who were coming down the road across the field, formed a line and returned fire.

Colonel Ludington quickly shouted, "Prime and load!"

As they reloaded the second company, under Ferris's command, crossed the wall and advanced a few yards past the Colonel and his men.

Ferris gave the orders for his men to stop. He yelled, "Take care!" Then he yelled, "Halt!" And they all stopped.

Ferris' men were already loaded so he gave them the orders, "Make Ready! Present! Fire!"

Ferris's men fired a volley which was immediately followed by the Crown Forces returning a volley.

When the Crown Forces returned fire some of Ferris' men were hit. Jesse Ganong was among those struck. He was thrown back and fell to the ground, seriously wounded.

Joseph was alarmed as he saw his friend Jesse fall. He ran over to help him. He could see Jesse was seriously wounded. He did his best to stop the bleeding from Jesse's wounds.

Colonel Ludington, Edmond Ogden, and the others in the first group, bravely advanced past Ferris' company.

They yelled a prolonged, *Huzzah* as they pressed forward to push the Crown Forces back. They stopped and fired again.

As soon as the Colonel's group fired, Ferris and his men advanced past them and continued the musket fire.

The Crown Forces retreated and took a different route. Muskets continued to fire. The smoke from the muskets filled the field with smoke and made it hard to see.

Patriot's Monument at Compo Beach
Made by H. Daniel Webster. 1910 cast by Tiffany & Co.
Photograph by Larry Maxwell, 2017

Chapter 42

The Smoke Clears
April 28, 1777 - Monday

It was Monday April 28, 1777. The battle which started near Saugatuck Bridge quickly shifted to Compo Beach. As soon as the first part of the Crown Forces were attacked the rest of their force stopped their advance. They turned aside and headed to Compo Beach another way, fording the river. That decision avoided many casualties.

General Benedict Arnold quickly deployed the artillery and the rest of his force to attack the Crown Forces on Compo Beach.

General William Erskine and his men fought valiantly, holding off the Rebel advance, while the rest of the Crown Forces boarded the ships.

General Arnold almost became a casualty. A musket ball passed through his coat, but he was not hit. Though he escaped injury he had another horse shot under him.

Colonel John Lamb was not as fortunate. Lamb was seriously wounded two years ago at the Battle for Quebec. During this battle he left his cannons under the command of one of his men and led an assault against one of the

British field pieces. He was climbing over a hastily erected barrier when he was struck down and seriously wounded again. He miraculously survived.

When the battle ended, and the smoke cleared, the surviving Crown Forces were aboard their ships heading back to New York City.

After the battle, Colonel Henry Ludington and his men went back to the stone wall where they left their horses and wagons. They found Joseph Angevine and Jesse Ganong along the stone wall. Joseph was caring for Jesse, who was badly wounded. He was very bloody and did not look well.

Friend Helping Wounded Soldier
Engraving from Harper's Weekly, June 28, 1858.

Colonel Ludington, along with Edmond Ogden, approached Joseph and Jesse.

Jesse was pale and very weak, yet looked up at the Colonel and asked, "Colonel? Did we win?"

The Colonel responded positively, "Yes, Jesse. Thanks to you we did."

He paused then said, "We drove them back to the sea like scared rabbits."

Jesse tried to smile but instead coughed up some blood and writhed in pain.

The Colonel leaned down close near Jesse. With much appreciation he said, "Thank you for taking a stand and helping us."

Jesse coughed again. A very concerned look came over his face. He had an important message he wanted the Colonel to convey. He struggled to get out each word, "Colonel ... please ... tell my father ... I am ... sorry."

As soon as Jesse said the last word he passed out and his body went limp. Joseph became distraught and cried bitterly for his friend.

The Colonel reverently took off his hat. Ogden did the same. He bowed his head and said, "No need to apologize Jesse, no need at all."

Two men came over with a two-wheel cart. They picked up Jesse's body and loaded it in the cart.

The rest of the men gathered their horses and wagons and began the long march home.

Everyone was deeply saddened that some fell. They were glad to know they did not fall in vain. They knew they took a stand for liberty and inflicted serious damage on the Crown Forces who dared to invade their land.

After this battle the war continued, yet the Crown never attempted another deep inland attack in Connecticut.

Chapter 43

The Return
April 30, 1777 - Wednesday

It was Wednesday, April 30, 1777. A lot happened since Sybil Ludington made her courageous all night, forty-mile ride in the rain, to call out the Militia.

Those whose loved ones responded to the alarm were anxiously waiting word of what happened.

Joseph Angevine's father Jacob was having a cup of tea with Abigail, Sybil, and Rebecca. He came to their house, the night of the alarm. He could not go with the militia, so he helped by staying and keeping guard at the Ludington's.

As they were having their tea, Abigail voiced her concern, "I wonder how much longer it will be until we hear some word?"

Jacob looked at her kindly and reassuringly as he said, "I think we will be hearing something soon."

Sybil emphatically interjected, "I hope they drove the Crown Forces back into the sea!"

Jacob smiled as he said. "I think my son Joseph, would try to do that on his own!"

Sybil had a determined look on her face as she said,

"And I would too!"

Rebecca wanted to show she felt the same as Sybil, so she enthusiastically added, "Me Too!"

As they were having their tea, there was a knock at the door. Jacob arose, grabbed a musket, and headed to the door. He was followed by Abigail and her daughter Sybil. When they opened the door there stood John Ganong, the uncommitted father, whose son Jesse responded to the call. John Ganong was normally dressed impeccable but looked quite disheveled as he stood there.

He was totally distraught as he humbly asked, "Any word yet?"

After his son Jesse left to help drive back the Crown Forces, John came to the Ludington's home each day, looking to see if there was any word about his son.

As the others stood there, Sybil spoke right up to answer his question, "No word yet, Mr. Ganong."

John shook his head in disappointment. He was feeling very penitent, "I was so wrong! I did not realize they would attack us like that!"

While they were talking, Archibald, one of Sybil's younger brothers, was intently looking out the window for any sign of his father. Suddenly his expression changed from a somber look to one of great joy.

Archibald quickly ran quickly past Jacob, his mother, his sister and Mr. Ganong, shouting excitedly, "Mother! Sybil! Everyone! Look! It is Father!"

They all looked up the road and saw Colonel Ludington on his horse and a whole group of others approaching. The

Colonel and his men looked tired and very dirty after marching two days, without much rest, to return home.

Soldiers Return from Battle

Members of the 2nd, 3rd, and 4th N.Y. Regiments.
Living History Guild Archival Photograph

His family were thrilled to see him. They all ran to greet him. He got off his horse and ran toward them.

Abigail was so elated. Tears of joy were streaming down her cheeks as she ran and hugged her husband. She joyfully said one word, "Henry!"

Sybil and her siblings ran up to their father and joined their mother hugging him. They all cheerfully yelled, "Father! Father!"

Edmond Ogden accompanied the Colonel home. He dismounted and stood back a few paces, smiling as he watched the happy reunion. Sybil looked inquisitively at him wondering who he was.

Colonel Ludington spoke, "Sybil! Thanks to you we

arrived at a time when we were able to provide much needed help."

Edmond Ogden interjected, "And we drove the Redcoats and Tories into the sea!"

Abigail and the others were elated. Abigail exclaimed, "Henry! That is wonderful news!"

Sybil was excited but was also very curious. She looked at Ogden inquisitively and asked, "Father, who is this?"

Edmond started to reply, "I am ... "

He was interrupted by Sybil's father before he could get his name out, "This is Edmond Ogden. He is a good man. He served bravely by my side."

Sybil smiled, she liked what she saw and liked that her father said Edmond was a good and brave man. She gave a curtsey and said, "My name is Sybil, pleased to meet you."

Ogden smiled, gave Sybil a bow and said, "So, Colonel, is this the amazingly brave daughter you were telling me about?"

That made a big smile appear on Sybil's face.

Colonel Ludington looked at Ogden, then looked at his daughters Sybil, Rebecca, and Mary. He wisely replied, "Yes Edmond, that is one of my amazing daughters."

Sybil, Rebecca, and Mary all smiled.

Ogden continued to speak, "Colonel, you did not tell me that she is as fair and beautiful as she is brave."

Sybil blushed, Rebecca and Mary giggled.

Ogden then looked at Abigail and continued speaking quite eloquently, "I can see she got her charm and good looks from her mother."

Abigail appreciated that compliment. She smiled and said, "Why, Henry! It is so nice you brought back such a fine gentleman."

The Colonel smiled and spoke in jest, which he was very fond of doing, "Yes, I thought I would bring back a suitable husband for Sybil!"

Abigail was shocked at what Henry said. Then she smiled when she realized he was jesting and said, "Henry!"

Sybil smiled and gave her father a push, as she sternly said, "Father!"

Ogden was surprised at the whole exchange. He looked at Henry and said inquisitively, "Colonel?"

The Colonel realized Ogden did not realize he was jesting. He put his hand on Edmond Ogden's shoulder and reassured him, "I am just kidding."

Ogden looked relieved, but his face showed he liked what he saw in Sybil. She also liked what she saw in him. They ended up liking each other so much, that a few years later Sybil became his wife.

While Colonel Ludington was having this nice reunion with his family, Jacob Angevine looked calmly down the line for his son while John Ganong was desperately looking over the line of returning soldiers for his son.

They finally saw Joseph Angevine pulling a cart. Jacob was elated. He ran over and embraced his son.

John knew Joseph was a friend of his son Jesse. He was extremely concerned when he noticed a body in the cart Joseph was pulling. The body had a hat over its face.

John stopped dead in his tracks. He looked totally

distraught when he realized the body in the cart was that of his son Jesse. He ran to the cart crying bitterly, "Oh no! My son! My son!"

Joseph stopped pulling the cart. He wiped his brow and nodded to John that it was Jesse in the cart.

John threw himself on Jesse crying. He was overwhelmed with emotion.

After a few moments John was startled beyond words as his son Jesse woke up. When Jesse saw his father he spoke weakly, "Father?"

John was startled and overjoyed. His sorrow was instantly replaced by ecstatic joy. He yelled, "Son! My son! You are alive!"

John tightly hugged Jesse.

Colonel Ludington, Edmond Ogden, Sybil and all the others came over to the cart.

Jesse spoke penitently to his father, "Forgive me, Father! I did not mean to dishonor you!"

John shook his head penitently as he said, "No! Forgive you?? Dishonor me? Oh, No! Son! Will you forgive me! I was an old fool! I had my head buried in the sand! I could not see! I was blinded to the tyranny!"

He paused then said, "But now, now I can finally see! Thanks to you! I know now there is a time to take a stand against tyranny, no matter how hard that may be."

John stopped, looked at Jesse and proclaimed, "Jesse, I am so proud of you!"

Henry put his arm around Abigail and Sybil and said, "Yes! Our children can make us very proud!"

Historical Background

Dates and Times Used in This Book

Some other books contain contradicting accounts as to the timing of events mentioned in this book. Many modern accounts are well-meaning but too often repeat incorrect information from well-meaning articles or books.

The dates and times used in this book were extrapolated from a variety of historical accounts. Other factors were also considered, such as: the influence of the weather on travel time between two points; travel times for an army marching in the rain at night, with artillery, on muddy dirt roads; the time of sunrise and sunset for the locations in this story; the time it would take a messenger to reach someone; and the amount of time it would take for the person receiving the message to respond and arrive at a particular place in 1777.

Historical accounts reviewed for this book include: contemporary newspaper articles which were published within days of the events; military reports; letters by participants; older reliable history books; and journal entries.

Newspaper articles were published in newspapers sympathetic to the Crown and in ones sympathetic to the Revolution. In some cases, it is unclear who the sources were for those articles. It must be understood; newspaper accounts are often flawed and reflect the paper's bias.

Contemporary letters, reports, and journals written by some of the participants provided valuable information. In some cases, they included contradictory or incorrect information. Authors wrote what they observed, perceived, or recalled, and in some cases, what others told them. That information was sometimes flawed.

Many histories incorrectly report the Crown Forces boarded ships on Friday, April 25, 1777. Journals and official military reports clearly show they boarded ships in New York on the afternoon of Tuesday, April 22, 1777, intending to arrive in Connecticut that evening. They were delayed by bad weather and were stuck on their ships until they arrived at Compo Beach three days later on Friday, April 25, 1777.

Historical Background for Chapter 1
Paul Revere's Dangerous Ride

This was a time of dangerous disagreement and dissension. People in the colonies were filled with anger at a series of laws enacted ten years prior to the events in this chapter by the Crown and Parliament. Many colonists felt they were being mistreated like unwanted stepchildren. They were no longer willing to be complacent. Some complained, some protested, and others resisted.

Those leading the British government were outraged at the ungrateful colonists. To bring their subjects in line they enacted more laws and imposed more taxes. Those actions had the opposite effect. Things went from bad to worse.

British Regular troops under the command of General Thomas Gates were sent to Boston to bring the wayward children in line. From 1763 until 1775, Gates was the British Military Commander in North America.

Opposition to the Stamp Act
*The Bostonian's paying the Excise Man.
Philip Dawe, London, 1774.*

Many historians say the conflict started in March 1765, ten years before the events in this chapter. That was two years after the war against the French and the Indians ended. England claimed they wanted the colonists to help pay for their share of conducting that war. They did that by passing the Stamp Act. The Stamp Act required colonists to pay a tax on every piece of printed paper. Many people used paper in some form, so the Crown saw this as a good way to raise a considerable amount of money.

The colonists were not opposed to helping pay for the war but were enraged at taxation imposed on them without having any representation or say in the matter. That caused clouds of unrest to form.

After passage of the Stamp Act, that same year a British aristocrat in the Hudson Valley of New York added insult to injury. Beverley Robinson claimed ownership of lands which settlers lived on for years. Some were lands the settlers leased from the Wappinger Tribe. He claimed the Philippse family, into which he married, owned that land. Yet they never made that claim. Robinson produced documents claiming the Philippse family bought the land many years prior to that. He persuaded the Royal Courts to allow him to forcefully displace settlers in Dutchess County, who refused to pay him rent. He replaced those people with his *Loyal Tenants*.

Instead of taking up the hatchet, Daniel Nimham, chief of the Wappingers whose tribe owned the lands, attempted a peaceful resolution. He challenged Robinson's land grab in court. He even went to England where he found support from William Petty, the Earl of Shelbourne, Southern Secretary to Prime Minister William Pitt. Petty agreed Robinson's claims were based on fraudulent documents. Petty was a Whig and later became Prime Minister in 1782 and negotiated peace with the United States. When Nimham returned from

England, Sir Henry Moore, the Royal Governor of New York, a friend of Robinson, was dealing with unrest in response to the Stamp Act. Though Moore agreed Petty was correct, he refused to overturn Robinson's claim because he believed it would upset things too much. He was very wrong.

The oppressed settlers responded with an aggressive approach. In November 1765, more than three hundred of them gathered at Samuel Towner's home in Fredericksburg, New York to express their outrage and resist Robinson. They vowed to reclaim their homes and not pay rent to Robinson.

Instead of discussing the matter with the dissatisfied parties, Governor Moore backed Beverley Robinson and sent in regiments of British Regulars from Poughkeepsie and from New York City, along with artillery. They were sent to forcibly put down what they called *The Settler's Revolt*. It was during this revolt British Regulars first fired upon American colonists. After several months of fighting, the Settlers were defeated, and the well-armed Regulars prevailed.

William Prendergast, one of the leaders of the Settler's Revolt, was finally arrested and taken to Poughkeepsie where he was tried in the Court of Assizes by the English aristocrats who controlled the court.

Prendergast was a Scottish-Irish-immigrant. The English looked down on people from Scotland and Ireland. They derogatorily called them the Scotch-Irish. Perhaps that is why, when the Court of Assizes found Prendergast guilty of High Treason, it gave him the same sentence English aristocrats passed upon the Scottish hero William Wallace. They invoked an old English statutory penalty from 1351 which allowed for men convicted of high treason to be hung but not killed and then to be drawn and quartered. That was his sentence.

In a desperate noble attempt to save her husband's life, his wife Mehitable Prendergast, borrowed a horse and made an inspiring 80-mile ride to New York City. She appealed to Governor Moore to spare her husband's life. She warned the Governor there would be a revolution if he allowed the execution of her husband. Moore responded to her appeal and spared William Prendergast's life on September 1, 1766. Despite this reprieve more ominous clouds formed.

When Samuel Adams saw reports of *The Settler's Revolt* and Prendergast's sentence in the Boston newspaper he was outraged and called for the *Sons of Liberty* to unite.

The Boston Massacre and Crispus Attucks
Crispus Attucks killed at Boston Massacre.
W.C. Nell, 1855

Unrest due to injustice spread among the colonies. In March 1770, civilians in Boston gathered to protest a continuing series of oppressive acts. British Regulars responded to the protest by firing upon the protestors and killing five of them. Among those slaughtered was Crispus Attucks, an African-American who died on the spot. That infamous day became known as the *Boston Massacre*. The clouds which were gathering grew very dark.

The unrest continued to grow greater. Sixteen months before the events in this chapter on December 17, 1773, Samuel Adams and other colonists refused to pay another tax, this time a tax on tea. *The Sons of Liberty* donned Indian clothing and went from *Faneuil Hall* in Boston to the nearby harbor. They boarded ships which were importing tea and defiantly threw 342 chests of tea into the water.

The Boston Tea Party

Engraving from 1773.
New York Public Library

The British responded to that act of rebellion with another series of coercive taxes and regulations which the colonists called *The Intolerable Acts*. The waters were dirtied by dissatisfaction and the dark clouds intensified.

Discontent and dissent continued to spread throughout the colonies. In 1774, one year before the events in this chapter, representatives from all thirteen colonies gathered together for the first *Continental Congress* to address their concerns about how they were being treated by Mother England. Now dark clouds of unrest covered most of America.

The British government did nothing to diffuse the tension. Instead, it escalated matters by sending additional British Regulars to Boston under the command of the Lord William Howe. Howe was there to put down the troublesome colonists. The colonists were forced to provide room and board to house those unwanted occupiers whom they viewed as oppressors. The dark clouds grew thicker and thicker and were ready to burst. Then came April 1775 at Lexington and Concord.

Paul Revere's Ride

Artist A. L. Ripley, 1935.
WPA Administration Project.
Lexington Massachusetts Post Office

Paul Revere's ride was immortalized in Henry Wadsworth Longfellow's imaginative poem, *The Midnight Ride of Paul Revere*, published in 1861. Though the poem is a literary masterpiece and though it is true Paul Revere made an important ride, the poem contains some information which is historically incorrect. Longfellow knew that but was using literary license to immortalize an American hero.

The biggest inaccuracy is not the fault of the poem but of those who never read it. Many people, including numerous historical textbooks, newspaper articles and websites often refer to the poem stating Paul Revere's famous words, "The British are Coming." Neither the poem nor Paul Revere ever uttered the words, "The British are coming."

The poem does not say what Paul Revere said on his ride. Historical accounts claim the riders who sounded the alarm said, "The Regulars are coming!"

The poem also says Revere rowed to Cambridge and there waited for a signal to appear in the steeple of the North Church which would let him know if the British would be coming by land or by sea. The reality is Revere was rowed across the Charles River by Joshua Bentley and Thomas Richardson. He did not wait on the other side for a signal. He knew the British Regulars were coming by sea as he was the one who had the signal placed in the church to alert others.

The poem also says Revere arrived in Lexington at one o'clock and was in Concord at two o'clock. Historical accounts place Revere's arrival in Lexington between midnight and one thirty. Though he did head to Concord, he was detained along the way and had his horse taken from him. He never made it to Concord.

The poem omits the fact there were other riders that night. William Dawes rode out across Boston Neck before Revere left. Dr. Samuel Prescott also rode, as well as many others whose names have not survived.

Larry A. Maxwell

Historical Background for Chapter 2
War Begins

This chapter presents the historically correct order of events which took place at Lexington, Massachusetts on April 19, 1775. This is based on careful review of contemporary accounts. Only the exact words spoken by the parties involved are used in this chapter.

The May 15, 1775 edition of *Dunlap's Pennsylvania Packet*, a newspaper published in Philadelphia, Pennsylvania, included numerous sworn affidavits taken on April 25, 1775, from more than fifty men present at the Battle in Lexington. The affidavits recounted what took place on April 19, 1775. Among those sworn affidavits was one from Captain John Parker, head of the Lexington Training Band.

All the people giving the affidavits swore the British Regulars took the first shots and British officers ordered their men to attack the Militia. Those men reported what they recollected. It is important to know they all collaborated on their testimonies and their accounts appeared in a publication which fully supported the Revolution.

The May 30, 1775 edition of *The Public Advertiser*, a newspaper published in London England, published a report dated April 26, 1775, about the events of April 19, 1775. It called the attack on Lexington and Concord "inhuman," and said it was conducted by a "Body of the Kings Troops."

The report stated, "the Regulars rushed on with great violence and first began Hostilities by firing on the said

Lexington Company whereby they killed eight and wounded several others; that the Regulars continued their Fire until those of said Company who were neither killed or wounded, made their Escape."

The Crown Forces, which participated in the attack on Lexington and Concord, were British Regular soldiers. Later in the Revolution the Crown Forces also included Loyalists and Hessians.

Most Regulars, according to the 1768 clothing warrant, wore white small clothes. That included white shirts, white breeches, and white waistcoats. In 1771, some of the Light Infantry were authorized to wear red waistcoats.

All Regulars involved in 1775 wore black neck stocks and carried cartridge boxes and British Long Land (1st model) Brown Bess muskets. The shortened Brown Bess muskets, known as the Short Land or 2nd Model Brown Bess did not arrive in America until 1776, when they were brought over to New York with some of the regiments.

Most people think the soldiers in the Crown Forces all wore the same uniform, that is not correct. Though most had the same items mentioned above, each regiment had its own distinctive uniform with the number of their regiment on the buttons of their regimental coats and waistcoats. The coats for each regiment had their own facing color and distinct lace around their buttons which differed from other regiments.

The two regiments at Lexington were the *4th Regiment of Foot* and the *10th Regiment of Foot*. The *4th Regiment of Foot* wore red coats faced dark blue and wore full gaiters. In contrast, the *10th Regiment of Foot* wore shorter red coats faced buff, red waistcoats and half gaiters.

After those two regiments left Lexington they joined the following regiments, which marched directly to Concord. Notice the different facing colors: the *1st Battalion of His Majesty's Marines* wore red coats faced white; the *5th Regiment of Foot* wore red coats faced buff, red waistcoats and tall bearskin caps; the *18th Regiment of Foot* (also known as *The Royal Irish*) wore red coats faced in dark blue and tall bearskin caps; the *23rd Regiment of Foot Fusiliers* wore a similar uniform to *18th Regiment of Foot*; the *38th Regiment of Foot* wore red coats faced yellow; the *43rd Regiment of Foot* wore red coats faced white; the *52nd Regiment of Foot* wore red coats faced buff; and the *59th Regiment of Foot* wore red coats faced red along with tall bearskin caps.

After leaving Concord the British Regulars returned to Cambridge and then back to Boston. The retreat is usually pictured in movies or books as a group of British Regulars quickly going down a road, fearing for their lives, being shot at by Militia hiding behind trees.

The report in the May 30, 1775 London edition of *The Public Advertiser*, spoke about the Regular's return to Cambridge. Though they retreated and were shot at, the article reported they apparently had time to behave shamefully.

The article states, "To give a Particular account of the Ravages of the Troops, as they retreated from Concord to Charles-town, would be very difficult, if not impracticable, let it suffice to say that a great Number of the Houses on the road were plundered and rendered unfit for Use, several were burnt, Women and Children were driven by the Soldiery naked into the Streets, old Men peacefully in their Houses were shot dead, and such Scenes exhibited as would disgrace the Annals of the most uncivilized Nations."

> the Regular Troops were killed and wounded.
> To give a particular Account of the Ravages of the Troops, as they retreated from Concord to Charles-Town, would be very difficult, if not impracticable; let it suffice to, say, that a great Number of the Houses on the Road were plundered and rendered unfit for Use, several were burnt, Women in Childbed were driven by the Soldiery naked into the Streets, old Men peaceably in their Houses were shot dead, and such Scenes exhibited as would disgrace the Annals of the most uncivilized Nations.
> These Brethren are Marks of ministerial

The Public Advertiser, May 30, 1775 edition

Account of the Regular's return march back to Cambridge. Published in London, England, 1775.

Historical Background for Chapter 3
Meet Sybil's Family

When the other colonies finally received the news about Lexington and Concord some people responded with great joy, others responded with fear and trepidation. The response to the message united some and divided others.

Tensions between England and the Colonies were rising for a long time. In September 1774, seven months before Lexington and Concord, twelve of the thirteen colonies met in Philadelphia, Pennsylvania. They formed the *First*

Continental Congress to address grievances between the colonies and England. England ignored their petitions.

First Continental Congress Opens in Prayer
Tompkins Harrison Matteson, 1848 - Granger Collection.

Just a few months later, on April 20, 1775, a Provincial Convention was held in New York City to address the specific grievances Yorkers had with the Crown and Parliament. Though that was just two days after the Battle of Lexington and Concord, word of the battles had not yet reached New York. When word about what happened at Lexington and Concord did reach that assembly, those present officially formed the *1st New York Provincial Congress*.

At that time, the Yorkers and many others, were not looking to separate from England, they just wanted to have their grievances resolved. Despite all the grievances between the Colonies and England many people envisioned a Grand Union between the two. A *Grand Union flag* was made which bore the King's Colors as a canton in the upper left-hand corner. It also had thirteen alternating red and white stripes which represented the thirteen colonies. The flag was a visual symbol representing a Grand Union between England and the thirteen colonies. After the *Declaration of Independence* was signed, the United States abandoned the *Grand Union flag*.

Raising the Continental Grand Union Flag
Clyde O'DeLand - Illustration 1897.

The *First New York Provincial Congress* selected delegates to meet with the other colonies at a *Second Continental Congress* in May 1775. Representatives from Quebec was also invited to attend.

The *Second Continental Congress* addressed not only the grievances between the Colonies and England but also dealt with the hostile attack by England against the Colonies. It held its meetings in Philadelphia, Pennsylvania, the same place where the *First Continental Congress* met.

The next year in July 1776, that *Second Continental Congress* issued America's founding document, the *Declaration of Independence*. After that, on July 10, 1776, New York proclaimed itself a state.

The Birth of New York State
Painting by G.A. Harker ca. 1912.

In this chapter it is April 22, 1775, three days after the Battle of Lexington and Concord. The location is Fredericksburg, New York, north of New York City.

During the French and Indian War, Colonel Henry Ludington faithfully served in the Crown Forces under Colonel Beverley Robinson. After the war ended, New York Governor William Tryon appointed Henry Ludington Colonel of the 7th

Regiment of the Dutchess County Militia.

It is very important to understand that while Henry Ludington and his friend Daniel Nimham, chief of the Wappinger Indians, and other men from Dutchess County were away fighting in the French and Indian War, Colonel Beverley Robinson, took actions which caused *The Settler's Revolt* and helped ignite the Revolution.

During *the Settler's Revolt,* Beverley Robinson and his associate Oliver Delancey worked to take the land away from the residents in Dutchess County. Later, when the Revolution started, Robinson and Delancey both raised regiments of *Loyalists* to advance their cause. That put them in a second confrontation with the men of Dutchess County.

This chapter recounts the heroic ride of Mehitable Wing Prendergast. Sybil Ludington was inspired by Mehitable's ride, 80 miles each way, in order to save her husband's life after English aristocrats convicted him to die a horrible death.

Historical Background for Chapter 4

A Plan to End the War

By June 1775, just two months after Lexington and Concord, some 1,200 volunteers from all walks of life, and from various colonies, came to Boston to join the fight and take a stand against Crown's tyranny. Rich and poor, white and black; as well as people from different religious backgrounds; along with Tribal Warriors, all stood shoulder to shoulder to fight for liberty.

Most of those who came to Boston were once loyal subjects of the Crown. They came to show they would no longer tolerate the intolerable actions of a government which to them seemed more interested in receiving revenue from the colonies than in governing them justly.

Many of them, like Daniel Nimham Chief of the Wappinger Tribe, fought valiantly on the side of the Crown in the last war. He and his son Abraham were now joined by warriors from Stockbridge and went to Boston to help the Revolution.

The Sons of Liberty learned the British planned to fortify Breed's Hill and Bunker Hill, the high ground on Charlestown Peninsular. The Crown Forces wanted to capture that ground and fortify it to give them a superior military position and greater control over Boston. That was unacceptable to the colonists.

On the evening of June 16, 1775, a rag tag army of colonists hastily occupied those hills, to give them the military advantage, before the British could claim the ground.

When the British Army learned the Rebels occupied the high ground, they decided they could not allow such a presence to remain. The British commanders decided to launch a full-frontal attack against the ill-equipped volunteer army. The Crown Forces greatly outnumbered the Rebels with 2,200 professional well-equipped soldiers.

The Rebels, who were on the high ground, did not rest that night. They dug entrenchments throughout the night and prepared for an attack which started the next morning.

The Rebel Army had very limited ammunition. They

needed to make every shot count. The command was given, "Do not shoot until you see the whites of their eyes."

A large force of British Regulars marched up the hill with their bayonets fixed. The colonists showed great restraint and waited until their enemy was uncomfortably close. Then, almost in unison, they set off a massive musket volley. A wall of musket balls cut down the front ranks of the British line killing both enlisted men and officers. The enemy withdrew back down the slopes.

Engraving of Battle of Bunker Hill

Engraving by John Lodge, based on a drawing by Millar. Published 1783 in England.

The Regulars reformed their ranks and attacked again. The Rebels allowed the Regulars to get uncomfortably close, and again, released another massive volley of musket fire. The Crown Forces took many casualties and withdrew again.

The Regulars refused to capitulate. They reformed their

lines and launched a third attack. By that time many of the colonists were out of ammunition. They did not have the fire power to hold back the attacking wave of soldiers and were pushed off both hills.

It was a bloody battle. There were more casualties inflicted on both sides at that battle, than in any other battle during the entire Revolution. Rebel causalities that day totaled 441, including thirty captured. Dr. Joseph Warren, President of the *Massachusetts Provincial Congress,* a key leader of the *Sons of Liberty* was killed. The British sustained the most significant losses with 1,054 casualties, including 19 officers killed and 62 officers wounded.

Peter Salem at Bunker Hill
William C. Nell, 1855.

The Battle became known as *The Battle of Bunker Hill.* Though the Crown Forces won the battle they took heavy losses. That galvanized the Rebel's resistance.

At the Battle of Bunker Hill at least a dozen free slaves fought on the Rebel side. One of them, Barzillai Lew is said to have kept the soldier's morale high as he played on his fife the song, *There's Nothing Makes the British Run, Like Yankee Doodle Dandy.*

Freed slave, Salem Poor is credited with mortally wounding British Lieutenant Colonel James Abercrombie at Bunker Hill. Former slave, Peter Salem killed Major John Pitcairn. It was Pitcairn who led the attack on Lexington.

General Howe Evacuating Boston
Engraving by M.A. Wegman and J. Godfrey.
Anne S.K. Brown Military Collection

After the battle, hundreds of Militiamen came from the other colonies to help lay siege to Boston. The British no longer dared to venture outside of the city.

A Militia captain from Connecticut led a group of men in

his Militia to Boston to help. His name was Benedict Arnold. He was quickly given a commission as an officer in the Continental Army. He plays a major role in this book.

Finally, in March of 1776, after a long winter siege the British boarded ships and evacuated Boston. Some people thought the war was over and rejoiced when the British left. General George Washington knew better. He knew the Crown would not accept defeat. He believed they retreated from an untenable position and would return and try to take New York City. Washington assembled his army, along with the Militia, and stationed them around New York City.

British Fleet Arrives in New York
Engraving, Harper's Magazine, Vol. 53, August 1876.

Washington was correct. The largest British Fleet ever to sail landed at Staten Island, New York on July 3, 1776, with 22,000 soldiers.

The day before their arrival on July 2, 1776, the *Second Continental Congress*, unaware of the impending British invasion, voted on and passed the *Declaration of Independence* in Philadelphia. It was proclaimed publicly on July 4, 1776. They did not sign it until August 2, 1776.

The Lord William Howe was Commander of the British Forces in America. In August 1777, Howe turned forty-seven years old. He was a *Whig* and a member of Parliament.

There were two factions in England at that time: the *Whigs,* and the Tories. The *Whigs* were sympathetic with the call from the American Colonies for greater representation.

By August 1776, the number of Crown Forces on Staten Island, and on ships around New York, swelled to 32,000. That included Hessian soldiers. They were not mercenaries, but men impressed into service by their lords. The Battle for New York began in earnest.

Over the next few weeks Washington and his troops, being heavily outnumbered by the Crown Forces, were forced to retreat from Brooklyn and then Manhattan. The British occupied New York City and held it for the next seven years.

In early 1777, Howe, came up with a plan to end the Revolution. He believed if they could take control of the Hudson River, that would sever the Colonies in half and the war would end. To do that, he first needed to destroy the Rebel Supply Depots.

In this chapter it is March 1, 1777. Almost two years passed since Lexington and Concord and eight months since the Battle for New York. The Lord Howe held a meeting with four generals to tell them of his plan to divide the colonies by launching a raid on the Rebel Supply Depot at Danbury, Connecticut. That meeting included: Governor William Tryon; General James Agnew; General William Erskine; and General Montfort Browne.

Governor William Tryon was a professional soldier. He served as the Royal Governor of North Carolina then became the Royal Governor of New York. When the Revolution started, the *New York Provincial Congress* choose their own governor to replace Tryon. Tryon was then given a commission as a general in the Army. He would turn forty-eight years old in June 1777.

General James Agnew was a career military officer born into a Scottish military family. He was in Boston in late 1775 and was part of the Battle for New York in 1776. He commanded the combined force of Grenadiers from the 23rd, 44th and 64th Regiments. He was fifty-eight years old in 1777. General Agnew died in October 1777, six months after the raid on Danbury, while he was leading his troops into battle during the Battle of Germantown.

General William Erskine was fifty-eight-years old. Like Agnew, he was a Scottish career officer. Unlike many Scots, he sided with the Crown. He was the Quartermaster General for the British Army in North America.

General Montfort Browne was a wealthy English landowner from Ireland, and a developer with interests in Florida and the Bahamas. King George appointed him Governor of Florida, then of the Bahamas. When the Revolution started he was captured by the Continental Army. While held a prisoner he secretly raised a Loyalist Regiment, mainly comprised of Connecticut Loyalists. He called it the *Prince of Wales American Regiment*. He was released as part of a prisoner release. After his release he was made a general. He was known for being pompous. He liked the title *General* better than *Governor*. Like the men in his Loyalist Regiment, Browne wore a green regimental coat faced white.

Howe's plan, which was implemented in this chapter, did not work. In 1778, the year following the events in this book, Howe resigned as Commander of the British Forces in North America. He claimed he did not receive the support he needed. Members of the Tory faction in England alleged Howe, who was a Whig, did not end the Revolution because he was sympathetic with the Colonials. Upon returning to England he lost his re-election bid in Parliament.

Historical Background for Chapter 5
Enoch Crosby the Spy

Enoch Crosby was a spy for the Continental Army. He answered to John Jay who became the head of the United States counterintelligence. Jay later became the first Chief Justice of the United States and later the second Governor of New York State.

Some claim John Jay's neighbor, James Fenimore Cooper, used Enoch Crosby as the basis of his character Harvey Birch in *The Spy, a Tale of the Neutral Ground*.

Larry A. Maxwell

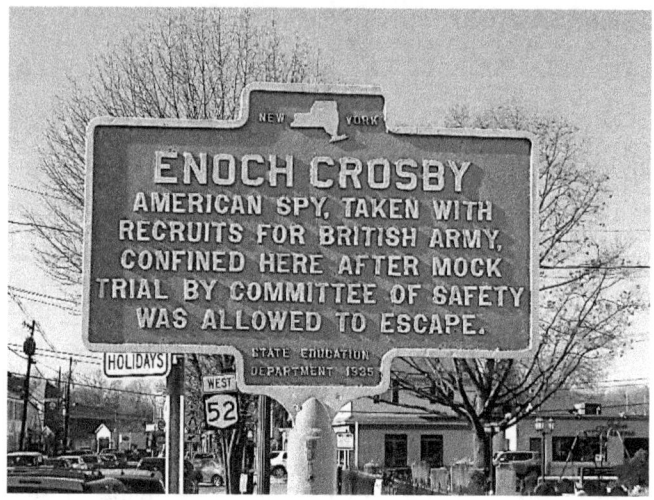

Enoch Crosby Historic Marker - Fishkill
Route 52 & Route 9, Fishkill, New York.
Photograph by Larry A. Maxwell, 2017

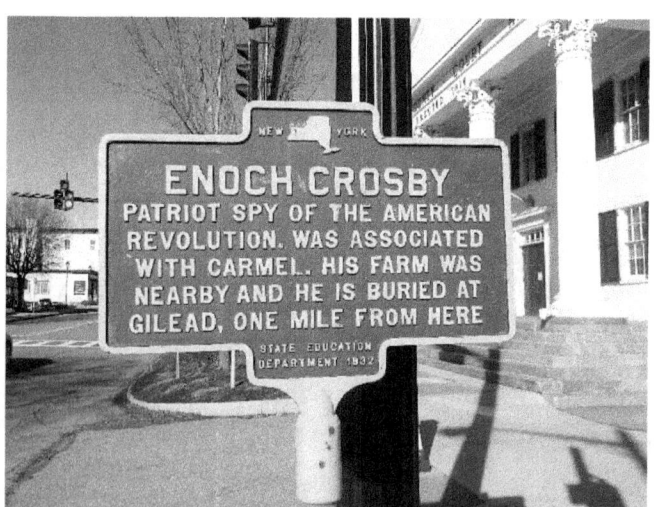

Enoch Crosby Historic Marker - Carmel
Gleneida Ave., Carmel, New York.
Photograph by Larry A. Maxwell, 2017

Nathaniel Sackett, who worked with John Jay coordinating spies for the Continentals, mentioned Enoch Crosby in his letters.

Crosby was so convincing in his role portraying a Loyalist that Dr. Jonathan Prosser, a hard-core Loyalist, confided in him. That helped save Colonel Henry Ludington.

In the 20th Century, a handwritten note, written during the Revolution, was found in an old abandoned brick oven in the Town of Carmel, New York. It identified Enoch Crosby as someone faithful to the Revolution. The purpose of the note was to help clear Crosby's name in case he was tried for being a Loyalist, if there was no one alive who could vouch for him.

In this chapter we also meet Jacob and Joseph Angevine. Jacob was a freed Black Man who earned his freedom while fighting in the French and Indian War. He took the surname of his owner. The Angevines were a French Huguenot family who fled persecution in France and helped settle New Rochelle, New York.

When many people think of slavery they think of the South and the War Between the States, not the Revolution. When the Revolution started there were some half-a-million slaves in the thirteen colonies. Some may be surprised to known studies indicate half the population of New York City were slaves. During the Revolution there were some 400 free Blacks in Dutchess County. Years later, Dutchess County became an important stop on the Underground Railroad.

Those of African descent faced a dilemma during the Revolutionary War. Both sides offered freedom to slaves of owners on the other side. Both armies were integrated.

Larry A. Maxwell

Historical Background for Chapter 6
The Loyalists Plot

After the *Declaration of Independence* was issued in July 1776, the states were concerned about where people's loyalties laid. To deal with the question of where one's loyalties laid some states came up with an *Oath of Loyalty* or *Oath of Allegiance* which they required everyone to sign.

Local *Committees of Safety* were established to help provide homeland security. They administered the *Oath of Loyalty* and often put together *Watch Lists* of people they monitored. In some places those who refused to sign the oaths, were arrested and their lands were confiscated. Some *Loyalists* signed the oaths, feigning loyalty to the Revolution.

> Province of   Day of   1779.
>
> I do hereby profefs and declare my Loyalty and Allegiance to his Majefty King George the Third, and do hereby engage, that when ever I can be protected againft the prefent rebellious and ufurped Government in this Province, I will take up Arms, in Defence of his Majefty, and the Laws of the faid Province; and that I will in the mean Time, promote his Majefty's Intereft, by every Means in my Power, confiftent with my prefent Safety.

Affirmation of Loyalty
Document confirming loyalty to the "American Cause."
Dated December 1777.

Those loyal to the Crown were called *Loyalists* or *Royalists* because they supported the monarchy. They were called *patriots* by the Crown because they were loyal to their mother country, England.

The April 25, 1770 issue of *The Public Advertiser,* London England, stated, "A true Patriot must necessarily be a good Subject, because he will make the Laws of his Country the Rule and Measure of his Actions."

Oath of Loyalty to the King
*Document confirming loyalty to King George the Third.
Dated December 1779.*

Historical Background for Chapter 7
Enoch Crosby Warns Ludington

Colonel Henry Ludington and his friends were chopping wood in this chapter. Wood was the sole source of heat and was necessary for cooking in most homes in the Hudson Valley. That required a steady source of firewood. It was an essential task to chop wood for the fireplace.

Most houses had one fireplace. Larger houses had more

than one fireplace. Even with more than one fireplace, most of the rooms in a house, such as bedrooms, were usually unheated.

In warmer weather, back then, a person might only wear their small clothes inside their home. Small clothes consisted of a shirt, breeches (pants) and a waistcoat (vest). A man's shirt and a woman' shift was considered their underwear.

People often wore the same shirt or shift during the day and to bed at night. Affluent people often had a separate nightshirt. No one wore just a shirt and breeches inside, and definitely not outside, as that was considered immodest. They made sure they had on a waistcoat or a heavier work shirt over their small clothes.

In colder weather, it was necessary to wear warm clothing to keep warm inside a house. That usually meant men would wear an additional shirt called an over shirt or frock.

Men and women usually wore hats inside, especially in their home and even in some churches. It was uncommon to see a man or woman with an uncovered head. The one exception was, most men removed their hat to pray.

Historical Background for Chapter 8
Attempt to Capture Ludington

Those who went with Dr. Prosser to attempt to capture Colonel Ludington had a variety of motives. Some were ultraistic and saw Ludington as a threat. Others were opportunists and saw apprehending Ludington as a way to prosper financially. Some may have had both motives.

The Great Swamp, where Dr. Prosser hid the muskets, has always been a significant resource in Fredericksburg. The Wappingers used it for their hunting and fishing grounds. It is now a wildlife refuge and recreational resource used for canoeing and kayaking.

The Ludington's lived in a two-story house with a porch and a separate millhouse located next door. The mill was built in 1776 and burned down in 1972. The house was built before 1776 and was torn down in 1838, before photography was available. When Interstate Route 84 was built, it went right through the Ludington property.

The way Sybil and her siblings fooled the Loyalists may have inspired a scene in the movie, *"Home Alone,"* where the main character used shadows to fool two would-be-robbers into thinking there were more people in the house. Dr. Prosser and his men were apprehended shortly after this incident.

Historical Background for Chapter 9
Conflict at the Ganong's House

Some people claim one-third of the colonists favored the fight for independence, one-third wanted to remain part of Great Britain, and the other third did not care. There were surely people who fell into those three categories, but those percentages are merely conjecture.

People's business dealings and associates often had a strong influence on which side they fell. People with business dealings which depended on trade with England often found themselves on the Loyalist side. There were many like that in New York City.

People's religious affiliation also affected which side they fell on. Those who were active members of the *Anglican Church (The Church of England)* often fell on the Loyalist side. George Washington, an Anglican, was an exception.

Catholics were forbidden to practice their religion in England and in most English colonies such as New York, so they easily fell on the Rebel side.

Baptists, Presbyterians, Congregationalists, Separatists, and *Jews* were all at odds with *The Church of England*, so many of them aligned themselves with the Rebels.

Ambrose Serele, Secretary to William Howe, wrote to the British Secretary of State in 1776 that the Revolution was a religious war and could not be sustained in America were it not for the Presbyterian ministers who breed it.

Hessian Captain Johann Heinrich wrote the following to a friend in Germany on January 18, 1778, "call this war, dearest friend, by whatsoever name you may, only call it not an American Revolution, it is nothing more nor less than an Irish-Scotch Presbyterian Rebellion."

Andrew Hammond, an Anglican and British commander of *H.M.S. Roebuck*, arrived in America in 1776. He wrote, "It is the Presbyterians that have brought about this revolt, and aim at getting the government of America into their hands."

Historical Background for Chapter 10
Sybil's Birthday Party

This chapter emphasizes the fact Sybil turned sixteen years old just before her fateful ride. A sixteen-year old was no longer considered a child. This birthday party features some important, yet lesser-known historical characters, who played a role in the Revolution.

One of the guests at Sybil's party was Rev. John Gano, the pastor of the *First Baptist Church of New York City*. When the Crown Forces occupied New York City they turned Gano's church into a stable. Gano became chaplain for the Continental Army in New York State, then for the whole Northern Department.

Rev. John Gano Baptizing George Washington
1908 Portrait on Display at William Jewell College

Gano was a confident of General George Washington. Some historical reports claim Washington, an Anglican who was christened as an infant, asked Gano to administer to him Believer's Baptism by immersion. Gano's great-grandson, billionaire Howard Hughes, claimed he investigated the reports and found them valid. Others discount that claim.

On April 19, 1783, Washington humbly had Gano read the notice of the British Surrender to the troops.

Many history books sadly leave out the influence of two important groups represented in this chapter: the Jews and the American Indians. Those two groups are often discriminated against in America History.

Contributors to The Cause U.S. Stamps
Unites States Postal Service, 1975.

Haym Salomon, a friend of John Gano, was a Polish immigrant and member of the Jewish Synagogue in New York City and an active member of the *Sons of Liberty*. Salomon was arrested twice by the British as a spy. He helped find much needed financing for the Revolution, personally guaranteeing loans. After the war he died bankrupt, an unsung hero.

Haym Salomon, Salem Poor and Sybil Ludington were all honored by the U.S. Postal Service in 1975 along with Peter Francisco, as part of the *Contributors to the Cause* Bicentennial Stamp Series.

One group, which has never been honored properly for the role they played in the Revolution are the Tribal People.

Daniel and Abraham Nimham and their brave band of Wappinger and Stockbridge warriors were American heroes who served bravely in the Continental Army from Bunker Hill to the Battle of Monmouth and until their untimely death.

Daniel Nimham, Sachem of the Wappingers
Statue by Michael Keropian, Kent, N.Y.

Enoch Crosby mentioned the prison ships to Colonel Ludington. They were awful places. Men were kept below deck and not feed properly. No sanitary facilities were provided. Starvation, venomous rats, and disease spread rapidly. When prisoners died their bodies were thrown overboard. More people died on prison ships than in all the battles in the Revolution.

Lists survive of 8,000 prisoners held on the *H.M.S Jersey*, a British Prison Ship harbored in New York. When the war ended, and the Crown Forces evacuated New York City, they set the H.M.S. Jersey on fire, killing all the prisoners aboard.

British Prison Ship H.M.S. Jersey
1855 Engraving by Felix O. C. Darcey.
When the Crown Forces left New York, they burned the HMS Jersey with prisoners still on board.

Historical Background for Chapter 11
British Embark for Norwalk

The Crown Forces boarded a fleet of twenty-six ships on Tuesday afternoon, April 22, 1777. They planned to arrive at Compo Beach near Norwalk, Connecticut, that evening. Their plan was to disembark that night and march undetected to Danbury. Little did they realize severe weather would strand them on their ships for three days.

New York City in 1776

George William Sheldon, 1882.
New York Public Library

Captain Henry Duncan was given command of the fleet. In some records he is incorrectly called Commodore Duncan.

The invasion force was headed by Governor William Tryon. His generals included: General James Agnew, General William Erskine, and General Montfort Browne.

The invasion force included about two thousand soldiers with two-hundred soldiers from each of the following regiments: the 4th Regiment of Foot; the 15th Regiment of Foot, the 23rd Regiment of Foot (also known as The Royal Welsh

Fusiliers); the 27th Regiment of Foot (Irish); the 44th Regiment of Foot; and the 64th Regiment of Foot. There was also a group of men from the 17th Regiment Light Dragoons.

In 1775, when the British occupied Boston, the 64th Regiment of Foot was stationed as the garrison unit, to protect the city. Therefore, they did not partake in the Battles of Lexington and Concord, nor Bunker Hill, but they saw the aftermath and participated in the Battle of New York.

During the raid on Danbury, people reported seeing Hessian soldiers. No Hessians took place in the raid. People mistook the 64th Regiment of Foot for Hessians because of the tall bearskin hats their Grenadiers wore.

The 4th Regiment of Foot was at the Battle of Lexington. They were joined by the 23rd Regiment of Foot at Concord. Both regiments saw many of their men killed as they retreated to Boston and then again at the Battle of Bunker Hill. As they retreated to their ships during the Danbury Raid, they would have a similar experience as they were attacked by Rebels.

17th Light Dragoons Emblem
Illustration by John W. 1841.

There were also mounted men from the 17th Light Dragoons. They did scouting duty on horseback. They wore caps with a metallic plate, with the intimidating image of a death's head (similar to that later worn by Nazis S.S. Troops) along with the words, *Or Glory*.

Some modern accounts incorrectly say the Crown Forces brought along twelve-pound and twenty-five-pound cannons. That is incorrect. There were not any twelve-pound cannons in America during the Revolution. Twenty-five pounders are not light artillery and were not brought on an inland raid.

Some contemporary accounts from the Danbury Raid and the Battle of Ridgefield, claim the British fired on them with six-pounder cannons (the weight of the cannon ball). That did not happen. Official British military reports state six companies of light artillery from the 4th Royal Artillery, each brought along a three-pounder cannon.

One of the three-pound cannon balls, used in the battle, ended up lodged in a wall at the Keeler Tavern in Ridgefield, Connecticut, where it can still be seen by visitors.

Cannonball in Keeler Tavern
Ridgefield, Connecticut.
Photograph by Larry A. Maxwell - 2018

A Loyalist Regiment was involved in the raid. It was called the *Prince of Wales American Regiment* under the command of General Montfort Browne. Unlike the British Regulars, who wore red regimental coats, those Loyalists wore green regimental coats with white facings. They carried older Long Land Pattern Brown Bess muskets, also called a 1st Model Bess.

Historical Background for Chapter 12
Sybil & Friends
Shooting Muskets

This is the beginning of the back and forth chapters. In some cases the chapters talk about concurrent events. From this point on some of the chapters are very short because they recount a shorter historical incident.

At this point in the story the British Fleet is on its way to Norwalk yet none of the Rebels know that yet.

Joseph Angevine was a member of the 7th Regiment Dutchess County Militia commanded by Sybil's father, Colonel Henry Ludington. The Militia drilled regularly on the training ground located across from the Colonel's house.

Starting in the 1600's, most *colonies* had laws which required all men age fifteen, up to age fifty, to belong to the local Militia.

On January 11, 1676, New York passed a law saying the head of each household had to own one good firelock/musket or pay a fine.

During and after the French and Indian War (1754-1763),

most colonies passed a *Militia Act* requiring every male age fifteen to fifty, to own a firelock/musket. New York's law required men to own a good firelock/musket and a sword.

On August 22, 1775, New York passed a law requiring every male, age sixteen to fifty to own a good firelock, a bayonet, and a sword or tomahawk, or they had to pay a fine.

The purpose of a *Militia Act* was to make sure citizens were armed with the same weapons as the military, so they could help protect their families and their colony. Unlike other countries the weapons were owned by individuals and kept in their homes rather than owned by the government and kept in armories. That sentiment was included as a national law in the *Second Amendment to the United States Constitution*.

Even though the law required it, most people did not own muskets and certainly did not own a bayonet. Muskets were basically military weapons. They were expensive and owning a military weapon served little practical purpose.

Some people think everyone hunted in Colonial days, and hence, everyone had a musket. Hunting was time consuming. Most people's occupations kept them too busy to hunt.

In this chapter we see the very specific sequence for loading a musket. That sequence was part of the Militia drill. The loading sequence had commands which were usually called out step-by-step. The whole company would simultaneous carry out the order. When the *Fire* command was given to a company, the whole company would fire together. That was called a *volley*.

A musket volley was very intimidating yet muskets were smooth-bore and very inaccurate. Studies show that at about thirty yards a Brown Bess Musket was about ten percent accurate if the shooter and target were not moving. That meant if you stood still while the other side shot at you there was a ninety percent chance you would leave a battle unscathed. If you moved, your chances of being hit were less.

Rifles were different. They had groves in the barrel which made the bullet leave in a more accurate manner. At the beginning of the Revolution very few soldiers on either side had rifles. They were considered immoral because they were too accurate. It is important to understand the purpose for warfare was not to kill people but to take the ground.

In this chapter, when Jesse arrived, Joseph and he exchanged handshakes, but he did not shake hands with Sybil. Back then it was considered disrespectful to shake a woman's hand. It was considered more respectful to bow to a woman and for the women to respond with a curtsey. The depth of the bow and curtsey indicated the amount of respect shown.

Kissing was a very strong symbol of affection. Kisses were not given lightly. The only person someone would kiss in public would be a spouse or family member and that would usually only be on the cheek or forehead.

Historical Background for Chapter 13
Crown Forces
Land at Norwalk

Cedar Point at Compo Beach was where the British fleet landed. This book refers to Compo Beach as in, or near

Norwalk because during the Revolution Compo Beach was part of the Town of Norwalk, Connecticut. In 1835, when the Town of Westport was officially incorporated, Compo Beach became part of Westport.

When the British fleet landed at Compo Beach on April 25, 1777, there were not any docks suitable for large war ships.

Compo Beach is located in a very large cove which is shallow at low tide. The entire army, including the six cannons they brought with them, needed to take landing craft to get to the shore. That made the landing take a few hours.

The size of the British fleet, coupled with the members of the Loyalist Regiment who showed up to support the fleet, discouraged Rebel resistance in Norwalk. Resistance against such a large force would have meant certain death.

Historical Background for Chapter 14
Conflict Between Father and Son

During the Revolution conflicts between family members occurred because choosing different sides was not uncommon. That resulted in some families being separated after the war.

Benjamin Franklin's family was an example of this. Though Benjamin Franklin took a strong stand for independence his only son, William Franklin remained a Loyalist. William became Royal Governor of New Jersey. He was arrested as a Loyalist. His wife died while he was a prisoner. He and his father Benjamin never reconciled.

Larry A. Maxwell

Historical Background for Chapter 15
Confrontation at Bethel

It was a wet muddy march for the Crown Forces between Redding and Bethel. As each cannon crew advanced their heavy cannons made deep ruts in the mud. That made it more difficult for the next crew to advance. That is one reason the artillery was kept at the rear of the army.

The inspiring story of Luther Holcomb appeared in the very esteemed book, *Connecticut Historical Collections* by John Warner Barber in 1826. Barber spoke with eyewitnesses when he put together his book. The account of Luther Holcomb was mentioned in four other books in the 1800's.

Luther Holcomb was a twenty-five-year-old resident of Bethel Parish in Danbury. He was a member of the Danbury Militia. His actions at Bethel were daring, bold and brilliant.

Grave of Luther Holcomb
North Afton Cemetery, Afton, New York.
Photograph submitted by Shane and Ashley Clark-Butler

Luther Holcomb rode to the crest of the Hoyt's Hill where he acted like a general, riding back and forth, waving his sword, shouting commands to his invisible army.

Holcomb's actions made the Crown Forces stop to hold their ground and call the cannons forward. To not advance was a prudent move for the British generals because there was no way for them to know it was only one young man.

According to his Revolutionary War pension application, Luther Holcomb went on to fight in the Battle of Ridgefield and at Compo Beach. After the war he moved to Chenango County, New York. When he died, he was buried in the North Afton Cemetery in Afton, New York.

Historical Background for Chapter 16
Danbury Attacked

When General Erskine entered Danbury he and his troops were confronted by men wearing red regimental coats with white facings. That was disconcerting because in the British Army those colors were only worn by royal regiments.

Most people think the British Regulars all wore red coats, which looked the same and the Continental Army wore blue coats. That is not correct. There were more than 70 different variation of the British regimental coat used by different soldiers in the Revolutionary War and more than 100 variations of regimental coats worn by the Continental Army.

Most people are surprised when they learn some American

Rebel Regiments in both the Militia and Continental Army wore red coats similar to, and sometimes exactly like, those worn by British Regulars as late as 1779. Some had those uniforms from before the war and some wore captured coats.

Most Militia were responsible to provide their own clothing which resulted in little conformity. However, there were some Militia in more affluent areas who were issued matching uniforms. Before the Revolution and during the early part of the war some of the Connecticut Militia units wore red coats. Three regiments in the Connecticut Continental Line wore red coats as late as 1779. That confused the Crown Forces. Some speculate that was intentional.

The 1st Connecticut Regiment of the Continental Line was stationed at Danbury, where Colonel Joseph Platt Cooke was in charge. They carried on the early war practice of wearing red regimental coats faced white.

Prior to the Revolution Joseph Platt Cooke served in the Connecticut Assembly and as a Justice in Danbury. In 1771, he was Colonel of the *16th Connecticut Regiment of Militia*. In 1777, he was forty-seven years old. The fact he was both a government official and an officer in the Militia prior to the Revolution, it is very likely he had a red officer's regimental coat with white facing. He built a home on Main Street in Danbury, before the Revolution. It was partially destroyed by a fire set by the Crown Forces during the Danbury Raid.

In 1775, after Lexington and Concord, Noble Benedict organized a Militia in Danbury to oppose the Crown. A total of ninety-eight men joined. The first recruit was a shoemaker named Enoch Crosby. Crosby later became a spy for the

Continental Army and played an important role in this story.

Thomas Starr, another recruit enlisted by Benedict, became a captain in the Danbury Militia. In 1777, he was 57-years old. He was badly wounded by the Crown Forces during the Danbury Raid. In June 1777, he was commissioned Ensign in the *7th Regiment of the Connecticut Continental Line*. Like the *1st Connecticut Regiment* which was at Danbury, the *7th Regiment* wore red regimental coats with white facings.

One of the first flags carried by the American Rebels during the Revolution, and used throughout much of the war, was called the *Liberty Flag*. It had thirteen stripes, alternating between seven red and six white stripes, representing the thirteen colonies. It looked like a modern American flag without a canton, the box in the upper corner.

The Liberty Flag
Don Hewitt, 1932 Postcard.

Historical Background for Chapter 17
American Officers Meet at Redding

Three American Rebel generals met at Redding, Connecticut, late Saturday afternoon on April 26, 1777. Each was leading a group of men in pursuit of the Crown Forces.

The first was Brigadier General Gold Selleck Silliman, from Fairfield, Connecticut. He was a Yale graduate and an attorney. He was a Commander in the Connecticut Militia and came with the most men. No known portraits of him exist.

He lived in Fairfield, not far from Compo Beach, and was the first general to learn of the raid. He wrote a dispatch at 8 a.m. on April 26, 1777, informing others and requesting help.

Two years after the events in this book, on May 1, 1779, Regulars and Loyalists captured Silliman during a raid on Fairfield, led by Tryon. He was put him in prison and held until May 1780 when he was released in a prisoner exchange.

The second general was from New Haven, Connecticut. Unlike the others he did not attend college or complete any formal education. When he was young his father's business failed. He had to drop out of school and went to work as an apprentice apothecary with his cousins. His name was Benedict Arnold.

He served in the French and Indian War then became a merchant. The *Stamp Act* and *Sugar Act* impacted his business, so he smuggled goods to avoid the taxes and joined the *Sons of Liberty*.

Before the Revolution, Arnold became very popular and

was elected Captain of the elite *Governor's Guards*. It was an independent Militia company comprised of some of the most zealous young men in New Haven, Connecticut.

His passion and ability to strategize helped him quickly rise through the ranks. He distinguished himself in battle, earned a commission as a General in the Continental Army, and was considered a hero by many.

Arnold loved military titles. He expected people to respect him because of his position. He often made decisions which seemed right to him, without consulting others. That offended other officers who then questioned his integrity.

On February 19, 1777, the Continental Congress promoted five officers, junior to Arnold, and failed to give him the promotion he thought he deserved. He viewed that as a rebuke and became angry and contemplated resigning. He went to New Haven, Connecticut to visit his three sons, who were being raised by his sister. His first wife, Margaret died on June 19, 1775, while he was away serving in the army. He would later marry a second Margaret, Margaret "Peggy" Shippen, who was part of a powerful Loyalist family in Philadelphia.

When he received the message from General Silliman on April 26, 1777, Arnold gathered some men and rode rapidly to rendezvous with Silliman in Redding. He was a valuable asset during this campaign. He served valiantly and inspired others. Later, he became America's most notorious traitor.

The only artist known to do an actual contemporary portrait of Arnold was Pierre Eugene Du Simitiere. All other portraits, claiming to be Arnold, are only artist conceptions.

The third American general in this campaign was Major

General David Wooster. He was the oldest of the three and held the highest rank among the Connecticut Militia Officers. He arrived in Redding with about one hundred men.

Like Silliman, Wooster was a Yale graduate. He was a hero from the French and Indian War and Major General over all the Connecticut Militia.

Wooster and Arnold's relationship started two years earlier with a confrontation on April 21, 1775. Wooster was General of the Militia at New Haven and Arnold was Captain of the *Governor's Guard*. When word of the Battle of Lexington and Concord reached New Haven, Arnold rallied his men, along with some students from Yale. He then went to the local town leaders and demanded they give him weapons and ammunition. They told Arnold to wait for regular orders. Wooster was in charge of the munitions and refused access to Arnold. Arnold threatened to have his men brake open the doors and seize the supplies. Wooster gave him the keys.

A few months later in the Fall of 1775, Wooster was a Brigadier General over the Connecticut Troops and a leader in the Canadian Campaign. During that campaign, Arnold's daring service earned Wooster's respect. Wooster was one of the few who wrote to Washington complimenting Arnold. Arnold appreciated that.

Unlike Arnold, who loved to be in charge, Wooster was known to be very humble and gracious.

Officers for both the Continental Army and Militia had to provide their own uniforms. Officers in the Continental Army had to provide uniforms for their men. They were to be reimbursed for supplies by the State or Congress, often they were not. The lack of reimbursement for his expenses became one of Arnold's chief complaints.

By 1777, many officers in the Continental Army wore blue regimental coats faced buff, similar to that worn by General George Washington. Some speculate Washington choose those colors because they were the colors of the Dutch, from whom he sought financial support. The Dutch guilder was the strongest currency in the world. They had powerful banks and the *Dutch East India Company* had trade routes throughout the world. Washington appealed to their long-standing quarrel with England.

The Dutch East India Company Shipyard
Joseph Mulder, Engraving, 1726.

The attack on Danbury was dangerous. The June 30, 1777 edition of *The Public Advertiser*, printed in London, England, reported Sir William Erskine narrowly escaped. Two people, next to him, were shot and killed.

Newspapers back then, like today, exaggerated or reported false news. *The Maryland Gazette* on June 5, 1777, reported Governor William Tryon was seriously wounded in the leg by a musket ball at Danbury. *Purdie's Virginia Gazette*, in its June 6, 1777, edition, reported Governor William Tryon died of wounds he received in Danbury. Both news stories were incorrect. Tryon was not wounded and did not die until 1788.

Historical Background for Chapter 18
Messenger Arrives at Ludington's

The messenger from Danbury had to maneuver out of town without being stopped by the Crown Forces and then navigate about fifteen miles of muddy roads on a cold, rainy, starless night to get to Colonel Ludington's home. It was a long treacherous ride. He finally arrived about 9 o'clock at night.

The men in the *7th Dutchess County Militia* needed someone to bring them a call to arms. Colonel Ludington needed to stay at his house to meet the men and then lead the first group to help drive back the invaders.

The messenger from Danbury could not give the alarm. He was exhausted and had no idea where the men lived.

It was not unusual Sybil was chosen to issue the call to arms. She was her father's oldest child and a trusted rider. Taking messages to the Militia was a normal task for her. She was familiar with the roads and knew where the men in her father's regiment lived.

The fact it was night and had been raining for two days made Sybil's ride more dangerous than usual.

She never bragged about her courageous ride. She did not ride to be recognized nor did she do it for financial gain. She did it because she considered it a necessary patriotic duty.

It appears William Dawes and Samuel Prescott had that same attitude when they rode throughout the countryside in 1775 to call out the Militia, the same night as Paul Revere.

On the other hand, Paul Revere, who ended up becoming the most famous of the three, did something none of the others did. He gave the Committee of Safety a bill for providing messenger services. The total bill was for 11 pounds, 1 shilling. That amount is equivalent to about $2000 in 2018 money. His bill was paid in full.

Paul Revere's Bill for His Messenger Service

Revere submitted this bill to the Committee of Safety.
Part of the bill was for his messenger service.
Massachusetts Archives

Larry A. Maxwell

Reverse Side of Paul Revere's Bill
Approved for payment on April 22, 1775.
Massachusetts Archives

According to the United States Postal Service two notable founding fathers considered Sybil's ride heroic. General George Washington visited the Ludington's in 1778 and personally thanked Sybil for her ride. Alexander Hamilton wrote her a letter thanking her for her heroic service. Hamilton was part of Colonel Lamb's Artillery which participated in the Battle at Compo Beach.

Some people challenge the historical authenticity of Sybil's ride. They claim the first mention of Sybil's ride was in 1907 in Willis Fletcher Johnson's book, *Colonel Henry Ludington, A Memoir*. Some claim it is a fictional story. They say Sybil never wrote about her ride and never mentioned it in her Revolutionary War Pension Application. Some of those who challenge the authenticity of her ride, claim it is not feasible to think one girl could ride forty miles in one night, as the historical reports claim Sybil did. Though I disagree with those objections, I mention them here to show how they are seriously flawed.

It is important to note Willis Fletcher Johnson was a respected historian. He was especially known and respected for his *History of New York University*, his two-volume *History of America's Public Relations*, his five-volume *History of Cuba*, and his biographies of William Tecumseh Sherman, Sitting Bull, and African explorer Henry M. Stanley.

His book was not the first to mention Sybil's ride. Long before 1907, historian Martha J. Lamb included the historical account of Sybil's Ride in her three volume *History of the City of New York* which she wrote in 1876 and published it in 1877. That was thirty years before Johnson's book about Ludington.

Lamb was born while Sybil Ludington was alive. She was known as one of the most outstanding historians of her day. She was renowned for her extensive research and her unwillingness to include anything in her books that she could not confirm from numerous historical records. That led her to be acclaimed as an outstanding historian by more than a dozen international historical societies.

The New York State Department of Education, comprised of some of the leading educators in America, as well as The United States Postal Service verified the historical authenticity of Sybil's ride.

The objection that Sybil did not mention her ride in her Revolutionary War Widow's Pension Application is silly because that pension was a widow's pension based only on her husband's Revolutionary War Service.

The fact that it appears Sybil never wrote about her ride

only shows her humility it does not disprove she rode. It is interesting to note Paul Revere, William Dawes, and Samuel Prescott never wrote about their heroic ride, nor were their names mentioned as riders in any contemporary newspaper. Most people would probably not know about Paul Revere had it not been for Longfellow's poem, published eighty-six years after his ride.

The conjecture that it is not feasible to think a sixteen-year-old girl could have done the forty-mile ride is insulting to women and is truly demeaning.

It is a clearly established historical fact Sybil Ludington did indeed ride to call out the Militia.

Sybil's Ride was also mentioned in the May 24, 1912 edition of *The Putnam County Courier* in a poem entitled, *"How Tryon was Driven Back,"* by Mr. Noble. He ended the poem with this line, *"But a braver deed you have never known, By man or maiden done, Than that plucky ride through the long, dark night, of Sybil Ludington."*

Historical Background for Chapter 19
Sybil Arrives at the First House

The Ludington's home was in the part of Fredericksburg, which would later (1817) be called the Town of Kent. Names of places where Sybil rode changed over the years. It did not take her long to reach the first house but took all night and into the morning before she reached the last home.

Approximate Route of Sybil's Ride
Approximation on David Burr's 1829 Map.

Sybil's ride took her south to the area which later became the Town of Carmel (1795). She rode past Shaw's Pond, which was later renamed Lake Gilead (1840's), then further south to the area later known as Mahopac (1812). In Mahopac, she turned west around Lake Mahopac to Red Mills. She then turned north to the area later called Kent Cliffs and Boyd's Corner, then to the area later known as Farmer's Mills. She then rode up to the area later called Stormville (1826). From Stormville she rode southeast to the area later called Pecksville and then back to her home.

The New York State Department of Education honored

Sybil's ride in 1932 and in 1934 by placing historic markers along the route she rode.

The Daughters of the American Revolution (DAR) honored Sybil with a monument in 1961 on Route 52, along Lake Gleneida in Carmel, New York. The monument shows Sybil on her horse issuing the call to the Militia.

They placed a smaller version of the monument at their national headquarters in Washington, D. C. and one at the Danbury Library.

Sybil Ludington Monument Dedication

Enoch Crosby Chapter of the Daughters of the American Revolution, Along Lake Gleneida, Carmel, New York, 1961.
Photo Courtesy of the Putnam County Historian's Office

Historical Background for Chapter 20
The Looting and Burning Continue

The Crown Forces looted and burned the supplies for the Continental Army they found in Danbury. That was one of the main goals of the expedition and was considered acceptable.

The soldiers also looted and burned the homes of Rebels in Danbury. Those actions and the drunkenness of the soldiers were not proper military protocol, yet those who engaged in those actions were not stopped and were never officially reprimanded by the Crown officers.

Historical Background for Chapter 21
Sybil and the Bandits

It was not unusual to encounter bandits along the roads in the Hudson Valley. Some bandits worked for either side. Many worked for their own profit. That made travel precarious.

One of the first uses of the word *cowboy* comes from the Revolutionary War and had a negative connotation. In the Hudson Valley those who stole cattle and horses were called *cowboys*. At first *cowboy* only applied to *Loyalist/Tory* marauders who stole from the Rebels and sold to the British.

Waite Vaughn was a Tory. He became a notorious *cowboy*. His uncle, Samuel Towner was one of the leaders in the Settler's Revolt and an ardent Rebel. Vaughn and his band of

Tory Cowboys frequently attacked people along the route between Fredericksburg, New York, and Connecticut.

Vaughn was shot and killed in 1782 in a confrontation with Captain William Pearse, and his Militia. Captain Pearse's brother Nathan was previously captured and whipped to death by Tories. Vaughn's story appears in Professor Warren H. Wilson's 1907 doctoral dissertation for Columbia University.

Those who stole from the Crown Forces or Loyalists were often called *Skinners*. That name may have come from Major John Skinner's *Connecticut Regiment of Light Horse* which operated around New York raiding the Crown Forces.

The distinction between *Cowboys* and *Skinners* was often blurred and eventually both terms came to mean thieves.

In a letter dated October 29, 1779, to General Washington, Abraham Woodhull, a spy for the Continentals, complained about *Skinners* raiding *Loyalists* for their own profit.

Capture of Major John Andre

By Paulding, Williams & VanWalt.
Lithograph by J. Baillie, 1845

It is alleged the men who caught Major John Andre, after he received the plans for West Point from Benedict Arnold, were *Skinners* out to rob whoever they came across. It appears by chance they stopped Major Andre. As they had Andre take off his expensive boots to steal them, they discovered the plans for West Point. They realized they had valuable information and went to take it to General Arnold at West Point for a reward. They did not know Arnold was the traitor who gave Andre the plans.

Historical Background for Chapter 22
Americans Arrive in Bethel

The bad weather caused it to take much longer than expected for the American Rebel Force to reach Bethel. Most reports agree they arrived in Bethel Parish around midnight. By that time, they were very wet, muddy, and exhausted.

Most armies did not engage in battle at night. Another factor which caused them to delay their attack was General Wooster realized their muskets would be useless because they were soaked from the rain and mud. Without working muskets the Rebels would have faced British bayonets. The Crown Forces had more training and experience using the bayonet and were deadly with them. Most Militia muskets did not have bayonets. If they engaged in a battle that night it would have resulted in the loss of many Rebel lives.

Larry A. Maxwell

Historical Background for Chapter 23

Sybil Arrives at Another Home

Most people were asleep by the time Sybil reached their homes. People did not have televisions to keep them awake.

Most people slept in the shirts they wore during the day. Affluent people might own a separate night shirt to sleep in.

It was unusual for someone to visit late at night. It was a common reaction to come to the door with a loaded musket and a lantern. On a rainy night the moon and stars were usually not visible, making it much darker and more important to have a lantern or candle to see who was calling.

Historical Background for Chapter 24
Making Ammunition

Muskets did not use pre-manufactured cartridges. The only way to get ammunition for a musket was for someone to make each cartridge by hand. Making cartridges was one way people who could not go off to fight were able to help.

Making musket balls was the most difficult part of making a cartridge. To make a musket ball, one melted lead hot some coals and then poured the lead into a mold which had to be the correct size for the musket. The resulting musket ball came out of the mold with a seam around the edge, which needed to be trimmed off.

The size of the musket ball had to be smaller than the caliber (diameter) of the musket barrel. The Long Land Pattern Brown Bess musket was 75 calibers. That meant the opening in the barrel was .75 inch. The musket ball needed to be slightly smaller than .75-inch to go down the barrel.

When a musket was fired the metal in the barrel became hot and expanded. That made the opening in the barrel smaller. The second and later musket balls needed to be much smaller than .75 inch, or they would be difficult to ram down the barrel. It was not unusual to make musket balls .69 inch so they would easily ram down the barrel. If you had a smaller caliber musket you needed smaller musket balls.

18th Century Musket Ball Mold & Tool
Musket Ball trimmer between handles.

Musket balls were put in paper tubes which were rolled, preferably using old newspapers. Newspapers were preferred because they were printed on much thinner paper than found in books or other paper. Thinner paper made them much easier on the teeth when you had to bite off the end of the cartridge to load your musket.

Larry A. Maxwell

Historical Background for Chapter 25
 Sybil Faces an Obstacle

Numerous rivers and streams ran along the route Sybil rode. Melting snow from the winter, coupled with two days of intense rain, made many of the streams overflow. Some streams turned into raging rivers. The current could knock over a person on foot or on horseback.

When streams overflowed their banks, fallen branches and rocks were hidden, and the ground became very soggy and treacherous to navigate. Those factors all combined to made it very difficult to cross a swollen stream.

Riding at night, especially a rainy night, made it much harder to find a way to cross a stream. If the rider's horse slipped while crossing a stream, it would most likely break a leg, ending the journey and usually the life of the horse.

Historical Background for Chapter 26
Militia Marches Off to Battle

The September 23, 1911 edition of *The Cold Spring Recorder* published an historical account of Colonel Henry Ludington. It said his name often appeared with the spelling, *Luddenton*. The account mentioned how he and his regiment helped compel Tryon and his troops, "to retreat from the vicinity of Danbury and embark on their boats to New York."

Like most armies during the Revolution, the Continental Army marched from one location to another by foot. That was not the case with some Militia. Many of the members of the Militia in the Hudson Valley lived quite a distance apart. Most owned horses and many had wagons. They responded to alarms on horseback or in their wagons. That allowed them to respond more quickly and to travel greater distances. Those who did not have a horse rode with those who owned wagons.

Revolutionary War Militiaman on Horse

This painting is called Israel Putnam Leaving His Plow. Most Militia were notified by a messenger on horseback.
Yale University Art Gallery, New Haven, CT.

Historical Background for Chapter 27
Sybil at the Ganong's

When Sybil recognized she was at the Ganong's house she almost did not approach the house because of John Ganong's

Loyalist leanings. Someone who was a Loyalist would not be interested in responding to help stop a raid on Rebel supplies led by Crown Forces, especially ones which included Loyalists.

She made the decision she must give the call to every house so she went to the front door and made the call. That resulted in her friend Jesse Ganong responding.

Like many others, Jesse did not have his own musket. Muskets cost about one month's wages and most people had little use for them. Sybil assured Jesse her father would provide one for him.

Historical Background for Chapter 28
Crown Forces Leave Danbury

The Crown Forces continued their looting and burning of Danbury throughout the night. Many of the Loyalists in the Danbury Raid were from Fairfield County, where Danbury is located.

Anyone suspected of being a Loyalist was constantly monitored by a local *Committee of Safety*. Some had their land confiscated. Most Loyalists had a deep-seated resentment for their Rebel neighbors. This raid was the first chance some of them had to take out their frustrations.

In the morning before leaving Danbury, Tryon ordered his men to make a pile of all the remaining supplies they could not fit in wagons and to burn them in the street.

Supplies which could not be burnt were disposed of in

other ways. The July 25, 1777 edition of the *Virginia Gazette* mentioned Dr. John Wood of Danbury, Connecticut found 400 cannon balls and 120 musket balls in his well. They were thrown in there by the enemy as they retreated.

Historical Background for Chapter 29
Sybil Rides as the Sun Rises

The area where Sybil rode was comprised of farms separated by woods with rolling hills and many streams.

Sunrise Over the Hills
Engraving by Andrews from Wheelock drawing, 1860.

Sunrise on April 27, 1777, in the Hudson Valley was at 5:02 in the morning. The sun rose and set as much as ten minutes later, depending on which side of a hill you were on.

The rising sun had a wonderful warming effect, especially on someone who was wet. That would reinvigorate a rider.

Larry A. Maxwell

Historical Background for Chapter 30
American Officers Plan Response

The American officers originally planned to attack the Crown Forces in Danbury. They changed their plans when they learned the Crown Forces left Danbury and were marching to Norwalk through Ridgefield.

General Arnold wrote a letter on April 27, 1777, to General Alexander McDougall, stating he believed the Crown Forces were going to march west from Danbury to Peekskill or Tarrytown. He later learned that was not their intention.

The route from Danbury to Peekskill would have taken the Crown Forces through Fishkill where the Rebels had their other Supply Depot but would also take them through the homeland of Colonel Henry Ludington and the *Dutchess County Militia*. It was much safer for them to head south through towns where Montfort Browne's Loyalists were from.

Historical Background for Chapter 31
Opposition South of Danbury

Small groups of Militia launched isolated attacks against the Crown Forces on their way to rendezvous with the rest of the Rebel Forces.

The Militiamen did not do a head-on face-to-face linear attack but launched surprise attacks from behind stone walls and trees and then quickly dispersed.

That type of attack was used by the Rebels when the Crown Forces retreated from Concord. It provided the Crown Forces little opportunity to effectively strike back.

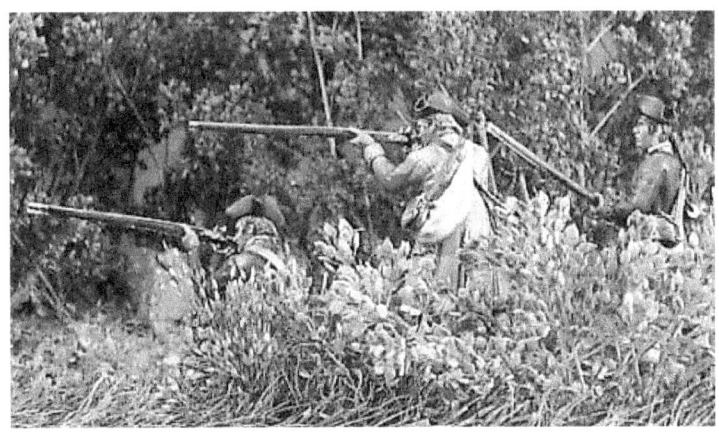

Militiamen Attack Crown Forces
Militia shoot then quickly disappear.
Living History Guild Achieve Photo

Historical Background for Chapter 32
 Sybil at the Last House

Many people rose early back in that time and did their chores before they had breakfast.

Most people in the Hudson Valley and surrounding areas were church going people back then. Many went to church every Sunday morning. Church services were often held late in the morning, so farmers could do their chores and the morning milking before they went to church.

Larry A. Maxwell

The family Sybil encountered in this chapter kindly offered Sybil breakfast. If she had not been riding all night it would have been proper for her to accept the invitation.

Historical Background for Chapter 33
Wooster Attacks The Crown Forces

General Wooster had the *1st Connecticut Regiment* with him. They were wearing red regimental coats with white facings. When they attacked it must have been disparaging for the Crown Forces to fire upon other men wearing red coats.

Wooster struck the enemy twice. The first time he and his men took some forty prisoners. During the second attack the Crown Forces were able to use their cannons. During that attack Wooster was mortally wounded.

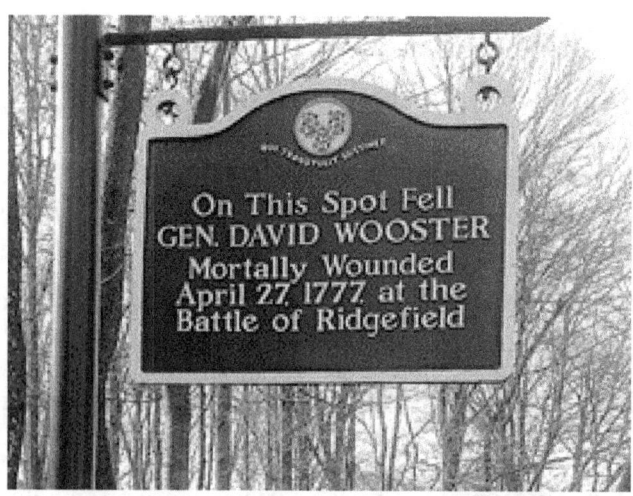

Historical Marker of Wooster's Death
North Salem Road, Ridgefield, CT.
Photograph by Larry Maxwell, 2018

Historical Background for Chapter 34
Sybil Returns Home

Sybil Ludington's Ride Ends

A historic monument was placed at this site on Route 52, in Kent by the New York State Department of Education in 1932. This was where the Ludington home stood. This is where Sybil ended her ride. That marker was damaged and then replaced in 2008.
Photograph by Larry A. Maxwell, 2018

Sybil's ride was an exhausting and incredible task. She is an inspiration as she persevered in spite of the dangers, difficulties, and obstacles.

The last of the Militia arrived shortly after Sybil returned from her ride. They then set off to join the rest of the regiment.

The fighting at Ridgefield and near Compo Beach was often referred to as the *Danbury Raid* or the *Battle of Ridgefield*, even though the fighting took place in different areas. It is important to remember that when reading other accounts.

Historical Background for Chapter 35
Barricades in Ridgefield

The times used in this book for the events related to the Battle in Ridgefield have been extrapolated from a careful review of reliable original records.

The Crown Forces left Danbury shortly after sunrise, which was six o'clock in the morning on Sunday, April 28, 1777. They were about nine miles northeast of Ridgefield. The road went west for about three miles toward Fredericksburg and then on to the Rebel Supply Depot at Fishkill. Close to that three-mile mark, another road turned south to Ridgefield. That point was about six miles north of Ridgefield.

The Crown Forces encountered some sporadic resistance from small groups of Militia on the way to Ridgefield.

The men from the *1st Ridgefield Militia*, together with the people in Ridgefield, started to build a barricade in the middle of the road on a ridge just north of the present-day center of town. A steep downward slope to the right of the barricades made it an ideal location. They used logs, rocks, carts, furniture and whatever else they could find.

The Town of Ridgefield, Connecticut is on the New York border. The *3rd Westchester County Militia* came from neighboring towns in New York. When they arrived they joined in building the barricade.

When Colonel Philip Burr Bradley of the *5th Connecticut Regiment of the Continental Army* arrived with his men, he was put in change and helped oversee the expansion of the barricade. That moved the authority for the engagement from the Connecticut Militia to the Continental Army.

Unlike the *1st Connecticut Regiment* which wore red regimental coats faced white, the *5th Connecticut Regiment* adopted a blue regimental coat with scarlet facings. Colonel Bradley wore the same color regimental coat as his men.

When General Arnold and General Silliman arrived, Colonel Bradley transferred command to Arnold who was the highest-ranking Continental officer.

Historical Background for Chapter 36
Battle in Ridgefield

From the time the Crown Forces left New York City, until they arrived at Danbury they tried to keep their mission a secret. When they reached Danbury they no longer needed to be secretive. They used military music to show they were in high spirits and to intimidate the Rebels. That was a favorite military tactic. As they approached Ridgefield they had their musicians play again.

Every British Regiment had its own musicians. The musicians were used to relay orders. Each regiment at its formation had 811 men. At least two of them were fifers. Each regiment was comprised of ten companies. Each company had at least one drummer.

The Danbury Raid included almost two thousand men, with 250 men from six different regiments. That is about three companies from each regiment. If each company brought one drummer there would have been eighteen drummers on the raid. It is likely each regiment sent along one fifer, which would put six fifers on the raid.

Participants at the Battle of Ridgefield said they heard the music from the Crown Forces as that army approached. Eighteen drummers and six fifers playing military music would be very loud and powerful and could be very intimidating as it approached Ridgefield.

Battle of Ridgefield

A Skirmish in America between the Kings Troops & Gen. Arnold. 1780 Engraving published in London by R. Sayer and J. Benet.

A common military tactic used back then was to enter a battle in companies forming two rows. The front row would fire, then while they reloaded, the second row would fire. That way one row was always loaded. That provided covering fire. That is the technique both sides used at Ridgefield.

If there was more than one company in a battle and the army was moving forward, the first company would fire then reload. The second company would advance past them and fire while the first company reloaded. That was the method they both used later at Compo Beach.

At the barricade in Ridgefield the Rebels followed a modification of the two-row formation with one row immediately behind the barricade and the second row behind them. After the first row fired, it stepped back and reloaded. The second row of men stepped forward, already loaded and fired on command. Then that row stepped back and reloaded, while the first row stepped up to the barricade and fired again.

After a few rounds of a whole row or company firing, it was common for the order, *Fire at Will* to be given. That did not mean you looked for someone named Will to shoot. It meant each man reloaded and fired at their own pace with an emphasis on shooting as quickly and as often as possible.

Soldiers Return Fire Under Cover
Franklyn Maxwell and Daniel Maxwell, 4th N.Y. Regiment.
Photograph by Larry Maxwell

Larry A. Maxwell

After the Revolutionary War, General Charles Cornwallis, who served as the British Commander General in America during the last years of the Revolution, wrote about the techniques he had his men use in the American Revolution. He wrote how there were engagements where he had his men, who were the best shots, stay behind a barrier and shoot at the enemy. The other men in the company reloaded muskets and handed those men a fully loaded musket after each shot. He said that was something he learned from the Americans during the French and Indian War. The Crown Forces were being pursued and did not use that method at Ridgefield.

Historical Background for Chapter 37
Crown Forces South of Ridgefield

Accounts say the Crown Forces stayed the night at the south end of Ridgefield. Some misinterpreted that to mean they stayed just outside of the part of town where the homes and businesses were located. That was close to where they fought the battle which lasted almost until the sun went down. That does not match with Erskine's report that some 50 to 60 of his men were killed in skirmishes that day after the battle. If they stayed in town it would also mean the next day they would not have enough time to march the seven miles to Wilton, stop there for breakfast, march another ten miles to Compo Beach, and arrive by 11:30 a.m. when the fighting started.

The Crown Forces did stay at the south end of Ridgefield, near the Wilton border. The Town of Wilton is located south of Ridgefield. During the Revolutionary War, Wilton was known as Wilton Parish and was part of the Town of Norwalk.

The *4th Regiment of Foot* and the *23rd Regiment of Foot* both participated in the Danbury Raid. They were at the Battle of Lexington and Concord. On their way back from Concord to Charlestown and then to Boston, they lost many men at the hands of the Rebel Militia. They were also at the Battle of Bunker Hill where they lost many more men. As they left Ridgefield they were again attacked by Militia and lost many men, that must have brought back bad memories for them.

Crown Forces Fall to Militia Attack from Woods
Lantern Slide from Story of the Revolution.
New York Public Library Image Collection

Historical Background for Chapter 38
Ludington Meets Arnold

Some historical accounts state Colonel Ludington and his men participated in the action against the Crown Forces at

Danbury. Other accounts state they were involved in the Battle of Ridgefield.

Colonel Ludington and his men set out for Danbury. On the way a messenger reached them and informed them the Crown Forces left Danbury and marched on to Ridgefield. They then continued east, until they reached the road which led them to Ridgefield, then went south.

It was not humanly possible for two hundred men to leave Fredericksburg, New York, when the Colonel and his men left, and arrive in Ridgefield, Connecticut in time for the battle.

Colonel Ludington and his men arrived in Ridgefield after the fighting, yet in time to join the rest of the forces by evening and to join in the battle the next day.

The accounts which state he and his men fought at Danbury or Ridgefield can be reconciled by the fact many historical accounts refer to the entire campaign as the *Danbury Raid* and the two days of fighting at Ridgefield and Norwalk as the *Battle of Ridgefield*.

Historical Background for Chapter 39
Back at the Ludington's Home

After riding all night Sybil was exhausted. It was not unusual for someone who completed such a physically and emotionally demanding task, as Sybil did, to sleep for an entire day and to wake up disoriented.

Historical Background for Chapter 40
British Officers Before Last Battle

The Crown Forces headed south to Compo Beach in the morning. They stopped in Wilton Parish for breakfast provided by local Loyalists. Little damage was done to Rebel homes in Wilton or Norwalk by the Crown Forces because they were trying to get back to Compo Beach as quickly as possible. They were concerned the Rebel Forces, which pursued them from Ridgefield, would be upon them at any moment. They did not know General Benedict Arnold led the Rebel Forces around them early that morning and was waiting to attack them before they could reach their ships.

General Montfort Browne's words to the other officers in this chapter provides a very important perspective on a mindset held by some Loyalists during the war.

Loyalists believed their neighbors were traitors. Those who lived in areas controlled by the Rebels were often imprisoned and had their lands confiscated if they did not sign an oath of allegiance.

There are no known records of anyone in England joining the Regular British Army so they could help stop the American Rebel's quest for independence. Being in the army was just looked upon by the common enlisted man as a job. Yet in America thousands of Loyalists joined Loyalist Regiments so they could help put an end to their struggle with their rebellious neighbors who dishonored them and the Crown. They fought with passion to restore order.

Historical Background for Chapter 41
Battle in Norwalk

The American Forces were able to go around the Crown Forces undetected. Their advantage was two-fold. They were familiar with the area and were not encumbered with cannons and wagons of confiscated goods as the Crown Forces were.

The Crown Forces had to travel on the larger roads which were muddied by days of rain. They were pulling six heavy cannons which slowed them down considerably. That provided the Rebels plenty of time to pass them on the smaller back roads and remain undetected.

Cannon Monument at Compo Beach

This monument honors the artillery who opposed the Crown Forces. These cannons were placed at Cedar Point at Compo Beach on July 4, 1901. These cannons are extremely larger than those used by the Rebels who fought there.
Photograph by Larry A. Maxwell, 2017

On Sunday evening, Colonel John Lamb's Continental artillery arrived with his three, three-pounder cannons. He met General Arnold during his reconnaissance in Norwalk.

Lamb positioned his artillery near the Saugatuck Bridge. They were joined by an artillery unit from Fairfield. They had plenty of time to see up an offensive position to oppose the Crown Forces in the morning.

Historical Background for Chapter 42
The Smoke Clears

The Battle near Saugatuck Bridge was very short. General Benedict Arnold and his men were located near Old Hill. When the front lines of the Crown Forces encountered the Rebel resistance the rest of their army changed course to avoid the Rebels and took a different route back to Compo Beach. They wadded across the Saugatuck River at Ford Road.

The Battle of Compo Hill by Hannan
Eugene E. Hannan, series of bas relief plaster 1936-1937.
Westport Schools Permanent Art Collection

Arnold had his men attack at the Kings Highway Bridge.

He then moved them to Compo Hill, overlooking the beach, and continued the battle as the enemy retreated to their ships.

Two twenty-two-foot-long bas reliefs depicting the Battle at Compo Beach were done during the Depression by Eugene E. Hannan. They were titled *The Battle of Compo Hill* and *The Battle of Cedar Point*. They are part of the Westport Schools Permanent Art Collection.

Left Section of The Battle of Compo Hill
Gen. Benedict Arnold shot leading a charge on horseback.

Right Section of The Battle of Compo Beach
Rebels advance on 64th Regiment of Foot behind stone wall.

The Battle of Cedar Point
Eugene E. Hannan - 22' long bas relief plaster 1936-1937.
Westport Schools Permanent Art Collection.

Left Section of The Battle of Cedar Point
64th Regiment of Foot.
British Fleet and Landing Craft in Background.

Right Section of The Battle of Cedar Point
Continentals & Militia.
British Fleet & landing Craft in Background.

The July 16, 1777 edition of *The Public Advertiser*, published in London, England, listed the huge amount of Rebel supplies the Crown Forces destroyed at Danbury. It was a significant loss to the Continental Army. That article compared the Danbury retreat of the Crown Forces to the retreat from Lexington. It said the Crown Forces had sixty-two men from the kings-troops killed and forty taken prisoner.

Though most newspapers which favored the Crown, gave glowing reports of the expedition, it had a negative impact on the Crown. That was reflected in a humorous advertisement in the August 4, 1777 edition of *The Public Advertiser* in London.

> ADVERTISEMENT.
>
> LOST, this Summer, in the Enclosures about New York in North America, The BRITISH ARMY. Whoever can give an Account of it to his Majesty's Secretary at War, shall not only receive a large Premium, but have the high Honour of killing his Majesty's Hand.—A Part of it is said to have been seen in the Spring near Danbury; but its Stay was so short, that its Tracks were not deep enough to be traced.

Newspaper Advertisement for Lost British Army
The Public Advertiser, August 4, 1777 edition, London.

It read as follows, "LOST, This Summer, in the Enclosures about New York in North America, The BRITISH ARMY. Whoever can give an account of it to His Majesty's Secretary of War, shall not only receive a large Premium, but have the high Honour of kissing his Majesty's Hand. – A Part of it is said to have been seen in the Spring near Danbury; but its Stay was so short that its Tracks were not deep enough to be traced."

Historical Background for Chapter 43
The Return

Colonel Ludington and his men returned home at a slower pace than they went to Ridgefield because they did not have an enemy to pursue. The trip back from Compo Beach to Colonel Ludington's home was about forty miles and would normally take two days by horse or in a wagon.

The loved ones back home had no idea what was happening with the Colonel or his men. There were no phones, telegraph, radios, or computers back then. The only way to communicate was by a messenger, but all the messengers were engaged in the conflict. Families anxiously waited for their loved ones to return with either good or bad news.

Though the Colonel and his men were not pursuing an enemy, or being pursued, they desired to get back to their loved ones who had no word from them since they left. They did not stop much along the way and arrived home very tired from the long journey. Everyone was very glad when they finally returned.

Howes plan to end the war failed and the war went on for another six years until 1783. Sybil Ludington continued to ride and take messages to the Militia for her father. Colonel Ludington and his men continued to respond and faithfully defended liberty against tyranny for the remainder of the war.

Just as the Crown Forces never returned to Lexington and Concord they never attacked Danbury again.

Many books incorrectly list the wrong name for Sybil's husband and misreport her children. Her husband was Edmond (Edmund) Ogden, and they had only one child, Henry Ogden. This is addressed clearly by Vincent Dacquino in his book, *Sybil Ludington, the Call to Arms*.

After the war, Sybil married Edmond Ogden. They moved to Catskill, New York. After he died, she moved to Unadilla, New York, where she later died. Her body was returned to Patterson, New York where she was buried next to her father Colonel Henry Ludington and her mother Abigail.

Sybil's grandson Edmund Augustus Ogden went to West Point Military Academy where he graduated in 1831. For the next twenty-four years he had an impeccable military career.

On May 30, 1848, he was issued the rank of Brevet Major for Meritorious Service in the War in Mexico.

In 1855, he was a captain in the *8th U.S. Infantry*. He oversaw the construction of Fort Riley in Kansas. A cholera epidemic struck and killed many people in the area. He contracted cholera while helping his men and died. He was honored with a monument.

Edmund Ogden is the only West Point graduate who has a monument erected to him as well as one erected in honor of his grandmother, Sybil Ludington.

Tombstones of Sybil & Colonel Henry Ludington
*Maple Avenue Cemetery, Route 311, Patterson, New York.
Sybil's name is spelled "Sibbell Ludington" on her stone.*
Photographs by Larry A. Maxwell, 2017

Edmund Augustus Ogden
Grandson of Sybil Ludington & Edmond Ogden.
New York Public Library Image Collection

Suggested Study Strategies

For those who want to use this book in the classroom or in a study group, unless you plan to do one session for each chapter, you will need to combine a few chapters per study session. The following are two suggested study combinations based on a logical connection between the content in chapters.

5 Sessions

Session 1	Chapter 1-8
Session 2	Chapter 9-15
Session 3	Chapter 16-28
Session 4	Chapter 29-37
Session 5	Chapter 38-43

10 Sessions

Session 1	Chapter 1-4
Session 2	Chapter 5-8
Session 3	Chapter 9-13
Session 4	Chapter 14-18
Session 5	Chapter 19-26
Session 6	Chapter 27-32
Session 7	Chapter 33-35
Session 8	Chapter 36-37
Session 9	Chapter 38-42
Session 10	Chapter 43

Projects & Questions

The fact Sybil Ludington is a teenage female heroine has earned her a place America's Core Curriculum and in many school's social studies curriculum. This section provides some Projects and Questions educators may want to use with their students to enhance their learning experience. These can also for used for personal study or by a reading group for discussion. All of these projects and question are based on information in the regular edition of *Sybil Rides*.

Projects

Some of these projects can be coordinated between English, Social Studies, and Art classes.

1. Make a map identifying all the places involved in the *Sybil Rides* book.

2. Write a paper contrasting the *Loyalist* and *Rebel* positions. Which side do you think you would have chosen and why?

3. Write a paper explaining what it meant to be a *Patriot* during the Revolutionary War. Did that change?

4. Write a paper showing some character traits of Sybil Ludington and what makes her a good role model.

5. Write a paper showing some character traits of General Benedict Arnold. Explain why he was a hero in this story. Are there any hints in this story as to why he later became a traitor?

6. Write a paper showing some of the character traits of Colonel Henry Ludington.

7. Write a story showing what you would have experienced if you were a British Regular soldier in the 4th Regiment of Foot, based on the facts from this story.

8. Write a paper contrasting some of the military officers

in this story.

9. Illustrate either the steps involved in making a cartridge for a musket or the procedure involved in the loading and firing sequence.

10. Write a paper about the military tactics used in the battles in this book.

11. Do a timeline of events, from this book, which led to the Revolution and then to Sybil's Ride.

12. Look up at least two newspaper accounts, included in the Bibliography for this book, and summarize how they reported on the events in this book. If there is a difference between the details they reported, and the events presented in this story speculate on why their reporting of events differs. Consider the bias of the publication.

13. Attend a Revolutionary War reenactment and write a paper of about some similarities between the reenactment, reenactors, and this book.

14. Put together a display of images showing the different uniforms worn by some of the soldiers on both sides in this story. Look up historical images and images of re-enactors. Highlight some of the differences.

15. Write a paper about one character in this story you would like to be like and why.

Questions

1. Why did riders go to Lexington on April 18, 1775? Who were those riders?

2. Who were some of the leaders of the *Sons of Liberty* mentioned in this book?

3. Why is the Battle of Lexington and Concord considered the first battle of the Revolutionary War? Who instigated it?

4. Who fired the first shot at Lexington?

5. How did the message about Lexington and Concord get to the rest of the colonies? How long did it take?
6. Who won the Battle of Bunker Hill? What were the results of that battle?
7. What did some people think when the British Forces withdrew from Boston?
8. Who was the commander of the Crown Forces in America in 1777?
9. When was the first time British Regulars fired upon American Colonists?
10. Who was Mehitable Prendergast and what did she do which inspired Sybil Ludington?
11. Why is Sybil Ludington called the *Female Paul Revere*?
12. Why did Colonel Henry Ludington have his daughter Sybil ride to call out the Militia?
13. What was the difference between a *Loyalist* and a *Rebel*?
14. What was the difference between the *Continental Army* and the *Militia*?
15. What was the difference between a *British Regular solider* and a *Loyalist solider*? What was the difference in their uniforms in this story?
16. Who were Jacob and John Angevine? How were they different from others in this story?
17. Why did a person like John Ganong not embrace the Rebel cause?
18. What background did John Ganong and Colonel Ludington have in common?
19. How did the Crown try to scare the colonists about an alliance with the French?
20. What made John Ganong, Jesse Ganong's father, change his mind?

21. Why did Dr. Jonathan Prosser and his men want to capture Colonel Henry Ludington?
22. Who were the British Generals in this story?
23. Why was there a conflict between General William Erskine and General Montfort Browne?
24. Who were Daniel and Abraham Nimham?
25. Who were John Gano and Haym Salomon? Which one was an immigrant and how did he help the Revolution?
26. Who were the officers mentioned in this story on the Rebel side?
27. What role did Sybil Ludington's mother, Abigail Ludington play in this story?
28. What role did Sybil Ludington's sister, Rebecca Ludington play in this story?
29. What role did Enoch Crosby play in this story? Why was that so important?
30. Is there any evidence that religion played any part in the lives of the characters in this story?
31. How did Sybil Ludington and her siblings foil the Loyalist plot to capture their father?
32. What was the purpose behind the Crown Forces raid on Danbury?
33. How did the Crown Forces get from New York City to Compo Beach? How long did it take and why?
34. How did Luther Holcomb delay the Crown Forces at Bethel? Why did that work?
35. Why did General Erskine hesitate when he saw Colonel Cooke and his men when he entered Danbury?
36. What let General Erskine know Colonel Cooke and his men were on the Rebel side?
37. Why did the Rebel forces stop at Bethel and not proceed immediately into Danbury?
38. What were the conditions like when Sybil rode to call

out the Militia? What obstacles did she face? How did she overcome them?

39. What happened to Loyalists in Danbury during the Danbury Raid?

40. What happened to Rebels in Danbury during the Danbury Raid?

41. What role did General David Wooster play in this story? How were his last words significant?

42. How were some townspeople in Ridgefield involved in this story?

43. What did the Crown Forces encounter when they reached Ridgefield?

44. What role did Colonel Ludington's Militia play in this story?

45. What was the similarity between the Crown Forces return from Lexington and Concord and their return to Norwalk from Danbury?

46. Why did the Crown Forces rest when they reached the south end of Ridgefield instead of going all the way back to their ships?

47. What made General William Erskine change his attitude about General Montfort Browne?

48. What similar thing happened to General Benedict Arnold in Ridgefield and at Compo Beach?

49. Who was Edmond Ogden?

50. What happened to Jesse Angevine?

Larry A. Maxwell

Some Vocabulary Words & Terms
Find the words in this book. Define or discuss them.

affidavit
aide
alliance
barricade
ammunition
bayonet
bounty
British
capture
cartridge
casualties
colony
Continental
Committee of Safety
Continental Congress
Crown Forces
curtsey
dragoon
enemy
fire at will
fleet
French & Indian War
Graces
Grand Union
Grenadiers
guineas
headquarters
Hessians
Huzzah
independence
Indian Regiment
King
lantern
liberty
Loyalist
Marine
military music
Militia
musket

needlework
nefarious
Oath of Loyalty
officer
Parliament
patriot
plundered
pompous
prison ship
prisoner
protocol
Rebel
rebellion
regiment
Regular
reins
rendezvous
resolve
Revolution
Sachem
salute
sentry
Settler's Revolt
shift
sibling
small clothes
Sons of Liberty
spoil
spy
supply depot
sympathizer
The Crown
Tory
traitor
vengeance
volley
waistcoat
wampum
Whig

Fun Facts & Trivia

1. **Did Sybil Ludington foam at the mouth when she made her famous ride?**

If you visit the Sybil Ludington monument in Carmel, New York it is not unusual to see her appear to be foaming at the mouth. Renowned sculptor Michael Keropian says that is not an intentional effect. When Anna Huntington made the monument, the plaster from the mold in the head was left in after they made the bronze casting. That is usually removed. Rain leaches into the monument and a clay foam-like residue leaks out making it appear Sybil is foaming at the mouth. Keropian offered to fix the monument but locals turned down his offer because it would require removing Sybil's head. If that were done, while her head was being fixed she might be mistaken for the legendary figure from nearby Sleepy Hollow.

2. **What modern sayings come from the muskets used during the Revolutionary War?**

The whole lock, stock, and barrel – The musket was made up of three parts: the *lock*, which is the firing mechanism; the *barrel*, which holds the charge; and the *stock*, which is the wooden part that holds it all together. Unless you had *the whole lock, stock and barrel,* your musket was useless.

Flash in the pan – To fire a musket, some black powder is placed in the pan on the lock. When the flint strikes the metal frizzen it makes a spark which causes the powder to ignite. To the left of the pan is a small touch hole which extends into the musket barrel. If that touch hole gets clogged, the ignition only causes a *flash in the pan* and the musket does not fire.

Half-cocked – The hammer on the musket lock, holds the flint. When a soldier went to battle they put the hammer in the *half-cocked* position. That helped the loading sequence. When you were *half-cocked* all you had to do was open the pan, put the powder in, close the pan, and then put the charge in the barrel. You should only be *half-cocked* when you are going to battle. When you are in a battle and want to fire the musket you need to move the hammer to the full-cocked position. If you are *half-cocked*, you cannot fire.

Keep your powder dry – To fire your musket, you needed your black powder to be dry. Wet powder will not ignite well.

3. **Who was the model for the Patriot's Monument at Compo Beach and is there a Robin Hood connection?**

The model for the Patriot's monument was Town of Westport First Selectman, Lewis Penfield Wakeman. He married Jennie Sherwood. Sherwood Island, which can be seen from Compo Beach was named after her family. Though there may appear to be a small forest on Sherwood Island, Robin Hood has never been seen there, though it is not unusual during the summer, to find some merry men there.

4. **In what television show was the Patriot's Monument at Compo Beach damaged?**

In the May 6, 1957 episode of *I Love Lucy*, Lucille Ball and her husband Ricky Ricardo were fictitiously invited to help dedicate the monument. In that episode, Lucy accidently destroyed it. She humorously tried to pose as the monument for the dedication. That was the final episode of *I Love Lucy*.

5. **Where are the two twenty-foot-long tributes located which depict the Battle at Compo Beach?**

Two twenty-two-foot-long plaster bas relief depictions of the battles which took place around Compo Beach, are in the entrance to the Saugatuck Elementary School in Westport, Connecticut. During the Great Depression (1929-1939), the United States Government had a program called the *Works Progress Administration* (WPA), which helped put people to work. As part of the WPA, artist Eugene E. Hannan made the two bas relief plaster images for the entrance to the Saugatuck High School between 1936-1937. The high school later became the Saugatuck Elementary School. At age two-and-half, Hannan contracted scarlet fever and became deaf. He attended Gallaudet College the first college for the deaf in America.

Bibliography

Almon, J. – *The Remembrancer, or The Impartial Repository of Public Events for the Year 1777*. London, UK: W. Haydon, 1778.

Amstel, Marsha - *Sybil Ludington's Midnight Ride*, Minneapolis, Minnesota: Carolrhoda Books, Inc., 2000.

Bailey, James Montgomery – *The History of Danbury, Connecticut 1684-1896*. New York: Burr Printing House, 1896.

Baldwin, Alice M., *The New England Clergy and the American Revolution*. New York: F. Ungar Publishing Co., 1958.

Baldwin, R. – *The London Magazine or Gentlemen's Monthly Intelligencer, Vol. 46*. London, UK, 1777.

Barber, John Warner – *Historical Collections of Connecticut*. New Haven: Durrie & Peck and J. Warner Barber, 1836.

Beatson, Robert – *Navy and Military Memoirs of Great Britain from 1727 to 1783, Vol. 4*. London, UK, 1804.

Berkin, Carol – *Revolutionary Mothers: Women in the Struggle for America's Independence*. New York, New York: Random House, 2005.

Berry, Erick – *Sybil Ludington's Ride*. New York: Viking Press, 1952.

Bosworth, Frank E. – *The Burning of Danbury, The Colonial Magazine, Vol. 1, No. 1*. Burlington, Vermont, The Colonial Magazine, 1895.

Braisted, Todd – *The History of the Prince of Wales American Regiment*. The Online Institute of Advanced Loyalist Studies, royalprovincial.com, 2001.

Burr, William Hanford. *The Invasion of Connecticut by the British*. Hartford, Connecticut: The Connecticut Magazine, 1906.

Cannon, Richard - *Historical Record of The Seventeenth Regiment of Light Dragoons*. London: John W. Parker, 1841.

Case, James R. - *An account of Tryon's Raid on Danbury in April 1777 also The Battle of Ridgefield and The Career of*

Gen. David Wooster. Danbury, Connecticut, 1927.

Chartrand, Rene – *American Loyalist Troops 1775-1784*. New York: Osprey Publications, 2008.

Company of Military Historians – *Military Uniform Plates (Drawings) Illustrating Uniforms, Plate 279 – Light Company, 4th Regiment of Foot (King's Own) In America; Plate 379 – British General and Staff Officers; Plate 382 – The Prince of Wales' American Regiment; Plate 453 – British Light Infantry [10th, 14th, & 1th Foot]; Plate 557 – New York Continental Artillery; Plate 845 – 1st Regiment of the Connecticut Continental Line*. Rutland, Massachusetts, The Company of Military Historians, 1966-2008.

Cooper, James Fenimore – *The Spy, a Tale of Neutral Ground*. New York: G.P. Putnam's Sons, 1821.

Dacquino, Vincent T. – *Sybil Ludington, The Call to Arms*. Fleischmanns, New York: Purple Mountain Press, 2000.

Darley, Stephen A. – *Call to Arms, The Patriot Militia in the 1777 British Raid on Danbury, Connecticut*. North Haven, Connecticut: Darley Books, 2015.

Davis, Ryan C. – *Sybil Ludington, An Encyclopedia of American Women at War From the Homefront to the Battlefields, Vol. 1, A-L*. Edited by Lisa Tendrich Frank, Santa Barbara, California: ABC-CLIO, 2013.

Dawson, Henry B. (Henry Barton). *The Expedition Against Danbury*. In *Battles of the United States, by Sea and Land: Embracing Those of the Revolutionary and Indian Wars, the War of 1812, and the Mexican War, with Official Documents*, 1:212–20. New York: Johnson, Fry, and Company, 1858.

Douglas, Damon Greenleaf. *The Bridge Not Taken, Benedict Arnold Outwitted*. Connecticut: Westport Historical Society, 2002.

Dunlap's Pennsylvania Packet, May 15, 1775 edition, pp. 1-4, Philadelphia, Pennsylvania, newspaper, 1775.

Edes, Benjamin - *The Boston-Gazette and Country Journal, May 19, 1777 Edition*. Boston, MA., newspaper, 1777.

Ellis, Edward Sylvester – *The Youths' History of the United States: From the Discovery of America by the Northmen, to the Present Time. Vol. II*. London: Cassell & Company, Ltd.,

1887

Fast, Howard – *Haym Salomon: Son of Liberty*. New York: Julian Messner, Inc., 1941.

Feldberg, Michael – *Haym Salomon: The Rest of the Story*. Jewish World Review, 2001.

Gano, John – *Biographical Memoirs of the Late John Gano of Frankfort, Kentucky, Formerly of City of New York*. New York: Hardwick and Southwick, 1806.

Gardiner, Richard - *The Presbyterian Rebellion?* Ph.D. Dissertation, Marquette University, Milwaukee, WI., 2005, re-published in *Journal of the American Revolution* https://allthingsliberty.com, September 5, 2013.

Green, Thomas & Samuel – *Connecticut Journal and New-Haven Poor-Boy, April 30, 1777, edition*. New Haven, Connecticut, newspaper, 1777.

Grumet, Robert S. - *The Nimhams of the Colonial Hudson Valley 1667-1783. The Hudson River Valley Review, Vol. 9, No. 2*. Poughkeepsie, New York: The Hudson River Valley Institute, 1992.

Hall, Marjory – *See The Red Sky*. Philadelphia: Westminster Press, 1963.

Hammond, A.S. Hammond - *Hammond Papers*. August 5, 1776, Charlottesville, Virginia: University of Virginia, Alderman Library, 1776.

Harper's Weekly Magazine, June 18, 1868 issue - New York.

Heinrichs, Johann - *Extracts from the Letter Book of Captain Johann Heinrichs of the Hessian Jager Corps, 1778-1780. Pennsylvania Magazine of History and Biography* 22 (1898). Philadelphia, Pennsylvania, 1898.

Herring, James – *General David Wooster, National Portrait Gallery of Distinguished Americans, Vol. 2*. New York: Monson Bancroft, 1832.

Hewitt, Don - *Flags of the American Revolution, A Salute to America's Bicentennial*. PA: Pittsburgh National Bank, booklet, 1968.

Huntington, E. B. – *Genealogical Memoir of the Huntington Family*, Stamford , Connecticut, 1863.

Historical and Genealogical Record Dutchess and Putnam

Counties New York. Poughkeepsie, New York: Press of the A. V. Haight Co., 1912.

Hunt, Paula – *Sybil Ludington – The Female Paul Revere: The Making of a Revolutionary War Heroine.* New England Quarterly, June 2015, Vol. 88, No.2, pp. 187-222, Boston, Massachusetts: University of Boston, 2015

Ives, J. Moss - *A Connecticut Battlefield in the American Revolution: Danbury-Captured and Burned by the British in 1777-Village Sacked by General Tryon. The Connecticut Magazine. Vol. 7, No. 5.* Hartford, Connecticut, 1902-1903.

Johnson, Justin - *Battle of Ridgefield, American Military History Podcast, Episode 031.* AmericanMilitaryHistoryPodcast.com

Johnson, Rossiter - *Appletons' Cyclopaedia of American Bibliography, Vol. 1.* New York: D. Appleton Company, 1886

Johnson, Willis Fletcher – *Colonel Henry Ludington, A Memoir.* New York, 1907.

Jones, Keith Marshall III – *Farmers Against the Crown.* Baltimore, Maryland, Gateway Books, 2002.

Journals of the Continental Congress. Washington, D.C: The Library of Congress, 1774-1789.

Kaimer, Jamie – *The Danbury Raid*, Connecticut: The Mercurial, Web Magazine and Gallery, 2011.

Katcher, Philip – *Uniforms of the Continental Army.* York, Pennsylvania: George Shumway Publisher, 1981.

Kochan, James L. & Coates, Earl – *Don Troiani's Soldiers in America 1754-1865.* Mechanicsburg, Pennsylvania: Stackpole Books, 1998.

Lamb, Martha J. – *History of the City of New York: It's Origins, Rise and Progress, Vol.2.* p. 159-60, vi, New York City, New York: A.S. Barnes & Co., 1876.

Laughton, J.J. - *Journals of Henry Duncan, Captain, Royal Navy 1776-1782, The Naval Miscellany, Vol. I.* Reading, UK: Navy Records Society, 1901.

Leake, Isaac Q. – *Memoir of the Life and Times of Colonel John Lamb.* Bedford, Massachusetts: Applewood Books, 1857.

Longfellow, William Wadsworth – *The Midnight Ride of Paul*

Revere. Boston: The Atlantic Magazine, 1861.

Lossing, Benson John - *Pictorial Field Book of the Revolution, Vol 2*. New York, New York: Harper Brothers, 1850.

MacCracken, Henry Noble – *Old Dutchess Forever. The Story of an American County*. New York, New York: Hastings House, 1956.

Marshall, Douglas W., & Peckham, Howard H. - *Campaigns of the American Revolution: An Atlas of Manuscript Maps*. Ann Arbor: University of Michigan Press, 1976.

Martin, James Kirby – *Benedict Arnold Revolutionary Hero*. New York: New York University Press, 1997.

Maxwell, Larry A. – *Engagements, Units and Uniforms in the American Revolutionary War*. Patterson, New York: Living History Publications, 2017.

McDevitt, Robert F. - *Connecticut Attacked, a British Viewpoint: Tryon's Raid on Danbury*. Chester, Connecticut: Pequot Press, 1974.

Miller, Harry Edward - *The Spy on Neutral Ground*. The New England Magazine, Vol. 18, Boston: Warren F. Kellogg, 1888.

Montresor, John – *Gov. Tryon's Expedition to Danbury, 1777, Map*. Washington, D.C.: Library of Congress, 1777.

Moore, Frank – *The Diary of the American Revolution*. New York: Charles Scribner, 1876.

Nell, William C. – *Colored Patriots of the American Revolution*. Boston, Massachusetts: Robert F. Wallcut, 1855.

New York Gazette, May 5, 1777 edition. New York, N.Y., newspaper, 1777.

Oshkosh Daily Northwesterner, June 18, 1891 edition, p. 1., Oshkosh, Wisconsin, newspaper, 1891.

Patrick, Lewis S. – *The Ludington Family, The First Name in America*. Marinette, Wisconsin: The Independent Press, 1886.

Pawling-Patterson News Chronicle, October 17, 1936 edition, Pawling, New York, newspaper, 1936.

Pelletreau, William – *History of Putnam County, New York*. Philadelphia, Pennsylvania: W.W. Preston & Co., 1886.

Prochnow, Gene – *Top 10 American Loyalist Officers*. Journal of the American Revolution, allthingsliberty.com, 2014.

Purdie's Virginia Gazette, June 6, 1777 edition, pg. 2. Williamsburg, Virginia, newspaper, 1777.

Reid, Stuart & Chappell, Paul – *King George's Army 1740-1793: (1) Infantry*. Northants, UK: Osprey Military, 1995.

Reid, Stuart & Chappell, Paul – *King George's Army 1740-1793: (2)*. Northants, UK: Osprey Military, 1995.

Reid, Stuart & Chappell, Paul – *King George's Army 1740-1793: (3)*. Northants. UK: Osprey Military, 1996.

Reid, Stuart & Zlatich, Marco – *Soldiers of the Revolutionary War*. Northants, UK: Osprey Military, 2000.

Pencak, William; Dennis, Matthew; and Newman, Simon P. - *Riot and Revelry in Early America*. University Park, Pennsylvania: the Pennsylvania State University Press, 2002.

Roberts, James. A. – *New York in the Revolution as Colony and State*. Albany, New York: New York State Comptroller's Office, 1888.

Robertson, Archibald. – *Lieutenant General Royal Engineers – His Diaries and Sketches in America, 1762-1780*. New York, New York Public Library - 1930.

Robins, G. – *The Lady's Magazine or Entertaining Companion for the Fair Sex, Vol. 8, 1777*. London, 1777.

Rosenblatt, Hon. Albert M. – *The Historical Society of the New York Courts, County Court History, Poughkeepsie, Crown vs. William Prendergast*, pp. 38-39. www.nycourts.gov.

Russell, Charles Edward – *Haym Salomon and the Revolution*. New York, Cosmopolitan Book, 1930.

Selleck, Rev. Charles M. – *Norwalk*. Norwalk, Connecticut, 1896.

Sheldon, George William - *The Story of the Volunteer Fire Department of the City of New York*. New York : Harper, 1882

Study Report for Proposed Local Historic Landmark Property Designation of Minute Man Monument at Intersection of Compo Road South and Compo Beach Road.

Westport, Connecticut: Westport Historic District -

Syrett, Harold C. & Cooke, Jacob E. - *The Papers of Alexander Hamilton, Vol. 1, 1767-1778.* New York: Columbia University Press, 1961.

Teller, Daniel W. – *The History of Ridgefield, Conn., From Its First Settlement to The Present Time.* Danbury: T. Donovon, 1878.

The Cold Spring Recorder, September 23,1911 edition, pg. 1. Cold Spring, New York, newspaper, 1911

The Bridgeport Sunday Post, September 28, 1975 edition, pg. 12. Bridgeport, Connecticut, newspaper, 1975.

The Maryland Gazette, May 8, 1777 edition, pg. 2.
The Maryland Gazette, May 15, 1777 edition, pp. 2-3.
The Maryland Gazette, May 22, 1777 edition, pg. 2.
The Maryland Gazette, June 5, 1777 edition, pg. 2.
The Maryland Gazette, June 12, 1777 edition, pp. 1-2.
Annapolis, Maryland, newspaper, 1777.

The Nebraska State Journal, June 19, 1899 edition. Lincoln, Nebraska, newspaper, 1899.

The North Carolina Weekly Gazette, July 4, 1777 edition, pg. 2. New Bern, North Carolina, 1777.

The Pawling Chronicle, June 1928 edition, pg.3.
The Pawling Chronicle, October 18, 1934 edition, pg.1.
Pawling, New York, newspaper, 1934

The Public Advertiser, April 25, 1770 edition, pg. 2.
The Public Advertiser, May 30, 1775 edition, pg. 2.
The Public Advertiser, June 9, 1777 edition, pg. 2.
The Public Advertiser, June 12, 1777 edition, pg. 2.
The Public Advertiser, June 10, 1777 edition, pg. 2.
The Public Advertiser, June 13, 1777 edition, pg. 2.
The Public Advertiser, June 25, 1777 edition, pg. 2.
The Public Advertiser, June 27, 1777 edition, pg. 2.
The Public Advertiser, June 30, 1777 edition, pg. 2.
The Public Advertiser, July 16, 1777 edition, pg. 3.
The Public Advertiser, August 4, 1777 edition, pg. 2.
The Public Advertiser, September 17, 1777 edition, pg. 2.
The Public Advertiser, October 11, 1777 edition, pg. 3.
London, England, newspaper, 1777.

The Putnam County Courier, May 24, 1912 edition.

The Putnam County Courier, July 19, 1929 edition
The Putnam County Courier, June 14, 1935 edition.
Carmel, New York, newspaper, 1912, 1935

The Virginia Gazette, May 23, 1777 edition, pg. 2.
The Virginia Gazette, June 20, 1777 edition, pg. 1.
The Virginia Gazette, July 25, 1777 edition, pg. 2.
Williamsburg, Virginia, newspaper, 1777.

The Waterford Chronicle, April 18, 1777 edition.
The Waterford Chronicle, June 13, 1777 edition, pg. 2.
The Waterford Chronicle, June 17, 1777 edition, pp. 1-2.
The Waterford Chronicle, July 1, 1777 edition, pg. 1.
The Waterford Chronicle, July 4, 1777 edition, pg. 2.
Waterford, Ireland, newspaper, 1777.

Troiani, Don & James L. Kochan – *Don Troiani's Soldiers of the American Revolution.* Mechanicsburg, Pennsylvania: Stackpole Books, 2007.

Ward, Christopher – *War of the Revolution.* Old Saybrook, Connecticut: Konecky & Konecky, 1952.

White, John Terry - *John Gano, The National Cyclopedia of American Biography, Volume X.* New York: James T. White & Co., 1909.

Wild, Patrick Tierney – *Historic Tales of Bethel Connecticut.* chapter 1, Charleston, South Carolina: The History Press, 2011.

Wilson, Warren H. – *Quaker Hill, A Sociological Study.* New York: Columbia University, doctoral dissertation, 1907.

World Heritage Encyclopedia, Battle of Ridgefield. World Heritage.org.

Young, Peter & Roffe, Michael – *George Washington's Army.* Berkshire, UK: Osprey Publishing Ltd., 1972.

About the Author
Larry A. Maxwell

Larry A. Maxwell is a historian and author. While working as a journalist he won the coveted Associated Press Writing Award.

He served as Chairman of the Company of Military Historians at West Point.

He is the New York State Town Historian for Patterson, New York. During the Revolutionary War, Patterson was part of Fredericksburg, Dutchess County, New York. Sybil Ludington and her family lived in Fredericksburg.

He has served for more than twenty years as Pastor of the *Patterson Baptist Church*. The church was originally called *The Baptist Church of Fredericksburg*. It is the oldest Baptist Church, still in existence, in New York State. The Ludington family donated the property where the church had its first building. Sybil Ludington and Edmond Ogden were married in the church. That church was part of the *Danbury Baptist Association* which wrote a letter to President Thomas Jefferson, to which he responded with his famous Separation of Church and State letter.

He is a re-enactor and historical tailor. He is the founder and director of *The Living History Guild*, an organization which helps re-enactors keep history alive. He is also commander of the 4th New York Regiment of the Continental Line.

He served as a historical advisor and costumer for film projects and appeared on screen in numerous productions.

He wrote a companion screenplay for this book. He also wrote a children's book about Sybil Ludington and some of the events in this book. It is called *Travels Through Time – A Revolutionary Adventure*.

He is available to speak at conferences and at historical or educational events or functions. He often speaks wearing historical attire.

www.ingramcontent.com/pod-product-compliance
Lightning Source LLC
Chambersburg PA
CBHW060048230426
43661CB00004B/704